WOMEN AND THE POWER WITHIN

WOMEN AND THE POWER WITHIN

To See Life Steadily and See It Whole

Edited by
Dawn Hall Anderson
and Marie Cornwall

Deseret Book Company
Salt Lake City, Utah

Library of Congress Cataloging-in-Publication Data

Women and the power within : to see life steadily and see it whole /
edited by Dawn Hall Anderson and Marie Cornwall.

    p.   cm.

   Includes index.

   ISBN 0-87579-520-X

   1. Women—United States—Congresses. 2. Women—United States—
Psychology—Congresses. 3. Women in the Mormon Church—Congresses.
4. Women, Mormon—Religious life—Congresses. I. Anderson, Dawn
Hall. II. Cornwall, Marie. 1949–
HQ1403.W583 1991
305.42'0973—dc20   90-26622

Printed in the United States of America

10   9   8   7   6   5   4   3   2   1

Contents

Contents

Preface

This book is the fifth in the series from the annual Brigham Young University Women's Conference. Selections in this volume were presented in the 1990 conference. Our special thanks go to Carol Lee Hawkins, chair of the conference, and to her planning committee. This volume is possible only because of the support of the BYU administration and faculty and the many women and men who plan, organize, and participate in the conference each year.

We also thank the staff of the Women's Research Institute, who helped create this volume. Tosha Strickland transcribed hours of audio tape, coordinated transcripts back and forth from authors to editors, and produced the final manuscript. Greg Mueller and Julie Tait checked quotations and citations.

We thank the several authors who were willing to prepare their conference presentations for publication. We also thank Suzanne Brady of Deseret Book Publishing for creating the final product out of the manuscript we submitted.

WOMEN AND THE POWER WITHIN

"For God hath not given us the spirit of fear; but of power, and of love, and of a sound mind."

—2 Timothy 1:7

The Power Within: To See Life Steadily and See It Whole

REX E. LEE

The 1990 BYU Women's Conference continues a tradition begun in 1976. I want to compliment this year's chair, Carol Lee Hawkins, and the dedicated, perceptive women who have worked with her in putting together more than forty lectures, workshops, panel discussions, and performances. Their job has not been easy nor free from controversy, but few things that are really worthwhile enjoy either of those luxuries. We are grateful to them for their efforts.

As participants we differ widely in age, and even among those who are the same age, there is a sizable range to the challenges and circumstances that each of us faces. The conference committee has deliberately and conscientiously chosen session topics to cover a broad spectrum of individual needs and interests. I would be surprised, even a bit disappointed, if you agreed with everything said during the conference. I invite you, in the finest tradition of the gospel and the free and open society guaranteed by our Constitution, to approach each experience not only as an evaluator, an assessor, of the worth of what is said but also as one who is trying to learn from new ideas and new points of view — some of which you

Rex E. Lee is the tenth president of Brigham Young University. He was the founding dean of the J. Reuben Clark School of Law at Brigham Young University, served as the solicitor general of the United States, and maintains a private appellate law practice before the United States Supreme Court. His juris doctor degree is from the University of Chicago Law School, and he holds five honorary doctor of law degrees. He is married to Janet Griffin Lee. They have seven children and three grandchildren.

may disagree with. You may well conclude that although all the issues presented are important to you or to others, in some cases you will not be sure what the right attitudes or answers are. In other words, you may come away from this experience with new questions as well as new insights and answers.

Many of the sessions have been designed for men as well as for women. A justified complaint being voiced today by women — and some men — is that society has both erroneously and presumptuously assumed that social concerns are and should be the domain of woman. That is one of many gender-based generalizations with which I do not agree. Unfortunately, because women are not only discussing these issues but also acting upon them as well, most of the responsibility has fallen in their laps.

As I look over the topics for this conference — relationships with aging parents, self-esteem for children, providing aid for abuse victims, and dimensions of service — I see very clearly why Carol Lee and her committee would like more men to attend. These are not women's issues. They are people's issues. Women are making gigantic efforts to find solutions to these concerns, but they should not be expected to do it alone.

The theme of this year's conference is adapted from a poem Matthew Arnold wrote describing those authors who gave him solace and strength amidst the uncertainties and problems of his own day:

> be his
> My special thanks, whose even-balanced soul,
> From first youth tested up to extreme old age,
> Business could not make dull, nor passion wild;
> Who saw life steadily and saw it whole.[1]

The theme also derives in part from 2 Timothy 1:7: "For God hath not given us the spirit of fear; but of power, and of love, and of a sound mind."

In order "to grow in wisdom and knowledge" and to become like God, who is omnipotent, all-powerful, we are told that each of us—man and woman—must grow in power.

But what kind of power is godlike?

Karen Lynn Davidson helped answer that question for me in a talk she gave at a BYU Women's Conference several years ago. In her description of the Savior, she clarified how power can be a godlike attribute: "[The Savior] rejected the worldly notions of dominion, power, and bosshood. On the other hand, no one who has ever lived has shown more strength, more courage, more perseverance, more willingness to stand up for truth or rebuke wrong, even at tremendous cost, than has the Savior. He spoke up for unpopular causes. He was willing to speak the truth, even when it cost him his life. If his inner inspiration told him something was right, he did it. That confirmation was all he needed. He didn't need an okay from any of his friends. He had the strength to stand alone. He had absolute confidence in himself and in his Father—confidence to lead out in what was right."[2]

We are told that the power God shared with his Son, Jesus Christ, he shares willingly with all his children, as they develop increased faith in him. "Downright solid faith," said Elder A. Theodore Tuttle, "is the one thing that gives vitality and power to otherwise rather weak individuals."[3]

It is this power—the kind described by Karen, not by the world— that will help us meet and deal courageously with the uncertainties of life. It is power that will lift us up over our stumbling blocks, so that we may see life steadily and see it whole.

It is my testimony to you that each one of us has within us this power. The purpose of this conference is to explore and examine that gift.

Notes

1. Matthew Arnold, "To a Friend," *The Poems of Matthew Arnold*, 2d rev. ed., ed. Miriam Allott (New York: Longman Group Ltd., 1979), p. 111; as

quoted in the program of the Brigham Young University 1990 Women's Conference.

2. Karen Lynn Davidson, "The Savior: An Example for Everyone," in *Woman to Woman* (Salt Lake City: Deseret Book Co., 1986), pp. 102–3.

3. A. Theodore Tuttle, "Developing Faith," *Ensign*, Nov. 1986, p. 73.

Shipboard Surprises and Shoreline Gleanings

KAREN LYNN DAVIDSON

A few months ago I was called as stake Relief Society president. What worried me most was that the people who were the most surprised were the ones who knew me best. It isn't that my close friends and relatives think I'm such a shocking person; it's just that they know I don't come anywhere near the traditional Relief Society image. I'm afraid that when it comes to those domestic arts for which Latter-day Saint women are so famous, I am weighed in the balance and found sadly wanting. At mealtime, when people in my house ask, "Is this homemade?" they're hoping the answer is no. We are better off with something out of a can or a box.

In other ways, too, I am not typical of the ideal of Latter-day Saint womanhood. For example, I teach at a Catholic girls' school; I was single until I was thirty-eight years old; I have no children of my own—I'm that other kind of mother that usually has the adjective *wicked* in front of it—a stepmother. But paradoxically, I serve an important purpose by not fitting the traditional image. It would be difficult for someone in my

Karen Lynn Davidson received her bachelor's and master's degrees in English literature from Brigham Young University and her doctorate from the University of Southern California. She returned to BYU as a member of the English faculty and director of the honors program. She is the author of Our Latter-day Hymns: The Stories and the Messages *and* Thriving on Our Differences: A Book for LDS Women Who Feel like Outsiders. *She has served on the General Church Music Committee and is stake Relief Society president in the Pasadena, California, stake where she lives with her husband, David A. Davidson.*

stake to look me in the eye and say, "I just don't think I fit the Relief Society mold!" I'm a daily reminder to our stake, for the time I'm serving in my present calling, that the umbrella of The Church of Jesus Christ of Latter-day Saints is large and welcoming. It is not made to shelter one kind of woman only. I may lack some of the usual powers, but I may have some that are unique to me. There's room for all of us, and what happiness we can find as we use our individual powers to teach, bless, and strengthen one another!

It's difficult, of course, to be our most saintly selves in trying times. One Latter-day Saint mother I know commented that one New Year she made a great and high-minded resolution: "I will not yell at my teenagers." A couple of weeks into the new year, however, she found it necessary to modify this resolution. She changed "I will not yell at my teenagers" to "I will not yell at my teenagers between 8:30 A.M. and 3:00 P.M. on school days."

But often, in a time of stress, even a time of disaster, when we might expect anger and bitterness, men and women can find amazing powers within. In 1855, twenty-eight Latter-day Saint converts from Australia set sail, bound for Zion by way of San Francisco.[1] Two of the passengers were returning American missionaries. An Australian couple, Andrew and Elizabeth Anderson, boarded the ship with their eight children. One young family, the Harrises, could not afford passage for both adults, so Eliza Harris traveled on ahead with her two-year-old and six-month-old children to join the Saints, with her husband planning to follow as soon as he could earn his fare. Martha Humphries and her three children sailed without their husband and father for the same reason. Also aboard were an equal number of non–Latter-day Saints, including the captain, an American, by the name of Benjamin Franklin Pond. As the voyage began, the Saints gathered to sing "The Gallant Ship Is under Weigh," a hymn written by William W. Phelps to cheer the hearts of the immigrants and missionaries who were a constant part of the early Latter-day Saint scene. Here are two verses from that popular early hymn:

> The gallant ship is under weigh
> To bear me off to sea,
> And yonder floats the steamer gay
> That says she waits for me.
> The seamen dip the ready oar,
> As rippled waves oft tell,
> They bear me swiftly from the shore,
> My native land, farewell!
> I go, it is my Master's call,
> He's made my duty plain!
> No danger can the heart appall,
> When Jesus stoops to reign.
> And now the vessel's side we've made,
> The sails their bosoms swell,
> Thy beauties in the distance fade,
> My native land, farewell![2]

The passengers' farewell to friends and family in Australia was probably farewell forever. One of them wrote in his journal, it "sounded more like a funeral hymn." As John Devitry-Smith has pointed out, "Most of the adults had traveled from the British Isles to Australia and knew from prior experience the perils of the sea. Cramped quarters, poor food, and months of boredom awaited them, and the cool sea breeze rekindled these memories and created a chill of apprehension and anxiety."[3]

But their faith was strong. Sister Martha Humphries had written to her mother, "If I knew for a positive certainty, that when we [reach the land of Zion] persecutions, such as have been the portion of the saints before, awaited us, I would still insist upon going. What are a few short years in this present State, compared with Life Eternal?"[4]

After about a month at sea, the *Julia Ann* was in rough waters about midway between Australia and Hawaii. At 8:30 in the evening, after most of the children were asleep, the ship smashed head-on into a coral reef.

Captain Pond saw at once that the ship was finished; the only question remaining was whether any lives could be saved in the terrible storm. Passengers tried to cling to the railing around the deck, but some of the younger children could not keep a handhold as the huge waves swept over them; little Marion Anderson and Mary Humphries were washed overboard and never seen again.

The *Julia Ann* did not sink; it began to break into pieces on the rocks with the continual crashing of the waves. Only one lifeboat remained, but it was unmanageable in the storm. At the request of Captain Pond, a crew member volunteered to leap over the side and swim to the reef—hardly an inviting refuge, rough, jagged and partially submerged in the pounding waves; he managed to fasten a rope to one of the rocks, so that passengers could use the rope as a hand-over-hand lifeline and leave the ship. One by one the women and children were urged to try this means of escape, but some could not bring themselves to step off into the empty black night above the swirling water.

Eliza Harris bravely strapped her six-month-old baby to her breast and prepared to make her way to the rocks, but at the moment a huge wave engulfed them. Both mother and baby son were drowned. A young mother of seventeen managed to struggle to the rock, along with her husband who carried their baby strapped to his back. Another mother, urged by Captain Pond to save her own life since her six children could not possibly make it to the rocks, decided to remain on board rather than let her children face death alone.

Captain Pond later wrote, "At every surge of the sea, I expected the vessel would turn bottom up. . . . I urged those remaining to try to get to the reef, on the rope, before it parted—it was a desperate, but only chance for life. The women and children could not, and the men shr[a]nk from the yawning gulf as from certain death."[5]

At last only nineteen passengers remained on the boat, all of them parents and children who had decided to face death together. The captain and the remaining crew members, knowing they had done all they could, made their way along the rope to the reef. Then, at about 11 P.M., the ship broke into pieces. Miraculously, the part of the ship to which the passengers were clinging was carried up onto the reef, and the remaining passengers were saved. In all, of the fifty-six who had originally sailed on the ship, fifty-one survived.

And so they waited on the reef for the dawn, all of them injured and exhausted, up to their waists in water, threatened constantly by sharks. Yes, they were alive, but what was to happen now? One later wrote, "The ship's bell could be heard, tolled by the motion of the waves, as if it were our funeral dirge."[6] They were miles away from the route of passing ships and entirely without a supply of drinking water.

When the sun rose, they saw an island about eight miles distant. Making some quick repairs to the remaining lifeboat, the captain and some crew members rowed to the island. In the meantime, some of those remaining on the reef managed to build a raft and salvage a few supplies from the shipwreck. But when the captain and his men returned that afternoon, they brought a discouraging report: the island was really only a sandbar, with apparently neither water nor food.

Even so, the sandbar was preferable to the coral reef, and the entire company was eventually transported there. Their spirits rose when they found that some shallow wells would yield drinking water. They discovered crabs and coconuts. One of the young men wrote, "Too much cannot be said in commendation of the Saints in this very trying situation. I have seen a . . . lady of sixty years of age out at night hunting turtles."[7] With the kind of resourcefulness that we like to think is characteristic of Latter-day Saint women to the present day, the marooned sisters improvised a kind of pancake made with a little flour salvaged from the ship, shredded coconut, and turtle eggs.

11

Thus they lived for forty-seven days. They knew that their only chance for rescue lay in rowing the battered lifeboat for help. Either they had to take this gamble or resign themselves to remaining on the sandbar forever. So the captain and the crew set out. After four days of nonstop rowing, they reached the island of Bora-Bora. Captain Pond arranged for a rescue ship, and sixty days after the shipwreck the grateful passengers sighted the sails of the *Emma Packer*, sent to carry them to safety in Tahiti. One of the returning missionaries wrote, "I need not attempt to describe our feelings of gratitude and praise which we felt to give the God of Israel for His goodness and mercy in thus working a deliverance for us."[8] Eventually, various ones of these Saints helped to pioneer such settlements as Smithfield, Payson, and American Fork.

Imagine, if you will, how great the temptation must have been to heap curses and blame upon the head of the captain during these appalling experiences. How natural to lash out at him: how could you let us sail so near the reef? How could you let any of us attempt to get to the reef by rope, when as it turned out all would have been safe had we remained on the ship? But instead, they praised the captain for his courage and unselfishness. Brigham Young, remarking later on the incident, said, "All [the officers of the *Julia Ann*] are well spoken of by our brethren."[9]

Do we find these powers today? If you and your fellow ward members were shipwrecked on a reef, how would you fare? I think my own ward would do quite well. Let me tell you a little about us. Each of us has different powers, a different contribution. And what a cross-section of Latter-day Saint humanity is my ward in Pasadena, California! I sat there looking at us one Sunday and thought, "It's as if the members of this ward had been chosen by Central Casting to represent different incomes, talents, races, interests." Let me introduce some of them more specifically:

Josephine Sakhnini, born in Nazareth, is a native speaker of Arabic who was reared a Catholic. That's an unusual combination! She joined the Church about four years ago. We love her exotic pot-luck contributions.

Elizabeth Baker is a professional foster mother, specially licensed, in fact, to care for handicapped children and drug-addicted infants. Our bishop describes her as "a woman of perfect common sense."

Giovanna Racossta served a mission in her native Italy, and Jade Hoang served a mission in San Diego after coming to the United States from Vietnam. They moved into our ward as newlyweds and are now serving as stake missionaries.

Deborah Ludeman is a professional nightclub singer and our early-morning seminary teacher. "Only in California," I can hear you say!

Beth Erickson is one of our mentally handicapped young adults. We are all her family. In testimony meeting, when she asks for the microphone and bears a testimony that only our Father in Heaven can understand completely, that's fine with all of us.

I'm proud of my ward. I'm grateful that our Father in Heaven instructs us to prove our worthiness not by living as hermits in holy isolation but by forming communities through our branches, wards, stakes, Relief Society organization. In this way, our individual powers can supplement the powers that may be missing in someone else. I don't believe I have the talents of that foster mother; I *know* I don't have the talents of the nightclub entertainer; but together, we can combine our powers to make all kinds of things happen. Sometimes in our ward the events on a typical Sunday are not perfectly predictable, but I realized long ago that efficiency is not usually the highest priority of our Father in Heaven.

One of the delights of living in my ward, or probably in your ward, is to discover that someone has powers within that we didn't suspect were there. One dear sister, Mary Coleman, is greatly loved in our ward. She will soon be ninety-one years old. She so enjoys telling people the story of her life while she shows them some photographs that she always carries in her purse. And it's a fascinating story—her great-grandfather was a runaway slave who escaped to Canada. One day I was sitting across the table from Mary at a Relief Society luncheon, and Mary realized that seated next to her was a new sister—Helen Gentry. A new audience for her story! And sure enough, right on cue, out came the photographs. There was just one problem. Helen Gentry, our new sister, has been blind from birth. Mary didn't realize this; she began handing Helen the photos, and I thought, "This I've got to see." But it was wonderful. Helen Gentry is so ingenious, so gifted with courteous warmth, that she carried it off without the slightest hesitation: "This is your grandson, you say? How wonderful! You must be so proud of him!" Mary handed over photograph after photograph, Helen expressed loving enthusiasm, and everyone was perfectly happy. How glad I was that I hadn't interfered at the beginning and caused embarrassment, and how impressed I was to find out about some of the wonderful powers within Helen.

As we strive to see life steadily and see it whole, our job is to balance each part of our earthly lives—the past, the present, and the future. All time is as one to our Father, but while we are on this earth, we can know our lives only as a sequence: each event, each circumstance, belongs to the past, to the present, or to the future. And each one of these three segments can potentially overshadow and strangle the other two. Sadness from the past can linger on to blight the present and future. The present can distract and entice, resulting in a past with little substance and a future with little potential. The future may represent a false happiness, forever out of reach, forever robbing the present of its joy and purpose.

What about, first of all, the woman whose present and future are at the mercy of her past? Perhaps she carries a burden of past sin. Or bygone years may continue to cast their shadow not because of sin but because of disadvantage; her heart may ache as she compares herself with others whose families, education, and other good fortune have pointed them along a

14

happy path of self-esteem and achievement. Or there is a third possibility: perhaps she is the victim of real or imagined wrong-doing and is unable to forget that misfortune; some people, it seems, choose to fuel their lives with resentment and feel most alive when they are most angry, like Robert Burns's "sulky, sullen dame" in his poem "Tam O' Shanter," "Gathering her brows like gathering storm, / Nursing her wrath to keep it warm."[10]

I am continually impressed by the ways in which the women of our Church are able to rise above their past. Once a woman comes to understand the Atonement, she knows she does not have to live with past mistakes. Disadvantage and injustice need not drag us down. Our sisters find a way to go on, with faith and strength. The father of a friend of mine underwent what was thought to be a simple operation, but he was found to have inoperable cancer. The doctors told the family the terrible news. One of the man's daughters, in the immense distress of the moment, kept saying, "I can't go on! I can't go on!" Finally her sister said, "Well, what exactly do you plan to do instead?" Whether we are struggling pioneers or distraught family members in a modern hospital, we some-how manage to go on. As we strive to see life steadily and see it whole, we need not allow any dark moment of the past to dim the present or the future.

The present, also, can enslave and burden us. I see the allure of the present especially among young people. Many of the girls at the college preparatory high school where I teach tell me they don't have time to learn to type. The price they will pay tomorrow, the time they will lose as college students and perhaps as professionals, for not knowing the keyboard means nothing to them today. Whatever it is they are doing at the present moment, it's more important than learning to type. On a far more serious note, a young girl will fix upon the notion of herself as a bride — the beautiful white dress, the celebration, the attention. She may not particularly want to be a wife, just a bride — with little thought to the consequent

15

responsibilities and commitments. It may be the wrong time, the wrong place, the wrong groom; yet the vision of that wonderful wedding may outweigh all else.

But these are young girls. Among the adult Latter-day Saint women I know, how often do I see one so entranced with the pleasures of the moment that she forgets everything else? Frankly, not very often. I would be amazed to find very many LDS women who live for shallow superficial excitement. I believe that most of us have quite a different problem with the present. We tend to wish it away by looking ahead to a future moment that is going to give us more spirituality, more satisfaction, and fewer worries. We let thoughts of the future gobble up the contentment that we should feel in the present. How easy it is to pin our expectations upon some future circumstance that will somehow make everything better: "When I am set apart as a missionary so I can really concentrate on spiritual goals, when the school year starts and I can get on a schedule, when summer comes so I can have some time to myself, when I finish school, when that raise comes through, when I get married, when we can move, when the children are all in school, when the children all leave home, when retirement comes . . . then everything will be better!"

I admire the women who define their own present and make the present rewarding and fine, rather than just wishing the present to change. My friend Karen Church was rearing her young family in South Chicago, where her husband was serving as institute director. She might have preferred to be somewhere other than in that uneasy neighborhood. In the meantime, Chicago was home, there were some things to appreciate about Chicago, and she wanted her children to feel proud of where they lived. So she wrote her own verse to add to "This Land Is My Land," and she taught it to her children and the rest of the Primary. These are the words:

> The crisp breeze blows
> From off the Great Lakes;

The city skyline
A lovely sight makes.
Here in this country
Are my heart's keepsakes.
This land was made for you and me.[11]

Karen and her family now live in Pleasant Grove. To this day, those children probably wonder why they are the only ones who know all the verses to "This Land Is My Land"!

In England, I met Ruby Andrus. As the mother of an American military family, she was faced with having to move every couple of years. Every house was temporary. But with each move, she made sure she turned that house into an attractive home. The family moved into one large but rather drab residence in England and assigned each child a room to transform, giving each a certain budget to work within. In one bathroom, a room that happened to be the responsibility of the fifteen-year-old daughter Sandra, the pipes coming out of the toilet tank extended halfway up the bathroom wall. So Sandra got some paints. She painted the pipes bright green, painted some big green leaves on the wall beside them, and then at the top, some huge, bright blossoms. Those ugly pipes had turned into giant flowers. Ruby Andrus was teaching her family a valuable lesson: don't just suffer through the present, or just wait it out; enjoy each moment while it is here.

And think once more of the marooned passengers of the *Julia Ann*. They created their own present. The shipwreck was in the past; it couldn't be helped, and they wasted no energy in recriminations or anger. A joyful life among the Utah Saints was, they hoped, in the future, but they wasted no energy in fruitless daydreams. Instead, they hunted turtles, supported one another and their captain, and built shelters for their families.

Today in Lebanon eight Americans are still held hostage. They have been there for years. Imagine, seriously imagine, for just a moment, that you are such a prisoner. You remember certain moments, dreaming of someday being able to experience them again. I would like to suggest that the moments you would long to relive, the moments that would make you think "If only I could once more . . . " would not be the time you won the one-hundred-dollar gift certificate at Albertson's, or the time you had that wonderful ski vacation, or any other supposed high point. I believe you would dwell on the most ordinary pleasant moments, the ones that we scarcely notice when they happen. You would be thinking, for example, "I would give anything to be back home on a crisp autumn Sunday, sitting in Relief Society, singing a hymn with my friends." You would long for an ordinary lunch with your family or co-workers, an ordinary stop by the dry cleaners or the hardware store, the pleasure of opening the phone book and finding a number you need, an ordinary chance to enjoy flowers and trees.

One Latter-day Saint man *was* a prisoner in Hanoi for five and one-half years. Air Force pilot Major Jay Hess survived that awful experience, but how did he preserve himself as a human being? How, in that cell, did he manage to see life steadily and see it whole? He found power within from his memories of the hymns of this Church. He tells us in his own words exactly how he was able to keep his humanity, his perspective, and his balance in the POW camp:

"Phrases from . . . [hymns] gave me gospel lessons when I needed them. One such phrase was 'Come, come, ye Saints, no toil nor labor fear.' I would think of that song on days that were tough and say to myself, 'That is a great lesson for me right there. Don't fear, just do whatever you have to do.' And the last verse: 'And should we die before our journey's through, happy day!' There were a lot of days just like that. It would have been happiness to have died that day, but I knew that if I could make it through, then I was going to be really happy. . . .

"I remember once when I got hold of some paper and made a pen; using blue iodine for ink, I wrote down as many hymns as I could remember. I listed about a hundred. Hymns were used in my prayers, like the one the children sing in

18

Primary: 'Lead me, guide me, walk beside me. . . . ' However, I didn't apply the words to myself, but turned them around. Don't teach *me* or guide *me*; rather, lead my children and guide them."[12]

As Latter-day Saints, we tend to be oriented toward goals and results. The thought of a joyful future sustains us. You can tell that just by looking at a few of our hymns. Hope is always smiling brightly before us as we march on to glory, when all that was promised the Saints will be given, and soon we'll have this tale to tell—all is well. We like to work for results and to point to those results as proof that we have been wise and obedient. Wards like to point to their statistics. Mothers like to point to their beautiful families. Professionals like the tangible rewards of paychecks and promotions. The trouble is, in our preoccupation with the future, in looking forward to results and goals, we forget to enjoy the process of getting there.

People often ask Mother Teresa, "How about the millions of unfortunate people in India you are not helping? What you do is wonderful, but it hardly makes any difference in the total grim picture." Her simple reply is that the numbers are not important. She says, "To us what matters is an individual. To get to love the person we must come in close contact with him. If we must wait till we get the numbers, then we will be lost in the numbers."[13] To value the process, the present experience of carrying out our mission, is an important part of seeing life steadily and seeing it whole. The present moment is not something to hurry through or to leap over as a means to a future goal.

Many years ago, just after Spain had been opened to missionary work, we were traveling through Cordoba and met two elders. We asked them how the work was going—have you had any baptisms yet, we asked? No, they said, they hadn't had any. How about contacts—are you teaching anyone? They said no. They had had one contact, but he was a member of the Spanish Civil Guard, and he knew he would lose his job if he joined the Church. So the missionaries weren't teaching anyone at the moment. Yet as they told us how difficult and apparently unproductive the work was, these elders radiated cheerfulness and fulfillment. I'm sure they would have liked to baptize people. But in the meantime, they were enjoying the process of being in the service of the Lord; they were true to their mission.

The sisters and brothers who find the power within to perform amazing feats of courage, ingenuity, and faith have usually started out as ordinary people, probably unaware of their power until a challenge brought it forth. Each of us is entitled to the comfort and pride of knowing we have those powers within. Let us visualize the Savior at our side, reassuring us that the needed strength, the needed ideas, the needed serenity will be there for extraordinary times. And let us visualize him standing next to us at ordinary times, helping us to see life steadily and see it whole, calling our attention to the beauty of the life we enjoy every day. I pray that we may say with the psalmist, "This is the day which the Lord hath made; we will rejoice and be glad in it." (Psalm 118:24.)

Notes
1. John Devitry-Smith, "The Wreck of the *Julia Ann*," *BYU Studies* (Spring 1989): 5– 29.
2. *Latter-day Saint Hymns* (Salt Lake City: Deseret Book, 1927), no. 129.
3. Devitry-Smith, pp. 8–9.
4. Ibid., p. 9.
5. Ibid., p. 13.
6. Ibid., p. 15.
7. Ibid., p. 17.
8. Ibid., p. 22.
9. Brigham Young, Journal History, 10 Dec. 1856; quoted in Devitry-Smith, p. 23.
10. Robert Burns, "Tam O' Shanter," in *British Literature*, 2d ed., vol. 2, ed. Hazelton Spencer, Walter E. Houghton, and Herbert Barrows (Boston: D.C. Heath and Co., 1963), p. 39.
11. Used by permission of the author; not in print.
12. "Eternal Values Sustained Prisoner of War," *Ensign*, June 1973, p. 70.
13. Malcolm Muggeridge, *Something Beautiful for God* (New York: Ballantine Books), p. 97.

The Unknown Treasure

JUTTA BAUM BUSCHE

One evening in late summer of 1940, the Baum family—the mother, two sons, one adopted son, two daughters, and a little baby—gathered in their dining room in the absence of the father, who was a soldier in the war. The mother had been busy all afternoon improvising a supper from such limited supplies as dandelion greens, turnips, and potatoes. As she placed the food on the table and looked around at the children, she asked, "Where is Jutta?" Startled, the three boys looked at one another, and then one by one guiltily dropped their eyes. The mother repeated her question more urgently: "Where is Jutta?" Finally, one of the boys said in a subdued voice, "She is still tied to a tree in the forest. We forgot to loosen her. We were playing a war game."

This incident was typical of my childhood. At the time I was only five and already a tomboy. I grew up mainly among boys and enjoyed participating in their war games. I served principally as their "weapons carrier," though occasionally I stood in as "the enemy." I am grateful to my Heavenly Father that I was born at that time in Germany. Wartime was full of sacrifices, fear, panic, pain, and hardships, but it was also a time of vivid memories, learning, and growth, because real learning often happens only in times of hardship.

Jutta Baum Busche, born in Dortmund, Germany, married at age twenty F. Enzio Busche, a publisher and printer. They were converted to the Church in the first years of their marriage. She served in the various Church auxiliaries for children, youth, and women. In 1977 her husband was called as a member of the First Quorum of the Seventy. She has since served as the wife of a mission president and as a temple matron. The Busches moved to Utah in 1980. They are the parents of four children and the grandparents of nine.

During the war years, I remember, each evening as darkness came, I would take a small backpack containing some extra underclothing, a pair of stockings, and a pair of shoes, and walk about three kilometers (just under two miles) from home to a tunnel to spend the night alone in a compartment of a stationary train kept there to furnish shelter for civilians who were afraid of the almost nightly air raids. I also remember the first banana I ever had and how good it tasted. The war had just ended, and a merciful soldier from the occupying forces gave it to me. I remember very vividly our meager diet of water soups, nettle spinach, dandelion greens, turnips, and the molasses that people in our town were fortunate to obtain from a damaged railroad car. I remember very well the smell of sheep wool, which we sheared ourselves and spun into yarn, making sweaters and dresses for ourselves. I saw, as a consequence of our lack of food and medical assistance during those years, my sixteen-year-old sister and my nineteen-year-old brother become ill and finally die. The death of my brother, to whom I was very close, hurt me terribly and filled me with a deep awareness of how fragile life is.

In our home there was little religious education, although my parents were Protestant. My family simply did not talk about religion. But my father's brother was a Protestant minister. I remember a time when this uncle's wife came to visit. Before my aunt arrived, my father instructed us, "When she is here, we must have a prayer before we eat." I will never forget how comical and strange it was to hear my father offer a blessing on the food in words and tone of voice so unfamiliar to us that it struck me as hypocritical. Yet, as I grew up, frequently in the evening I knelt at my bedside on my own initiative to pray to my Heavenly Father because, even without religious instruction, I felt in my heart that there must be someone whom I could trust and love—someone who knew me and cared about me. What a privilege it would have been to be reared in a family that was well-grounded in the restored gospel!

When the missionaries first came to our door in Dortmund,

Germany, my husband and I had not been married long. Our first son was only three months old. I was and always will be grateful each minute of my life for the message that came to us through these young missionaries. I was impressed with many things about these young men. One was the loving way they talked about their families. Another was their attitude about their message. There was no facade. I sensed such humble honesty in their expressions of testimony that I was compelled to listen. What they told me about angels and golden plates intrigued me enough that I wanted to learn why such nice young men could believe in such strange things.

I learned from them that we are all children of a loving Heavenly Father and that we are here on this earth to learn, to grow, and to love. I learned that we lived with God as his spirit children, his sons and daughters. We walked and talked with him. We knew him and he still knows us. We raised our hands in support of the plan to come to this earth. Achieving our full potential in our journey here depends on our free choices. That message needs to penetrate every act of our daily lives.

I have since discovered that one great stumbling block to our progress in faith is rule-keeping that does not spring from an honest heart. Too many people imply in their attitude toward others that our Heavenly Father expects a perfect conformity to established rules. But Jesus Christ never condemned the honest in heart. His wrath was kindled against the hypocritically empty rule-keeping of the Pharisees. Jesus preached that through repentance we become free from sin; *however, only as we become honest, do we feel the necessity of repentance.*

When at age thirteen I was confirmed a member of a Protestant faith, the minister quoted John 8:32: "Ye shall know the truth and the truth shall make you free." This scripture had no meaning for me until I found the true gospel and learned the value of free agency—the right to make one's own decisions in one's own way. For me the truth that makes one free is twofold: the truths of the restored gospel, which provide a map of eternal realities, and the skill of being truthful with oneself and others, which leads to genuine repentance and integrity.

Self-honesty is the foundation for developing other spiritual strengths. Self-honesty will determine whether obstacles and problems we face in life are stepping stones leading to blessings or stumbling stones leading to spiritual graveyards. Marcus Aurelius, an ancient Roman philosopher, observed the connection between honesty and spiritual growth nearly two thousand years ago: "A man's true greatness lies in the consciousness of an honest purpose in life founded on a just estimate of himself and everything else, on frequent self-examinations, and a steady obedience to the rule which he knows to be right, without troubling himself about what others may think or say, or whether they do or do not do that which he thinks and says and does."[1] According to Marcus Aurelius, then, self-honesty is both a prerequisite to greatness and the core quality of integrity.

A time of great insight into the principle of self-honesty came for me when my husband accepted a full-time call in the Lord's service, making it necessary for us to say good-bye to all those whom we had grown to love in our home ward in Dortmund and everyone with whom we had been associated. The transition was not easy for us.

I remember well the adjustments we had to make when we came to live in Utah. My first call in our ward was to serve as a Relief Society teacher. I watched the other teachers very closely and was deeply impressed with their striving for perfection in their teaching. Even their hairdos and immaculate dress showed their striving for perfection. I admired how fluent and articulate they were in the English language. How could I, with my poor English, compete with them and be their teacher? I was eager to learn and was so glad to hear that there was a stake preparation class for Relief Society teachers.

When I attended the training meeting for the first time, I was full of high hopes. I was not prepared for the question I was asked about what kind of centerpiece I would use when I gave my lesson. How incompetent I felt! I had no idea what a centerpiece was or what its purpose in the presentation of a lesson could be. Negative feelings about myself began to undermine my confidence.

Other efforts to fit in were equally discouraging. I felt very intimidated by my many wonderful neighbors with their seven, eight, or nine children. I became very shy when I had to reply that we had only four, and I could not even mention to these people the deep hurt I had experienced when I found that for health reasons my family would have to be limited to four children.

I continued to feel inferior as I watched the sisters in my ward and saw them planting gardens and canning the produce. They exercised daily by jogging. They sewed and bargain-shopped. They went on heart-fund drives and served as PTA officers. They took dinners to new mothers and the sick in their neighborhoods. They took care of an aged parent, sometimes two. They climbed Mount Timpanogos. They drove their children to and from music or dancing lessons. They were faithful in doing temple work, and they worried about catching up on their journals.

Intimidated by examples of perfection all around me, I increased my efforts to be like my sisters, and I felt disappointed in myself and even guilty when I didn't run every morning, bake all my own bread, sew my own clothes, or go to the university. I felt that I needed to be like the women among whom I was living, and I felt that I was a failure because I was not able to adapt myself easily to their life-styles.

I could have benefited at this time from the story of a six-year-old who, when asked by a relative, "What do you want to be?" replied, "I think I'll just be myself. I have tried to be like someone else. I have failed each time!" Like this child, after repeated failure to be someone else, I finally learned that I should be myself. That is often not easy, however, because our desires to fit in, to compete and impress, or even simply to be approved of lead us to imitate others and devalue our own backgrounds, our own talents, and our own burdens and challenges. I had to learn not to worry about the behavior of others and their *code* of rules. I had to learn to overcome my anxious feeling that if I didn't conform, I simply did not measure up.

Two challenging passages in the Bible remind me that I must overcome self-doubts. One is Proverbs 23:7. "For as he thinketh in his heart, so is he." The other is Romans 12:2: "Be not conformed to this world: but be ye transformed by the renewing of your mind, that ye may prove what is that good, and acceptable, and perfect, will of God." When I tried to *conform,* it blocked my being *transformed* by the Spirit's renewing of my mind. When I tried to copy my wonderful sisters as I taught my class with a special centerpiece and other teaching techniques that were unfamiliar to me, I failed because the Spirit still talks to me in German, not in English. But when I got on my knees to ask for help, I learned to depend on the Spirit to guide me, secure in the knowledge that I am a daughter of God. I had to learn and *believe* that I did not need to compete with others to be loved and accepted by my Heavenly Father.

Another insight from Marcus Aurelius is, "Look within. Within is the fountain of good, and it will ever bubble up, if thou wilt ever dig."[2] Sometimes our great potential for good is veiled from us by the negative judgments of others. For instance, one day in Germany I had a meeting with our eleven-year-old son's school teacher. I was very saddened to hear that she judged our son to be lacking in sufficient intelligence to follow the course of mathematics of that school. I knew my son better than the teacher did; I knew that, on the contrary, mathematics was his real interest and within the scope of his capabilities. I left feeling very depressed. When I got home, I saw in the eyes of my son his high expectations as he enthusiastically inquired about what his teacher had said. I knew how devastated he would be if I were to tell him his teacher's exact words. It was the Spirit that gave me the wisdom to rephrase his teacher's concerns. I told him that the teacher recognized his great talent for mathematics and that only his lack of diligence would separate him from great achievements, for his teacher held high hopes for his future. My son took this to heart, and it did not take long before he became the best student of mathematics in his class. I do not even dare to think what would have become of him had I reported exactly the teacher's negative remarks.

God works through the positive power of his love. When we truly learn to love God, we learn to love all things — others, ourselves, all creation, because God is in all, with all, and through all. We need not be afraid, and we need not hide behind a facade of performance. When we come to understand this *unknown treasure* — the knowledge of who we really are — we will know that we are entitled to the power that comes from God. It will come when we ask for it and when we trust his leadership in our lives. Our efforts should not be to *perform* nor to *conform* but to be *transformed* by the Spirit. Again, "Be not conformed to this world: but be ye transformed by the renewing of your mind, that ye may prove what is that good, and acceptable, and perfect, will of God." (Romans 12:2.)

Many pressures bind us to the world. Being honest in heart frees us to discover God's will for our lives. I am always touched in our monthly ward testimony meetings where my faith is strengthened by my neighbors who tell how they have been *buoyed up* to meet the challenges and trials that have come their way. So often their testimonies reveal serious challenges they have had to face — challenges that are not evident unless one opens up one's heart to another. I know that as I walk down our street and pass all the beautifully tended homes of my neighbors, I am inclined to think that all is well with them, that they do not struggle as I do. It is through the honest testimonies they bear that I learn to see their hearts, and we become united in feelings of love.

We, the children of the covenant whose eyes have been opened, have a great responsibility to be always aware of who we are. Although we might be absorbed in meeting our daily challenges and opportunities for growth, we cannot afford to live one day or one minute without being aware of the power within us. What a privilege I had to serve as the first matron in the Frankfurt Temple! I had to depend constantly on the Spirit; otherwise, it would have been impossible to succeed. The challenge to establish a fully functioning temple seemed overwhelming, but the more overwhelming our tasks are, the more we understand that there is only One who can help, our Heavenly Father. Only when we draw unto him can we learn how real he is, how much he understands, and how much he is willing to help. He knows that we are not perfect and that we are struggling; and when we accept ourselves with our weaknesses in humility, sincerity, and complete honesty, then he is with us. As Paul told the Corinthians, "Eye hath not seen, nor ear heard, neither have entered into the heart of man, the things which God hath prepared for them that love him." (1 Corinthians 2:12.)

Notes

1. As quoted in *TNT: The Power within You,* ed. Claude M. Bristol and Harold Sherman (New York: Prentice-Hall Press, 1987), p. 52.
2. As quoted in *Great Books of the Western World,* vol. 12, ed. Robert Maynard Hutchins (Chicago: University of Chicago Press, 1952), p. 283.

To Cheer and Bless in Humanity's Name
ARDETH G. KAPP AND CAROLYN J. RASMUS

Ardeth Kapp

Our beloved President Spencer W. Kimball taught that the influence of righteous women would be critical during the winding-up scenes on this earth before the second coming of our Savior.[1] Carolyn and I want to share with you our understanding of *influence:* service, ministering to one another. This is our time to be a righteous influence. There are righteous women throughout the world with whom we need to unite. We need not wait for a calling but can be anxiously engaged of our own free will.

We wish not to make anyone feel encumbered or burdened but to point out that little things can mean so very much. Let me draw attention to Doctrine and Covenants 64:33, which says simply, "Wherefore, be not weary in well-doing, for ye are laying the foundation of a great work. And out of small things

Ardeth G. Kapp serves the Church as General President of the Young Women. She received her bachelor's degree from the University of Utah and her master's degree in education from Brigham Young University. She has served on the BYU faculty in the College of Education and has also served on the General Church Curriculum Planning Committee and Youth Correlation Committee. She is the author of six books. She is married to Heber B. Kapp.

Carolyn J. Rasmus serves as the administrative assistant to the Young Women General Presidency. She joined the Church while in graduate school at Brigham Young University. She subsequently earned her doctoral degree and became a professor of physical education at Brigham Young University. Later she served as executive assistant to BYU presidents Dallin H. Oaks and Jeffrey R. Holland.

proceedeth that which is great." Keep that in mind. Our intent is not to overwhelm but to suggest how much can happen with even small things.

In the April 1990 general conference, President Thomas S. Monson, quoting our prophet, President Ezra Taft Benson, said, "Your words, President, echo loud and clear: We must dedicate our strength to serving the needs, rather than the fears, of the world."[2] President Monson added, "Perhaps never in history has the need for cooperation, understanding, and goodwill among all people—and nations and individuals alike—been so urgent as today."[3] Others who spoke in the same session reminded us of the importance of caring for one another. "Service helps us overcome selfishness and sin. . . . [It] helps us cleanse ourselves and become purified and sanctified."[4] We must "live the example of the good Samaritan, who was free of prejudice and excuses and therefore truly loved his neighbor."[5] "When, for the moment, we ourselves are not being stretched on a particular cross, we ought to be at the foot of someone else's—full of empathy and proffering spiritual refreshment."[6]

The hymn "As Sisters in Zion" includes the line, "How vast is our purpose, how broad is our mission." (*Hymns,* no. 309.) What is our responsibility to bring relief within our own homes, our neighborhood, our community, our country, our world? To bring relief from illiteracy and poverty, to extend relief not only to the homeless but to those in spiritual darkness, depression, despair? Do we confine ourselves to our own comfort zones? Can we offer relief from rejection and abuse, relief from loneliness and isolation? Do we see service when it is close to home, across the street, down the aisle in the marketplace? Can we unite to bring relief from the devastation of drugs and alcohol and the addicting power of pornography? Our opportunity and our responsibility to cheer and to bless in humanity's name beckons us to service.

Elder John A. Widtsoe wrote, "In our preexistent state in the day of the great council, we made a certain agreement with the Almighty. The Lord posed a plan conceived by him. We accepted it. Since the plan is intended for all men [and women], we became parties to the salvation of every person under the plan. We agreed right then and there to not only be Saviors for ourselves but measurably Saviors for the whole human family. We went into a partnership with the Lord. The working out of the plan became not merely the Father's work and the Savior's work but also our work. The least of us, the humblest, is in partnership with the Almighty in achieving the purpose of the eternal plan of salvation. This places us in a very responsible attitude toward the whole human race."[7]

To bless and to cheer in humanity's name takes us beyond our immediate neighborhood. We must tear down fences and walls and build bridges. Recently I was invited to participate in a meeting of the National Women's Leadership Task Force, a coalition of women working to stamp out pornography. As you read the following from my notes of that meeting, will you ask yourself whether you would be willing to participate with these women in that cause.

"We must have a theological and ethical base: the New Testament refers to the beloved community where each one has dignity, value, and worth."

Another woman commented, "This is a calling. Yes, because we are Christian women, but also because we are citizens. This problem erodes that covenant base which is the fiber of our republic. This problem unleashes and distorts human passion."

One woman admitted to having misjudged another, "I saw her as being different. I had an ally, and I mistook her."

Another urged, "Broaden the base. One woman can be helpful, ten women influential, one hundred women powerful, one thousand women invincible. Train women to interact in the process, to work with excellence and respect, integrity and balance."

Then another woman, quiet in nature, said, "I've been praying to get out of it. God is keeping us in it to do something about it."

The person leading the group said, "I feel the Lord put this all together. If you let in the light, he will bring in what else is needed."

Alex DeTocqueville was quoted, "Righteous women in their circle of influence beginning in the home can turn the world around."

"When committed women are singing off the same song sheet," one woman said, "we can make a difference. We need to promote virtue. That is the bottom line. The Lord impressed upon my spirit that God will give voice to women who are standing for righteousness. I believe we are here, placed at a point in human history by God's design. My heart longs for the day when all women everywhere will stand up and speak out for righteousness that affects our homes, our communities, our nation, but most of all our families." She emphasized, "Before we do anything, however, we must have prayer support. This evil is out of the pits of hell. When the women of this nation become mobilized in righteous causes and converted into votes, when we put our heads together, pray together, put our shoulders to the wheel, we can turn this thing around. We have been called to be righteous women. Think of all you have accomplished and then ask yourself, what does God want me to do now?"

The chairman closed the meeting with this thought, "The Lord bless you and keep you and use you all for his glory, Amen."

It is not enough to strive only to promote what is good. Must we not also accept responsibility to unite our efforts and extend our influence to eradicate the bad? I would like to tell you of a Relief Society in Las Vegas that determined to break with tradition. Rather than the usual Relief Society birthday social, nine wards united to research their community. They identified twenty major projects that could affect, protect, and guard the homes in their community. Each of the nine wards chose one activity. The sisters from one ward participated in projects leading to the dedication of the temple in that area;

others focused their concern on the telephone directory, which contained twenty-five pages advertising escort services (i.e., women for hire). The pornographic language and pictures in the telephone directory ads defiled the homes they were placed in. While some sisters blessed their community by participating in the completion of a temple in their midst, others blessed their community by uniting their forces to remove porno-graphic material from their homes.

Our labors are needed on both fronts, to promote the good and to eradicate the bad. Often we hesitate, concerned that if we take a stand we will be criticized. But we need to take that risk; we need to articulate our values. There is a proper framework for voicing our opinion. When I went to Washington, D.C., to present a paper to the Meese Commission Against Pornography, I confess it was not comfortable. I was there with representatives from *Playboy* and other magazines. Sometimes taking a stand simply is not comfortable. But I think we can be a righteous influence with dignity, with propriety, with clarity, and in support of constitutional procedures, but not with tolerance for things we know to be wrong. Sometimes Mormon women fear that it may not be appropriate for them to enter a political arena even in issues that endanger the home; however, the assignments that I have received from our priest-hood leaders — our General Authorities — tell me that we may not have the luxury to sit on the sidelines and hope that some-one else will stand up and speak out for what we believe.

"Out of small things proceedeth that which is great." (D&C 64:33.) In another stake in Draper, Utah, the stake Relief Society president gathered women together and with quilting frames border to border in the entire cultural hall, they made two hundred quilts to cover the beds in the Primary Children's Hospital. Each sister may have felt that her small contribution would not make much difference, but I think of the words of Mother Teresa, "I always say I'm a little pencil in the hands of God. He does the thinking. He does the writing. He does everything — and it's really hard — sometimes it's a broken pencil. He has to sharpen it a little more. But be a little instrument in His hands so that He can use you anytime, anywhere. . . . We have only to say Yes to Him."[8]

When are the seeds for that kind of ministering planted and in what settings are they nourished? Among the Young Women Values is Good Works, which states, "We will nurture others and build the kingdom through righteous service." A letter from one young woman provides a prescription for all of us: it describes the steps and displays the fruits of service, which blesses both the server and the one being served. She writes: "Last year in my junior high school year I set a goal in Good Works; to try to help someone in some little way every day, whether it was something that I did or just said or an example that I set. I decided to do this prayerfully, so every day before I went to school I prayed and I asked Heavenly Father, let me have the influence of the Spirit to know what I should do or say." She reports that these small acts of service changed not only her attitude about herself but her attitude toward others. "I began to see how everything we do affects others. . . . I began to feel better about myself and at the same time more humble. . . . Through my actions I began to have a different outlook on all my brothers and my sisters. Everyone should be treated with respect. Through my daily efforts I feel as though I am beginning to understand what love can really be."

A feeling of wanting to reach out beyond ourselves falls like gentle rain on parched soil on those days when we may feel useless or worthless or unfulfilled or maybe even bored or lonely. It answers our deeper spiritual needs. With charity in our hearts, we can go out beyond the borders of our own comfort zone; we can let our influence be felt for righteousness in circles where we may not initially be familiar or at ease. Charity is the key. A prayerful heart gives the direction.

When we learn to listen to the Spirit in answer to our prayers, our service becomes customized by the Spirit and we'll do things that we might not otherwise have known to do. At Christmastime one year I talked to a widow on her doorstep. "My freezer is full of goodies," she said. "And obviously I don't need them," she added with a laugh as she looked down at her expanding waistline. Then she commented wistfully, "But you don't really see the lights on Temple Square unless you go there with a family." She would have traded all of the cakes and cookies for such an invitation. When we seek direction of the Spirit, our labors will be more meaningful — and maybe even require less effort.

The value and far-reaching effect of our service, however small, has nothing to do with our age or material wealth. It has to do with our willingness to give of our time and be led by the Spirit. Many lives will be healed and blessed when we reach out in a spirit of love and concern. I think of a little girl who visited a neighbor's house where her little friend had died. "Why did you go?" questioned her father. "To comfort her mother," she said. "What could you do to comfort her?" "I climbed into her lap and cried with her," she said.

Our "Jericho Roads" may be just across the street, but they're there for each of us as we travel toward home.

Carolyn J. Rasmus

In Nauvoo the Prophet Joseph Smith taught that life is like a huge wagon wheel. Like the wheel, all of us at some time will find ourselves on the bottom, needing someone to pull us up. But as life evolves, like the revolving wheel, there will be times when we're on top of the wheel and can reach down and help lift others up. These are times when we can cheer and bless in humanity's name.

I want to share the process that has caused me to look at the whole idea of welfare in a different way. When Elaine Jack was sustained as Relief Society General President in April Conference 1990, she paid tribute to Ardeth Kapp as "a great woman of vision, called by the Lord to lead the young women around the world at a most critical time."[9] I too believe that Ardeth is a woman of vision. Every August, after our July break, Sister

Kapp shares her vision of our work for the coming year. Last year she spoke of developing attitudes of welfare among our youth, of caring for one another, serving one another and reaching out to one another. "We must," she said, "instill an attitude of welfare among our youth. Youth are an incredible resource. They are a mighty force for righteousness. It is as if we have them in waiting — on hold. I see youth as a great reserve unit, a unit ready and trained in attitudes and ready for opportunities for service."

Then she talked about the enemies of our youth: feelings of isolation and loneliness, feelings of not being valued, feelings of worthlessness. Welfare activities answer that need. "Welfare activities," Sister Kapp explained, "can provide groupings that are not just social groupings. Activities which focus on helping people provide an ideal laboratory in which young men and young women may become better acquainted with each other." Welfare activities will also "instill feelings of provident living and caring for each other among our youth. Our youth won't come to a marriage relationship with an awareness of individuals and family welfare unless teachings begin at an early age."

Finally, she mentioned that we frequently speak of "service projects" and stressed the importance of focusing instead on an attitude of ministering instead of on just the "project." A service project is an activity: we do the activity, it is over, and nothing has changed — especially our hearts.

What Sister Kapp did on that day was to expand our vision of service. Often when we speak to youth or adults and say the word *service,* they respond, "Oooh no, not another service project." Part of that is the way we as leaders look at service: do we view it as a project, or do we promote ministering to others as an attitude — one which pervades our everyday relations with others? Can you imagine what would happen if everyone determined right now to do something that could bless and cheer in humanity's name?

You may ask, "How can I get a sixteen-year-old to want to be involved in any kind of service for anyone else when a sixteen-year-old's world typically revolves only around self? That can be a challenge, but it is usually done when the sixteen-year-olds are in groups where caring relationships can be built. Recently we received an outline of community service projects performed by Brazil area youth. We saw videos of young people: 250 young women and young men cleaned and planted trees at the police district; eighty cleaned the grounds of an avenue; 150 spent hours at the orphanage; 260 spent the day at a hospital playing with the sick children, some of whom had AIDS; 160 cleaned a public school, including the walls. We saw them working, and the change in the school was wonderful. Serving becomes fun when youth have opportunities to work together and to build caring relationships. Fun is an attitude, not an activity.

After our board meeting last August, I began to look at scriptures in a new way. I saw a pattern I had never seen before. In Mosiah 18 we read of Alma's preaching to a group gathered at the waters of Mormon. He preaches faith in the Lord, repentance, and redemption and asks if they are willing "to bear one another's burdens . . . to mourn with those that mourn . . . comfort those that stand in need of comfort, and to stand as witnesses of God at all times and in all things, and in all places." (Mosiah 18:7–9.)

Usually I stop there, but one day I continued reading, "Now I [Alma] say unto you, if this be the desire of your hearts, what have you against being baptized in the name of the Lord, as a witness before him that ye have entered into a covenant with him, that ye will serve him and will keep his commandments, that he may pour out his Spirit more abundantly upon you?" (V. 10.) In other words, when we are baptized, we make a covenant with the Lord. We covenant to "serve him and keep his commandments." We — those of us who are members of his church — have already made a covenant to serve.

In a recent conference address, Elder Derek A. Cuthbert responded to the question, "How may I become more spiritual?" by explaining that we experience the Spirit when we serve. He then described ten specific ways in which service changes people, making them more spiritual.[10] As Alma promised, "Serve him and keep his commandments, that he may pour out his Spirit more abundantly upon you." (Mosiah 18:10.)

Moroni teaches this same principle. Referring to requirements for baptism, Moroni says, "And none were received unto baptism save they took upon them the name of Christ, *having a determination to serve him to the end.*" (Moroni 6:3; italics added.) That is what each of us covenanted to do when we were baptized.

The pattern is repeated again in the Doctrine and Covenants. "And again, by way of commandment to the church concerning the manner of baptism — All those who humble themselves before God, and desire to be baptized, and come forth with broken hearts and contrite spirits, and witness before the church that they have truly repented of all their sins, and are willing to take upon them the name of Jesus Christ, *having a determination to serve him to the end* . . . shall be received by baptism into his church." (D&C 20:37; italics added.) The principle is repeated over and over: When we are baptized, we covenant to serve him and he covenants with us that he will pour out his Spirit upon us.

I began also to reread old articles in new ways. One of my very favorites is an article by President Spencer W. Kimball entitled "Small Acts of Service." Remember what Mother Teresa said about being a little pencil in God's hand? Listen to President Kimball's words: "God does notice us, and he watches over us. But it is usually through another person that he meets our needs."[11] Could you be that other person? Could you be used as an instrument in the hands of God to serve someone else?

Another article I read in a new light was a general conference address by William R. Bradford called "Selfless Service." The subheading summarized the message: "Many things are only interesting and enticing, while other things are important."

"What *does* matter? What *is* important?" I asked myself.

My friend Kathryn and I live together. We had planned to see *Driving Miss Daisy* on the last day of our vacations. Everyone was talking about that movie and wondering if it was going to win an Academy Award. We wanted to see it. Besides going to movies, one of the things I love to do when I have time off work is to bake bread. I got carried away; that afternoon I baked eight loaves instead of four. (There is something therapeutic about having my hands in dough. I think it replaces the mud we played in as children.) We had about thirty minutes before we were to leave for the movie. I said to Kathy, "It's going to take us a long time to eat eight loaves of bread. Why don't we take one over to the Campbells?" This was during the heated debate in the state legislature about teachers' salaries. Our across-the-street neighbor, Jim Campbell, was president of the Utah Education Association and the focus of a lot of controversy. We decided the Campbells could use a loaf of bread. We rang the doorbell; Jim's wife, Barbara, came to the door. As we handed her the bread, she started to cry. She was home alone and had been for several days and nights. She said to us, "*Please* come in." I wondered what we would talk about, but I needn't have—all we had to do was listen.

When we left we felt so good we said, "Let's give away another loaf of bread. We have time now before the *second* showing of the movie." We debated about going to our next-door neighbors because only two days before their son had been convicted of sexually molesting children and was in the state prison. What would we say to his parents? We didn't know, and, I suppose, to be honest, we took the bread as an excuse because we didn't know how to start a conversation. We rang the doorbell. The father came to the door and said, "Please, *please* come in. Nobody has talked to us. We've got to talk to somebody." We listened for more than an hour to a mother and father, whose hearts were breaking, tell us about their son. When we got ready to leave, they hugged us. As we returned home Kathy said, "We missed the second showing, but who cares!"

Listen to what Elder Bradford says about selfless service. "They are not one-time events based on entertainment, fun, and games. Selfless service is people to people projects, face to face, eye to eye, voice to ear, heart to heart, spirit to spirit, hand in hand, people to people."[12] I began thinking how I might change an attitude of "projects" to one of ministering.

My mother is a member of the Lutheran Church. In an effort to cheer and bolster her, I send her things I think will be uplifting. I try and put something in the mail every week — something from the *Ensign* or the *New Era* along with a few other "thoughts to ponder." A year ago I gave her a calendar book published by *Guideposts Magazine* simply titled *Guideposts*. Every day features a thought. I bought the same book for myself so I could read what I knew she would be reading. When I called her she would frequently say, "Did you read the thought on Tuesday?" Often she would ask for my thoughts about it; sometimes I would ask her. About midyear there were three pages in the middle of the book labeled, "Thank You Notes to God." On these pages were blank lines numbered one through thirty. I wondered if she would fill in these pages. I thought she might just skip over them, but about a week later she mailed to me those three pages torn from her book. My mother is eighty-five; my father is in a nursing home. Listen to what my mother wrote as her "Thank You Notes to God." Think about the "small acts of service" that made a difference in my mother's life:

A telephone call from Mildred

A visit from Anita

A magazine from Kay

A visit with a friendly person in the mall

My family

Carolyn's concern

Lunch at Kay's

A call from Mark

A call from Evelyn

A call from Vera

A visit from our cousins in Detroit
A day of rest
A telephone call from Anita
A card from Carolyn
Meals on wheels
A telephone call from Kay
I called a friend of a friend
I'm able to get around
I had a telephone visit with Mark
I'm thankful my sister can drive
Carolyn's call was what I needed
And the last note said simply, "Thank you for your love."

Each of the things my mother was thankful for cost little if any money and took practically no time. Mother called me this past Tuesday and said, "Mark [my brother] came and took the garbage out." Do you know what it is like to take garbage out when you are eighty-five and need to hold a cane in one hand? It may not seem like a big thing, but it was enough of an event for her to call me and tell me how grateful she was.

Where do we begin? Ardeth referred to Doctrine and Covenants 64:33: "Be not weary in well-doing, for ye are laying the foundation of a great work. And out of small things proceedeth that which is great." I want to focus on the next verse, which tells us, "Behold, the Lord requireth the heart and a willing mind." How do we begin? By simply being willing. Would you be *willing* to write a note? Would you be *willing* to make a phone call? In the next five seconds, would you jot down the name of one person whose life you could bless or cheer today?

If you wrote down a name, you're willing. That's all that is asked of us, to be willing. The scriptures admonish us to be "anxiously engaged in a good cause, . . . [that we might] bring to pass much righteousness." (D&C 58:27.) Look around. If each of us listened, or smiled, or wrote a note, or made a phone call to just one person, we will have blessed and cheered in humanity's name.

41

The following experiences reflect the attitude of ministering we are hoping to encourage.

Sister Kapp

Last fall I was away from my home during the period of time when it would have been nice to plant tulip bulbs and daffodils. I felt a bit sad as I looked at the dark earth and realized that no bulbs would burst forth and announce spring. But on my birthday, in the middle of March, I walked out into my front yard and saw three daffodils. I wondered how that happened. I didn't remember planting daffodils. When did they come up? The next day I found more daffodils and before long discovered tulips! They sprang up every day in different places, and every morning I ran out to see what was coming up out of my ground, which to my knowledge was void of bulbs or seeds. Those seeds of love had been planted in the fall by a friend. Different plants continued coming up to delight and surprise me for about two weeks, and then a little card arrived that said, "Happy Birthday! I thought the flowers would be an announcement for spring and wanted to share spring with you this year." What a surprise. What a gift of love and service.

Sister Rasmus

Not long ago I participated in a Young Women event in Hooper, Utah, where a sixteen-year-old girl spoke. I was so impressed with what she said that I asked her to write it down and send it to me. I share with you what Kristy McCarther learned about serving others:

"Sometimes we think that the only recognition is either a certificate or book or a necklace. But the experience and knowledge you gain from serving others is far better than any award you could receive. This last summer I set a goal to help both my grandmas keep their lawns mowed and watered. Even though they would not accept at first that I only wanted to do it to help them, they were always waiting and expected me to come. At times it wasn't my favorite thing to do, but I knew they wanted me there and that helped me know that it was right. . . . I learned the value of giving good works and service to others. I'm thankful for the Young Women program."

Sister Kapp

I have a friend in San Francisco who has had a kidney transplant. She has been on a dialysis machine for a number of years. She keeps track of everyone from the confines of her home. Two or three weeks ago I received a letter from Irene. Inside the letter was a greeting card that was addressed to Freda Harms. Irene enclosed a note to me:

"Dear Ardie,

"I know you're busy, so you may not be aware that our dear Sister Harms in her older years is suffering from a severe illness. I know she would love to have a card from you. I have addressed and stamped it. Would you just sign your name and send it on?"

Sister Rasmus

There are people with needs and there are people with resources; the challenge is getting them together. I had a need. I was going to be away on an assignment in Australia for three weeks and my mother, with whom I talk on the phone several times a week, couldn't imagine how she was going to survive without hearing from me. I prayed to know how we could stay close while we didn't have telephone contact.

For years I have been asking her to write her family history. I had given her a journal, I had given her blank books, and I had given her loose-leaf pages. She kept saying, "I don't know what to write. Who cares about my life?" Before I left for Australia I sat at the computer and typed about fifty questions. They were simple things like, "What was it like when you went to school?" "What do you remember about your grandmother?" "Do you remember your first Christmas tree?" and on and on. With the questions I sent her about fifty stamped postcards that were addressed to me but blank on the other side. Can you imagine what it meant to me when I got home from Australia to find twenty-four postcards in my mail box? They were all in my mother's handwriting. Last year she wrote on each postcard a precious memory, a bit of important history.

Somehow I wanted to share this heritage with my brother and my niece and nephew. I typed the information, had the pages bound, and titled the resulting book *Post Card Jottings,* by Ella P. Rasmus. I added "Volume I" because I did not want Mother to think she was finished with this project. It has made a difference to me, and I find it has made a difference to her as she thinks back on wonderful things that have happened in her life. She sent me another postcard just a couple of weeks ago. She is working on Volume II — what she remembers about my brother and me when we were children.

"When Carolyn was about one year old, two ladies came to our door selling a set of children's books. They said, 'You should have been reading to your baby the day you came home from the hospital.' I was really worried. Was it too late? So I ordered the set and really read to her, making up for lost time. I guess that is why you came to be such an avid reader. Much love, your mother."

Sister Kapp

Two years ago at Christmastime, when the calendar was full and the schedules were tight and the streets were full of people rushing here and there, I was invited to go to the rest home to visit some elderly people. I looked at my busy calendar and thought, "If I can just rush over and give a quick message, I can get back and hardly lose a minute." I rushed to the rest home, turned my car off, ran in, caught my breath just as I got to the door, and walked into a place where time was moving at a different pace — if it was moving at all. I was ushered into a room where tired shoulders were covered with shawls and tired feet were enclosed in slippers and heads drooped. I gave my short message and wondered what I could have said that might have made any difference at all.

I was ready to rush back into the busy world when a woman who was there visiting her grandmother asked apologetically, "Would you have a minute to talk to my grandmother? She thinks she knows you." Her look told me that she felt her grandmother's mind was perhaps even more tired than her body. I said, "Certainly I would." I followed them as they shuffled down the hall together. I hadn't noticed this woman in the audience. When we got to her room she plopped her tired body down onto the bed and raised her eyes to meet mine. I said, "Sister Dudley! Sister Dudley, you were my Primary teacher." She tugged on her granddaughter's jacket. "See, I told you she would know me." And then more memories came tumbling back and I said, "I remember when you made carrot juice for my mother. I remember when you wore that maroon dress with the big sleeves that waved back and forth when you taught us songs in Primary." She tugged on her granddaughter's jacket again. "I told you she would know me." Then she opened her arms and drew me close to her, and I felt like a child in the arms of my Primary teacher again. She asked, "Did you come all the way from Canada to see me?" "Oh, Sister Dudley," I said, "it has been forty years, but I'm here." "I knew you would know me," she whispered as she held me close.

I lingered. I left more slowly. I had a new insight, and as I walked out and sat in my car for a moment, I thought of Sister Dudley. Sister Dudley knew me because she had served me. And I knew Sister Dudley because she had served me. I began to ponder another time in the future when we will give an accounting. I think our Father will know us because we have served him. And equally important, we will know our Father because we have served him — each of us in our own way, appropriate to our own circumstance. One day we might all say, "I told you he would know me."

Sister Rasmus

I share a note from Elder and Sister Humphreys, a missionary couple serving in eastern Nigeria:

45

"Shortly after our arrival in Etinan, I was practicing on a portable organ when Otobong came to our apartment door to visit a former missionary couple. Otobong showed a real interest in the organ and I seized the opportunity when she indicated a desire to play. My invitation to Otobong was, 'Let us learn together.' Otobong came every Tuesday for a lesson and at least four times each week to practice. This wonderful sixteen-year-old sister learned very quickly and soon could read the notes and play the melody line. Within three weeks Otobong could play the tune as I sang along to help keep the correct time. The chords were learned quickly and in eight weeks Otobong was playing approximately ten hymns without any hesitation."

Because a young woman showed an interest and a woman took time, this young sister now plays the piano and serves her branch as organist. "Sister Otobong continues to play and teach others not only in her branch but throughout her own and other districts."

Sister Kapp

Sometimes we feel that we need to do it all—and all at once. But that is not the case. When we give what we have according to our time, according to our energy, according to where we are at this moment in our development, then the Lord will take what we have to offer and he will make up the difference. That is the grace of God.

The dictionary in the LDS edition of the King James Bible defines *grace* as "an enabling power that allows women and men to lay hold of eternal life and exaltation after they have expended their own best efforts." (P. 697.) So whenever you read in your scriptures the word *grace,* replace it with the words *enabling power.* We know that it is by grace that we are saved after all that we can do, and the Lord knows how far, how much, and what is appropriate for us to do. He will guide us, bring peace to our heart, and remove the guilt, because there will be other seasons to do other things.

On one occasion I remember feeling overwhelmed by my sister who had ten children. I wondered, what am I doing that matters? And my father's voice came into my mind, as though he were sitting with me, though he had been dead for years (maybe it was his mission to be a ministering angel to me that day), "My dear, don't worry about the little things; just do the big things you agreed to before you came." God bless us to keep our eye on the big things that we agreed to and not be distracted by the little things that will not strengthen us spiritually. May God bless us to experience the joy of service in this great sisterhood and find the peace "that passeth all understanding" in the gospel of Jesus Christ.

Sister Rasmus

As you read your scriptures, be mindful of a phrase that is repeated again and again, usually at times of battle when the people of the Lord were so outnumbered that there appeared to be no way they could ever win the battle. The phrase is simply, "And they went forth in the strength of the Lord." That is how we will win our battles today, be they personal or societal. Of this I have a strong witness and a testimony. We are empowered and enabled and strengthened beyond all we can do because of our faith in our Lord, Jesus Christ. In his strength we can do all things.

Notes

1. Spencer W. Kimball, "Privileges and Responsibilities of Sisters," *Ensign*, Nov. 1978, p. 103.
2. Ezra Taft Benson, *Teachings of Ezra Taft Benson* (Salt Lake City: Bookcraft, 1988), p. 261.
3. Thomas S. Monson, "Conference Is Here," *Ensign*, May 1990, pp. 4–5.
4. Derek A. Cuthbert, "The Spirituality of Service," *Ensign*, May 1990, pp. 12–13.
5. Hans B. Ringger, "Choose You This Day," *Ensign*, May 1990, p. 26.
6. Neal A. Maxwell, "Endure It Well," *Ensign*, May 1990, p. 34.
7. John A. Widtsoe, "The Worth of Souls," *Utah Genealogical and Historical Magazine*, Oct. 1934, p. 189.

8. Mother Teresa, "Love: A Fruit Always in Season," *Daily Meditations* (San Francisco: Ignatius Press, 1987), p. 243.

9. Elaine L. Jack, "I will Go and Do," *Ensign*, May 1990, p. 78.

10. Cuthbert, "The Spirituality of Service," pp. 12–13.

11. Spencer W. Kimball, "Small Acts of Service," *Ensign*, Dec. 1974, p. 5.

12. William R. Bradford, "Selfless Service," *Ensign*, Nov. 1987, p. 75.

Eve's Role in the Creation and the Fall to Mortality

JOLENE EDMUNDS ROCKWOOD

For more than two thousand years, Eve has been blamed for woes ranging from the origin of sin to the presumed inferiority of the female sex. Much of this tradition has been so ingrained in our Judeo-Christian culture that we are often unaware of its presence or origin. Because of Eve, women have been cursed, their subordination to man has been justified, and their feminine weaknesses have been stereotyped—all because of a short section of Hebrew poetry in Genesis 1–3 which tells the highly symbolic story of the beginnings of time.

Like Genesis, the Latter-day Saint scriptural accounts in Moses and Abraham are figurative rather than historical stories. We know that the Creation and the Fall did occur and that Adam and Eve were real people, but all the other elements of the story—the serpent, the tree, the fruit, the rib story—all are symbols.

Church leaders have reiterated this truth numerous times. Spencer W. Kimball, for instance, as president of the Church, stated that the rib story was figurative.[1] Brigham Young, Joseph Smith, Joseph Fielding Smith, and others stated that Adam and Eve's bodies were engendered and born by natural sexual functioning and that they were placed in Eden as adult beings.[2]

Jolene Edmunds Rockwood received her master of theological studies from the Harvard Divinity School. She is a widely known lecturer and coauthor of Sisters in Spirit. *She is the founder and president of the Rural Alliance for the Arts in Indiana. Sister Rockwood is a homemaker and resides with her husband, Fred, and their six children in Batesville, Indiana, where she serves as her ward's Young Women president.*

Orson Pratt and, more recently, Hugh Nibley taught that the pair were tempted on numerous occasions, not only by the serpent but by other "beings" who had been "angels of light and truth" in the premortal existence but had then become followers of Satan.³ Other Latter-day Saint authorities have taught that Adam and Eve became mortal by eating a substance that was poisonous to their immortal systems and that the tree and the fruit were symbols representing the process by which the Fall came about.⁴

Symbolism has always been used to focus attention away from historical facts to the meaning behind the events. What, then, was the intended meaning of the Adam and Eve story? An examination of the original Hebrew text of Genesis 1–5 answers this question as it brings out some very interesting points that can help us understand Eve and the role she played in the Creation and the Fall.

First, Adam and Eve were created symbolically as two equal parts of one unified whole and were united in all their actions. The word translated as *man* is the Hebrew *'adam,* meaning "humankind," or man in a collective sense.⁵ It is used throughout most of the story rather than the more specific Hebrew noun *'ish,* meaning "one man," or "husband." The plural sense of *ha-'adam* is seen when it is used with "them," a plural pronoun, in "Let us make *man* in our image . . . and let *them* have dominion. . . . So God created *man* . . . male and female created he *them.*" (Genesis 1:26–27.)⁶

Many verses in the Book of Mormon indicate similar usage of *adam* and *man* as plural nouns. In 2 Nephi 9:6, *man* is used as a plural for the first couple, just as in the Hebrew version of Genesis: "And because *man* became fallen *they* were cut off from the presence of the Lord" (italics added).

Church authorities have also generally affirmed that the Genesis account describes the first couple as united in their actions in Eden and have recognized *'adam* as a plural word representing both the man and the woman. For example, Erastus Snow, a member of the Quorum of the Twelve, said

50

in 1878: "Male and female created he them and called their name Adam, which in the original in which these scriptures were written by Moses, signifies 'the first man.' There was no effort at distinguishing between the one half and the other, and calling one man and the other woman. This was an after distinction, but the explanation of it is—one man, one being, and he called their name Adam."[7] Spencer W. Kimball made a similar scriptural gloss in 1976:

"'And I, God, blessed them [Man here is always in the plural. It was plural from the beginning.] . . . ' (Moses 2:27–28.) . . .

"'And I, God said unto mine Only Begotten, which was with me from the beginning: Let us make man [not a separate man, but a complete man, which is husband and wife] in our image . . . ' (Moses 2:26.) . . .

"'Male and female created he them; and blessed them, and called their name Adam [Mr. and Mrs. Adam, I suppose, or Brother and Sister Adam], in the day when they were created.' (Gen. 5:12.)."[8]

The unity of Adam and Eve is further clarified in the "rib" story where the Hebrew words translated *help meet* and *rib* shed light on the author's intent.

The Lord states, "It is not good that the man [collective] should be alone; I will make him an help meet for him." (Genesis 2:18.) This phrase "help meet" (Hebrew *'ezer kenegdo*) is an interesting one. *'Ezer*, which in this context is translated as "help" (meaning "helper"), has the unfortunate connotation in English of an assistant of lesser status, a subordinate, or inferior—for instance, a willing but not very competent child.[9] In Hebrew, however, the word describes an equal, if not a superior. The other usages of *'ezer* in the Old Testament show that in most cases God is an *'ezer* to human beings,[10] a fact which makes us question whether "helper" is an accurate translation in *any* of the instances it is used. A more accurate translation in this context would be "strength" or "power." Evidence indicates that the word *'ezer* originally had two roots, each beginning with different guttural sounds.[11] Over time, the two gutturals were merged into one word, but the two meanings, "to save" and "to be strong," remained. Later, the meanings also merged into one word, "to help." Therefore, if we use the more archaic meanings of *'ezer,* and translate *'ezer* as either "savior" or "strength," we clarify not only the context we are discussing but also the other passages in the Old Testament where *'ezer* is used, especially when *'ezer* refers to God in his relationship with humankind.

'Ezer translated as "strength" or "power" also fits in nicely with the second word in the phrase, *kenegdo*, which has traditionally been translated as "meet for" or "fit for." Because *kenegdo* appears only this one time in the Old Testament, earlier translators had little upon which to base their translations. An important clue to the meaning of this word is found in its usage in Mishnaic Hebrew, where the root means "equal." *Kenegdo*, then, means "equal to" and the entire phrase *'ezer kenegdo* means "power or strength equal to." Thus, when God makes *ha-'adam* into two beings, he creates woman, a power or strength equal to man.

The King James translation of *kenegdo* as "meet for" is based on the seventeenth-century meaning of *meet*, "worthy of," a meaning no longer in current English usage. This archaic translation has led uninformed readers over the years to hyphenate the noun and adjective as "help-meet," detach the sense of "meet for," and then develop the neologism "help-mate," a term that never existed either in the original Hebrew or in the King James version. The phrase has, however, become so much a part of the Christian vernacular that references to wives as help-meets and help-mates are common.

The Lord then removes a "rib" from which he forms man's companion. (Genesis 2:21–22.) The Hebrew *sela'* is used more than forty times in the Old Testament to mean "side"; only in this passage has it been translated as "rib." Nearly every other usage gives construction details for the tabernacle or temple (i.e., *side* of the tabernacle, *side* of the altar, etc.).[12]

Sela' in Genesis 1:21–22 thus should be similarly read as construction information, though the object being constructed is a life form. The Lord, as master builder, takes the "side" (*sela'*) of the human and uses it to "build" (*banah*) another person. Reading *sela'* as "side" rather than as "rib" also better dramatizes the unity of the man and the woman, enhances the phrase "power equal to him," and makes the man's later characterization of woman as "bone of my bone and flesh of my flesh" even more meaningful. Thus, when God causes the human to sleep, he takes one of his sides and creates two beings out of one.

When the two are presented to one another as companions, the man seems to react with surprise and delight[13]: "This is now bone of my bones, and flesh of my flesh: she shall be called Woman, because she was taken out of Man." (Genesis 2:23.) Up to this point, the human has been *ha-'adam*. Now the words *man* (*'ish*) and *woman* (*'ishah*) are used for the first time. These are definite nouns that signify man and woman as separate individuals with gender. In addition, the man uses the feminine *zo't* ("this") for the first time: ("This is now bone of my bones").[14] The man at this point is not naming the woman, however. *Issah* is not a name; it is a common noun that designates gender. The word appears also in the previous verse. The man is actually making a pun on the origin of woman. As the human (*ha-'adam*) received his existence from the earth (*ha-'adamah*), now the man (*'ish*) has been used to form the woman (*'ishah*).[15]

The honorific and descriptive title *Eve* (or *Life*) is found in the book of Moses. The Lord states: "And worlds without number have I created; . . . And the first man of all men have I called Adam, which is *many*. . . . And Adam called his wife's name Eve, because she was the mother of all living; for thus have I, the Lord God, called the first of all women, which are *many*."(Moses 1:33–34; 4:26; italics added.) *Adam* and *Eve* appear to be general titles that the Creator had used numerous times to signify the first parents of a world. Adam, then, did

53

not name Eve. Adam uses her title in a way similar to the Near Eastern formula for titles given to goddesses.[16] He was calling her by her title, previously conferred by God. In the book of Moses, Moses calls the woman Eve even before Adam does. (Moses 4:6.)

It is significant that the man calls the woman "bone of my bones, and flesh of my flesh," a statement he could not have made about the animals. In Hebrew, these phrases indicate a closeness, a blood relationship between the two parties, and in this case a unified companionship between the man and the woman. But the phrases are also used in other places in the Old Testament to describe two parties who are not necessarily blood relatives but who have made a covenant with David, their new king, confirming it by saying, "Behold, we are thy bone and thy flesh." (2 Samuel 5:1.) David makes a similar covenant with the elders of Judah: "Ye are my brethren, ye are my bones and my flesh," referring to a covenant the two parties have made with each other. (2 Samuel 19:12.)[17]

The word for *bone* in Hebrew symbolizes power, and the word for *flesh* signifies weakness. "Bone of my bones and flesh of my flesh" thus becomes a ritual pledge to be bound in the best of circumstances (power) as well as in the worst (weakness). The man's use of this phrase in Genesis 2:23 implies a covenant similar to a marriage agreement and is, in fact, reminiscent of the phrase "for better or for worse" used in marriage vows. Thus it would be a mistake to read this verse as an expression of Eve's "subordination" (totally "derived" from Adam) or as an expression of Adam's possessiveness (she is "his" because she is part of him). Instead it acknowledges a total union of two creatures who have both strength and weakness.

Latter-day Saint authorities have persistently taught that Adam and Eve were sealed by an eternal marriage covenant, paralleling the Hebrew sense of the phrase "bone of my bones." Orson Pratt, an apostle, preached in 1875 that God himself officiated in a "marriage for eternity" linking Adam and Eve.[18]

"What a beautiful partnership!" exclaimed Spencer W. Kimball in 1975. "Adam and Eve were married for eternity by the Lord. Such a marriage extends beyond the grave."[19]

Another interesting point in the Hebrew is that until the woman and the man actually partake of the fruit, the use of plural Hebrew pronouns in the text indicates a union in their actions. The serpent addresses the woman with the plural Hebrew *you* form, and she replies with the plural *we* and *us*: "And he [the serpent] said unto the woman, Yea, hath God said, *Ye* [plural Hebrew] shall not eat of every tree of the garden? And the woman said unto the serpent, *We* may eat of the fruit of the trees of the garden: But of the fruit of the tree which is in the midst of the garden, God hath said, *Ye* [Hebrew plural] shall not eat of it, neither shall *ye* touch it, lest *ye* [Hebrew plural] die. And the serpent said unto the woman, *Ye* [Hebrew plural] shall not surely die." (Genesis 3:1–4.) After she partook of the fruit, she then gave some to "her man" (King James Version, *husband*) who was "with her." (Genesis 3:6.)[20]

The use of the plural pronouns *you, we,* and *us* and the phrase "her man" and "[who was] with her" imply that they are still united in thought and action. We can infer, consequently, that whatever action one would take, the other would take also. The same wording appears in the book of Moses as in the Hebrew text. (Moses 4:7–12.)

In Genesis 3:8–24, after the fruit has been eaten, the unity of the man and woman becomes suddenly separateness. Adam and Eve use the singular Hebrew pronouns for the first time as the Lord confronts them: "*I* heard thy voice in the garden, and *I* was afraid, because *I* was naked; and *I* hid *myself*," explains Adam, speaking only for himself. (Genesis 3:10.) Adam's shift to first person singular is even more interesting when we realize that both the man and the woman heard God's voice, both were afraid, and both of them hid. Although their actions are identical, their unity is ruptured. Eve also uses the first person singular to answer the Lord's question: "the serpent beguiled *me*, and *I* did eat." (Genesis 3:13.)

55

Thus, the Hebrew text clearly indicates that Adam and Eve were united in their actions before the Fall. Latter-day Saint church leaders as well have generally affirmed that the Genesis account describes the first couple as united in their actions in Eden. Because Latter-day Saint doctrine regards the Fall to mortality as an essential part of the premortal plan and finds the first parents "sacrificing" their immortality that mankind might be, both the man and the woman have been treated as equally responsible for the transgression. Brigham Young and others taught that Adam had a knowledge of the plan of salvation dating to his premortal existence as a spirit without a body and was foreordained to partake of the fruit as the "design of the Lord."[21] Eve must also have been foreordained for, as we have seen, they acted in unison. Elder Bruce McConkie stated that "Christ and Mary, Adam and Eve, Abraham and Sarah, and a host of mighty men and equally glorious women comprised that group of 'the noble and great ones,' to whom the Lord Jesus said: '*We* will go down, for there is space there, and *we* will take of these materials, and *we* will make an earth whereon these may dwell.' (Abraham 3:22–24.)"[22]

Many Church authorities have stated that both Adam and Eve shared the transgression in Eden. Throughout the Book of Mormon, the transgression is almost always referred to as Adam's, suggesting that '*adam* was probably used in the Hebrew sense to designate the first couple as a unit.[23] In 2 Nephi 2:18–26, Eve is singled out, but as the object of temptation by Satan, to whom the guilt is assigned. Doctrine and Covenants 29:36, 40 states that "*Adam* [was] tempted of the devil" and "partook of the forbidden fruit" (italics added), indicating that the name is being used as a collective word for Adam and Eve as a unit. Because of this unity, who was tempted first or who yielded first becomes irrelevant; they both were acting as one.

The judgments the Lord pronounced upon them after they partook of the fruit were essentially the same. The serpent is the only one who is directly cursed. When we view this text as a structural element of the story, these judgments are shown to be statements of cause and effect, which describe the result of the mortal condition. God's descriptions of mortality parallel the earlier warning in Genesis 2:17 that mortality will result in a knowledge of good and evil (thus a loss of innocence), and death. Here he instructs them more about their new state: the man must now labor by the sweat of his brow to survive. That is so because not only the man but all orders of creation fell to a mortal existence. The earth is now cursed (fallen) and will no longer automatically supply the man with all his needs. The plant kingdom will provide not only fruitful trees but also thistles and thorns. Subject to death, the man is told "unto dust shalt thou return." (Genesis 3:19.) Likewise, the woman has become mortal and must suffer the hardship and pain of bearing children.

Brigham Young University specialist in ancient scriptures, Hugh Nibley, felt the judgments the man and the woman received were identical: "To our surprise," he remarks, "the *identical* curse was placed on Adam [and Eve]. . . . For Eve, God 'will greatly multiply thy sorrow and thy conception. In sorrow shalt thou bring forth children.' The key is the word for sorrow, *tsavadh*, meaning to labor, to toil, to sweat, to do something very hard. To *multiply* does not mean to add or increase but to repeat over and over again; . . . Both the conception and the labor of Eve will be multiple; she will have many children. Then the Lord says to Adam, 'In *sorrow* shalt thou eat of [the bread of your labor] all the days of thy life.' . . . The identical word is used in both cases, the root meaning is to work hard . . . ; both the man and the woman must sorrow and both must labor. It means not to be sorry, but to have a hard time. . . . Both of them bring forth life with sweat and tears, and Adam is not the favored party. If his labor is not as severe as hers, it is more protracted."[24]

The "curse" for both the man and the woman, then, simply amounts to feeling the results of mortality, which made them imperfect, "carnal," and subject to temptation and sin. Many scriptures from the Book of Mormon state the same philosophy:

with mortality came sin, but the effects of sin can be overcome. In Mosiah 3:19 we read: "For the natural man is an enemy to God, and has been from the fall of Adam, and will be, forever and ever, unless he yields to the enticings of the Holy Spirit, and putteth off the natural man and becometh a saint through the atonement of Christ the Lord." That verse continues, enumerating the characteristics of the redeemed person; he or she "becometh as a child, submissive, meek, humble, patient, full of love, willing to submit to all things which the Lord seeth fit to inflict upon him [or her], even as a child doth submit to his [or her] father." The "natural" or fallen person does not spontaneously have these traits, for with mortality comes inequality in our relationships, pride, and a tendency toward selfishness rather than love.

Needless to say, all of these traits tend to create differences where there were none, to magnify small differences into great differences, and to reinforce the tendency toward hierarchy, division, and the rule of the "superior" over the perceived inferior. Any relationship in which one member "rules" over the other seems to be associated more with the fallen state than with the redeemed state.

Spencer W. Kimball, in discussing Genesis 3:16, redefined it: "I have a question about the word *rule*. It gives the wrong impression. I would prefer to use the word *preside* because that's what he does. A righteous husband presides over his wife and family."[25]

Doctrine and Covenants 121 sheds some light on the distinction between the words *rule* and *preside*. Oft-quoted as relevant to any situation in which a priesthood holder might be presumed to have some authority, whether ecclesiastically, maritally, paternally, or socially, it begins with a warning: "We have learned by sad experience that it is the nature and disposition of almost all men, as soon as they get a little authority, as they suppose, they will immediately begin to exercise unrighteous dominion." (V. 39.)

The contrasting "righteous dominion" is described a few

verses later: "No power or influence can or ought to be maintained by virtue of the priesthood, only by persuasion, by long-suffering, by gentleness and meekness, and by love un-feigned; By kindness, and pure knowledge, which shall greatly enlarge the soul without hypocrisy, and without guile.... Let thy bowels also be full of charity towards all men, and to the household of faith, and let virtue garnish thy thoughts un-ceasingly; then shall thy confidence wax strong in the presence of God; and the doctrine of the priesthood shall distill upon thy soul as the dew from heaven. The Holy Ghost shall be thy constant companion, and thy scepter an unchanging scepter of righteousness and truth; and thy dominion shall be an ever-lasting dominion, and without compulsory means it shall flow unto thee forever and ever." (Vv. 41–42, 45–46.)

Dominion based on "righteousness and truth ... *without compulsory means*" does not describe a relationship of sub-ordination. The goal of mortality is to overcome such "carnal" tendencies as unrighteous dominion and to strive for oneness in relationships with others and with God.

This is the Hebrew meaning for the heavily symbolic Adam and Eve story: that Adam and Eve were created as two incom-plete halves of one united whole, that they were united in their actions, and that both mutually sacrificed their immortality to bring about the Fall.

Genesis 2:24 summarizes their mortal situation: "Therefore shall a man leave his father and his mother, and shall cleave unto his wife: and they shall be one flesh." The man and the woman, who have just been created, have no physical father or mother in the story. But they symbolically represent all men and women. Male and female were created from one flesh; as separate individuals who are now companions to one another, they strive to again become as one in their relationship. Note that it is the man who leaves his parents and cleaves unto his wife. (Genesis 2:24.) In view of the patriarchal society in which this passage was written, one would instead expect to hear the reverse: a woman leaves her parents and cleaves unto her husband. Three important insights are, then, encapsulated in this summary statement: the woman is an independent and equal creation, marriage does not make her the possession of the man, and achieving oneness should be the common goal of both.

The book of Moses supplies more details about Adam and Eve after they were sent from the Garden of Eden. In Moses 5:1 we see Eve working alongside Adam in the fields; likewise in 5:12 we see Adam participating in the child rearing. The text further states that they prayed together, had children together, rejoiced for revelations, and grieved for their disobedient children together. Neither is silent; both speak freely. Neither blames the other for the transgression, but both share a view of the Fall as a great blessing: "Blessed be the name of God," rejoices Adam, "for because of *my* [not Eve's] transgression my eyes are opened, and in this life I shall have joy, and again in the flesh I shall see God. And Eve, his wife, heard all these things and was glad, saying: Were it not for our transgression we never should have had seed, and never should have known good and evil, and the joy of our redemption, and the eternal life which God giveth unto all the obedient." (Moses 5:2, 4, 10–11, 16, 27.)

Adam and Eve did not feel cursed; they recognized that the great blessings of mortality were now theirs. This sense of oneness and purpose has permeated Latter-day Saint doctrine since the beginning: from the oneness of the celestialized Father and Mother in Heaven, to the oneness of the Godhead, to the oneness that must exist among the Saints before Zion can be established before the second coming of Christ. "And the Lord called his people ZION because they were of one heart and one mind, and dwelt in righteousness." (Moses 7:18.)

Ida Smith, then director of the Brigham Young University Women's Research Institute, speaking at the BYU Women's Conference in 1980, said that a relationship in which inequality exists cannot be a celestial relationship: "A just God would not require the yoking of two unequal beings for eternity. . . . It is important for a woman to learn in this life her eternal role so that when she is sealed she will be prepared and ready — with all her heart — to function in and glorify that role. That means being ready and prepared to function as a full partner in a celestial team — without having to look *up* because of any feeling of inferiority, or look *down* because of any feeling of superiority, but look *across* into the eyes of an equally prepared, equally magnificent eternal mate." She maintained that the gospel of Christ should free men and women from the sexual stereotypes we sometimes attach to one another in mortality and pointed out that Christ openly displayed traits which have often been thought of as "feminine": he embraced children, openly wept, was gentle and compassionate. We have also many examples of intelligence, wisdom, and initiative, sometimes presumed to be masculine traits, in the great women of the Church.[26] Carolyn J. Rasmus, then administrative assistant to the president of BYU, in another address given at the same conference, corroborated: "The differences between men and women are designed to be complementary and unifying, not divisive and separating. The ultimate plan is for achievement of a perfect balance, with neither sex to be unduly emphasized."[27]

In conclusion, then, the Adam and Eve account in Genesis 1–3 must be viewed as a symbolic representation rather than as an historical account. Before the Fall the man and woman are united in equal stature before their creator. The rib (or side) story is symbolic of the completeness and perfection of their union. They both were mutually responsible for the Fall to mortality.

The judgments pronounced upon them by the Lord were not curses but symbolic statements about the essential characteristics of mortality for all humanity. To say that because of Eve all women are cursed is not only a misunderstanding of the intent of the Genesis story but also a misunderstanding of the eternal doctrine of free agency and personal responsibility. As a literal tenet of Latter-day Saint faith, Mormons "believe

61

that men [and women] will be punished for their own sins, and not for Adam's [and Eve's] transgression." (Articles of Faith 1:2.) Women and men feel the results of that transgression in that they are mortal and subject to imperfections of the flesh — sin, illness, fatigue, pain, etc. If we conclude that the judgments enumerated in Genesis 3:4–20 are results of the mortal condition, the implications are that first, these imperfections, such as pain in childbirth or man's "ruling" over woman, did not exist before the Fall and cannot be assumed to continue after mortality, and second, that we, like Adam and Eve, can strive to overcome our mortal weaknesses while still in mortality by understanding Christ's atonement and by obeying his commandments. The promise is that we will eventually be able to return to a state of unity and oneness with God and with others, similar to Adam and Eve's unity before the Fall.

Much depends on our pondering Eve's role in the Creation and the Fall to mortality. For only when we understand the real purpose and significance of the events in Eden can we truly appreciate the magnitude of the opportunity and challenge Jesus Christ gave to the sons and daughters of Adam and Eve when he commanded: "I say unto you, be one; and if ye are not one ye are not mine." (Doctrine and Covenants 38:27.)

Notes

1. Spencer W. Kimball, "The Blessings and Responsibilities of Womanhood," *Ensign*, Mar. 1976, p. 71.
2. Brigham Young, 9 Apr. 1852, in *Journal of Discourses*, 1:50; 23 Oct. 1853, in *Journal of Discourses*, 2:6; 20 Apr. 1856, in *Journal of Discourses*, 3:319; 9 Oct. 1859, in *Journal of Discourses*, 7:285; Orson Pratt, 13 Apr. 1856, in *Journal of Discourses*, 3:344; Joseph Fielding Smith, *Doctrines of Salvation*, 3 vols., comp. Bruce R. McConkie (Salt Lake City, Utah: Bookcraft, 1954–56) 1:97. The reader may note here and in many following instances that teachings in the doctrine of the Church and the accounts given in the books of Moses, Abraham, and Genesis may seem to differ from the depiction of the Creation and the Fall in the temple ceremony. The intent of the temple ceremony seems to be much the same as the intent of the Genesis account: to present ideas

through symbols and figurative language, which have many layers of meaning. It is perhaps appropriate that the Creation story in the temple is presented in a symbolic fashion, as the rest of the endowment is highly ritualistic and has numerous levels of meaning. To interpret the visual (film) depiction of the Creation and the Fall as only history rather than also as a figurative representation of underlying truths would deviate from the intent of the temple experience as a whole. One part cannot be interpreted as strictly symbolic and another as strictly historical. (See Boyd K. Packer, *The Holy Temple* [Salt Lake City, Utah: Bookcraft, 1980], pp. 38–41, on the symbolic nature of temple instruction.) Hyrum Andrus, in noting the difference between the temple portrayal and the books of Abraham and Moses said: "A study of the problem suggests that the temple ceremony gives merely a general *portrayal* and not an actual *account* of the creation." Hyrum Andrus, *God, Man and the Universe*, 2d ed., 4 vols. (Salt Lake City, Utah: Bookcraft, 1970), 1:333–34, footnote. This footnote does not appear in later editions. See also Packer, *Holy Temple,* pp. 191–94; John K. Edmunds, *Through Temple Doors*, 4th ed. (Salt Lake City, Utah: Bookcraft, 1979), pp. 73–74.

3. Orson Pratt, 22 Nov. 1873, in *Journal of Discourses,* 16:318; Hugh Nibley, "Patriarchy and Matriarchy," in *Blueprints for Living*, ed. Maren M. Mouritsen (Provo, Utah: Brigham Young University, 1980), p. 46.

4. See, for instance, Erastus Snow, 3 Mar. 1878, in *Journal of Discourses,* 19:271–72.

5. In English, *'adam* could have several different meanings, and ambiguity leading to inconsistency in English translations of Genesis. If *'adam* appears alone without the Hebrew definitive article *ha-* preceding it, it could mean either "man" as a collective (mankind, humanity) or "Adam" as a proper name. There are only two places in the text where it definitely occurs this way, and in both places the context dictates translation as a collective humankind: one is in Gen. 1:27 where *'adam* is used with a plural pronoun "them," and the other is in Gen. 2:5, where the presence of the negative before *'adam* would make translation of *'adam* as a proper name awkward: "there was not a man to till the ground." Three other places in the text are uncertain because the word *'adam* is preceded by a preposition which in Hebrew would eliminate the *ha:* 2:20, 3:17, and 3:21. See John Ellington, "Man and Adam in Genesis 1–5," *The Bible Translator* 30 (April 1979): 210–15; Gerhard Von Rad, *Genesis*, 2d Lussier, " *'Adam* in Genesis 1, 1–4, 24": 137–39.

6. *Ha-'adam* in the King James translation has been inconsistently translated, most often as a proper name, Adam. See Lussier, "*'Adam* in Genesis 1, 1–4,24": 137–39. For more extensive discussion of this and other issues relating to Hebrew usage, see Jolene Rockwood, "The Redemption of

Eve," in *Sisters in Spirit*, ed. Maureen Ursenbach Beecher and Lavina Fielding Anderson (Urbana and Chicago: University of Illinois Press, 1987), pp. 3–36.

7. Erastus Snow, 3 Mar. 1878, in *Journal of Discourses*, 19:269.

8. Kimball, p. 71; bracketed interpolations his.

9. Phyllis Trible, *God and the Rhetoric of Sexuality* (Philadelphia: Fortress Press, 1978), p. 90; also John L. McKenzie, "The Literary Characteristics of Genesis 2–3," *Theological Studies* 15 (1954):559; Clarence J. Voz, *Woman in Old Testament Worship* (Amsterdam: N.V. Verenigde Drukkerijen Judels and Brinkman-Delft, n.d.), p. 16.

10. From Voz, *Woman in Old Testament Worship*, p. 16: "Besides Genesis 2:18, 20, this word ['ezer] appears in the Old Testament nineteen times. Of these it is used once in a question. (Ps. 121:1—the answer to the question is given in the following verse in which it is said that one's help comes from the Lord.) It is used three times of man as a help, (Is. 30:5; Ezk. 12:14; Dn. 11:34), but in each instance it is clear that man's help is not effectual. (Dn. 11:34 could refer to God); fifteen times it is used of God as the one who brings succor to the needy and desperate. Thus, if one excluded Gen. 2:18, 20, it could be said that only God gives effectual help ('ezer) to man. . . . Viewing woman as created to be a subordinate assistant to man finds no basis in the word ('ezer)." See also Jean Higgins, "Anastasius Sinaita and the Superiority of the Woman," *Journal of Biblical Literature* 97, No. 2 (1978):255: "Of forty-five occurrences of the word in the LXX. [Septuagint], forty-two unmistakably refer to help from a stronger one."

11. R. David Freedman, "Woman, a Power Equal to Man," *Biblical Archaeology Review* 9 (January-February 1983):56–58.

12. A complete listing of usages is found in George V. Wigram, *The Englishman's Hebrew and Chaldee Concordance of the Old Testament*, 5th ed. (Grand Rapids, Mich.: Zondervan Publishing House, 1980), pp. 1073–74; see also Walter Brueggemann, "Of the Same Flesh and Bone (Gn. 2, 23a)" *Catholic Biblical Quarterly* 32 (1970): 532–42. Only two other usages refer to a human being: Job 18:12, where it is translated as "side" ("destruction shall be ready at his side"), and Jeremiah 20:10, which has uncertain meaning ("all my familiars [friends] watched for *my* halting [KJV], "for my *fall*" [RSV], or, "at my *side*"). *Sela'* refers to the side of a hill in 2 Samuel 16:13, but every other usage gives construction details for the tabernacle or temple.

13. James N. Robinson, ed., "The Apochryphan of John" and "The Gospel of Philip," in *The Nag Hammadi Library* (San Francisco: Harper & Row, 1977), pp. 110, 141; Louis Ginzberg, *The Legends of the Jews*, 12th ed., 7 vols. (1909; Philadelphia: Jewish Publication Society of America, 1937), 1:66.

14. Genesis 2:23; Trible, p. 97; John A. Bailey, "Initiation and the Primal Woman in Gilgamesh and Genesis 2–3," *Journal of Biblical Literature* 89 (1970): 142–43.
15. Trible, pp. 98, 100; McKenzie, pp. 556–59.
16. Isaac M. Kikawada, "Two Notes on Eve," *Journal of Biblical Literature* 91 (1972):33–37.
17. Brueggemann, pp. 532–42.
18. Orson Pratt, 11 July 1875, in *Journal of Discourses,* 18:48; see also Joseph Fielding Smith, *Doctrines of Salvation,* 1:115.
19. Kimball, p. 72.
20. Trible, pp. 112–13; Jean M. Higgins, "The Myth of Eve: The Temptress," *Journal of the American Academy of Religion* 44 (1976): 645–47.
21. Brigham Young, 3 June 1855, in *Journal of Discourses,* 2:302; Edward W. Tullidge, *The Women of Mormondom* (New York: Tullidge and Crandall, 1877), pp. 197–99, stated that Mother Eve chose to be the first to partake of the fruit to symbolize the great maternal sacrifice.
22. Bruce R. McConkie, "Eve and the Fall," in *Woman* (Salt Lake City, Utah: Deseret Book, 1979), p. 59.
23. See, for example, Mosiah 3:11, 19; 4:7; Alma 12:21–23; 22:12–14; 42:2–4; Helaman 14:16–17; Mormon 9:12. In some of these references, Adam and Eve are mentioned together as the first parents. See also 1 Nephi 5:11; Mosiah 16:3–4.
24. Hugh Nibley, pp. 45–46. *The Holy Scriptures According to the Masoretic Text,* 47th ed. (Philadelphia: Jewish Publication Society of America, 1964), states a similar meaning in its translation of Genesis 3:16, 17: "Unto the woman He said: I will greatly multiply thy pain and thy travail; in pain thou shalt bring forth children . . . And unto Adam He said . . . cursed is the ground for thy sake; in toil thou shalt eat of it."
25. Kimball, p. 72.
26. Ida Smith, "The Lord As a Role Model for Men and Women," *Ensign,* Aug. 1980, pp. 66–67.
27. Carolyn J. Rasmus, "Mormon Women: A Convert's Perspective," *Ensign,* Aug. 1980, p. 69.

WOMEN, MARRIAGE, AND CHILDREN

The beauty of the gospel is that people can change. Our children can change, and we can change! So if we have done things that destroy our children's self-esteem or don't do enough to build it, we can learn new, positive ways to influence children. And sometimes we can have a second chance with another generation.

—Michaelene P. Grassli

Did Grandmother Have a Happy Marriage? Myths and Realities of American Families

MARY E. STOVALL

A commonly heard cry, which often rises to a shriek, is that the American family is falling apart. Somehow, according to this scenario, the family has fallen from grace—from the stability of a two-parent household, in which the husband is the breadwinner and the wife the homemaker, who devotes herself to home and her numerous children, all of whom are invariably neat, polite, and well-behaved. Under the rosy glow of nostalgia, we picture this nuclear group in a snug, comfortable home surrounded by the homes of loving grandparents and other kin, upon whom one could call for aid at any time and who gather for dinner every Sunday and holiday. Contrast this, say the contemporary critics, with the present situation: a rising divorce rate, increasing incidence of child and wife abuse, the growing frequency and societal acceptance of extramarital sexual relationships and a resultant rise in the rate of illegitimate births, and an increase in the number of unconventional and unsanctioned unions, both heterosexual and homosexual. Further, families in our mobile society are now often widely scattered from Maine to California with few opportunities for interaction other than by telephone or letter.

These are, without doubt, serious problems for American families that should not be minimized. Yet, few of them are unique to the present. Further, by placing late twentieth-

Mary E. Stovall earned her Ph.D. at the University of Chicago in American history, with specializations in Southern and family history. She is an assistant professor of history at Brigham Young University. Formerly the director of the Women's Research Institute, she chaired the BYU women's conferences for four years.

century families in their historical context, we may see a little more clearly the dynamics behind the current situation. By studying the past, we may illuminate the present. One of a historian's main tasks is to find a pattern in experience so that a meaning can be drawn from it. As the great social historian Arthur Mann has stated, a historian desires "to recreate the dead and make them talk to the living in ways that the living can understand."[1]

First, I should define at the outset the parameters of this essay. There is no such entity as *the* American family. Diversity has characterized American families since Jamestown and has only increased as the population has embraced immigrants from every nation on earth. *The* American family is actually the families of blacks, American Indians, Orientals, Hispanics, and the numerous other ethnic groups we lump together as white families. Even within each subgroup there are innumerable individual variations, yet, collectively, there are sufficient similarities for us to make meaningful generalizations about families. Nonetheless, much of family history is biased toward the middle and upper classes because diaries and letters are available, naturally, only for the literate. Family historians have made concerted efforts to overcome this limitation by using statistical data from census records, tax rolls, marriage, land, and other records to offer insights into the demographic shape of families, but numbers do not yield interior dynamics. Thus, much of this essay will, of necessity, focus more on the experiences of those who have left records, although I will supplement those when the data allow. Because of the restrictions of space, I have also made an arbitrary decision to limit discussion to white families.

There has never been a period in American history—from the founding of Jamestown in 1607 to the present day—in which American families have fulfilled our longings for what William J. Goode has labeled the "classical family of Western nostalgia."[2] Indeed, seventeenth-century families suffered under heavy burdens: an extremely high mortality rate, particularly for children, a short life expectancy, high incidence of disease, and few extended kin. A seventeenth-century Puritan woman could, on average, expect to marry between ages twenty and twenty-two, to bear nine children, of whom three would die before reaching maturity, and to apprentice out for seven years both her sons and daughters when they were about age ten, partly because of economic considerations and partly because the sternness of Calvinism made parents fearful of spoiling their children by showing them too great affection. Not all parents had the luxury of living to see their children grown, however. Historian John Demos has calculated that every fifth woman in Plymouth Colony died from causes associated with childbirth. Life expectancy at birth for both men and women was about thirty-five years, although in some small towns in New England as many as 50 percent of men lived to their seventies. In Boston, however, smallpox epidemics regularly ravaged the population, killing as many as one-fifth of Boston's entire population during a particularly severe epidemic in 1677–1678.[3]

In the Southern colonies, life was, if anything, much more difficult. The first sizable group of white women did not arrive in Jamestown, Virginia, until twelve years after its settlement, and the unequal sex ratio throughout much of the seventeenth century—as many as six men to one woman in the 1630s, improving to 2.5 to one by the end of the seventeenth century—did not contribute to stable family life. Further, life was particularly fragile in the South—even more so than in New England—because of epidemics of yellow fever and malaria that killed off part of the population and weakened resistance to other diseases among those left alive. Infant and childhood mortality were horrendous—as high as 45 percent in some counties in Virginia and Maryland. Adults were also affected, as only 15 percent of white male immigrants to Maryland in the late seventeenth century survived to age sixty. Such figures, however, would have been welcomed as blessings in the early eighteenth century in South Carolina's Christ Church Parish, where 86 percent of all those whose births and deaths are recorded died before age twenty, with 33 percent of the girls and almost 70 percent of the boys dying before age five. It is little wonder that a contemporary English proverb counseled, " 'Those who want to die quickly, go to Carolina.' " Such realities were not lost on children. As William Fitzhugh of Virginia wrote to his mother in 1698, " 'Before I was ten years old . . . I look'd upon this life here as but going to an Inn, no permanent being by God's will . . . . therefore am always prepared for my certain Dissolution which I can't be persuaded to prolong by a wish.' " Because of such high mortality rates, one scholar has claimed that seventeenth-century Southern parents, particularly fathers, invested little of their emotional life in their children in order to cushion their reactions to their children's almost expected deaths. Puritan parents, likewise, were reminded in sermons to avoid becoming too fond of their children and too familiar with them.[4]

This emotional distance was compounded by the fact that seventeenth-century Southern families, although nuclear in structure, might contain few people related by blood. In addition to the high infant and childhood mortality, one of every two men and women died before age fifty. The results made for convoluted relationships in families. For example, a man and a woman might marry when the woman was in her early twenties and the man in his late twenties; after the birth of two or three children, the wife died either of complications attendant to childbirth or from general disability as a result of closely spaced pregnancies combined with endemic diseases. The husband remarried rather quickly, and then he and his new wife, who might be a widow with two or three children of her own, had additional children. At age forty the husband died. The remarriage of the second wife and the bearing of more children resulted in an entirely new family with no blood connection to the children from the original marriage. This is not simply a hypothetical example. Two scholars studying seventeenth-century Virginia found one such "chain of marriages and remarriages" from 1655 to 1693 that included six marriages among seven people and produced twenty-five children, some of whom did not share any parents. Further, the high mortality rates precluded the establishment of extensive kin networks, which did not become well developed until the eighteenth century.[5]

While life expectancies increased during the eighteenth century, family ties were still very much subject to the capriciousness of disease and death. Scholars have estimated that not more than one-third of all husbands and wives enjoyed a marriage that lasted more than ten years. And, not all enjoyed their marriages. For many the colonial period was not a "golden age of family relations." In the South a double standard of sexual behavior for men and women became institutionalized early. Men could openly keep mistresses and still remain respectable. Women were advised to look the other way, forgive, and forget, yet remain completely chaste themselves. Marital friction was often displayed in the large number of advertisements in the newspapers for runaway wives, often juxtaposed to advertisements for fugitive slaves and lost horses. Although the alleged purpose for a husband to place such a notice was to repudiate his wife's debts, it is clear that many sought as well to humiliate their wives. One husband accused his wife of " 'robbing' " him of " 'all her Wearing Apparel, a fine Pair of English Cotton Curtains, a Chintz Counterpane . . . two Pillow Cases, three . . . Napkins, a large . . . Table-Cloth . . . and a Side Saddle.' " And, according to the property laws in most colonies, she *had* robbed him, because a wife's wearing apparel and household effects were her husband's property until his death, when they were passed to her.[6]

Strife also appeared among the Puritans, but the Puritans had an advantage: one of the basic commandments required of all good Puritans was to love and live peacefully with one's husband or wife. Those who failed to do so found themselves fined or punished in court, although the court sometimes moderated sentences if there were extenuating circumstances. As

Edmund Morgan relates, "The wife of Christopher Collins was presented for railing at her husband and calling him 'Gurley gutted divill.' Apparently the court agreed with her, for although the fact was proved by two witnesses, she was discharged. On another occasion Jacob Pudeator, who had been fined for striking and kicking his wife, had the sentence moderated when the court was informed that she was a woman 'of great provocation.' "[7]

Puritan marriages were more frequently based on reason rather than on emotion; love was a result of the marital bond, not the cause of it. Nevertheless, both partners were warned against loving inordinately because death would soon part them. Puritan ministers constantly reminded their flock that their first and highest love was reserved for God; to love one of God's creations more than God himself was to border on idolatry. As Margaret Winthrop wrote her husband John, let us not " 'forget our selves and love this world too much, and not set our affections on heaven where all true happyness is for ever.' " For those couples for whom limiting their affections was not the problem but loving sufficiently was, Puritan ministers exhorted them that love could be controlled by the force of will. Couples were counseled to lower their expectations, for true bliss was possible only with God. John Oxenbridge reminded his congregation that they marry a " 'child of Adam,' " one that is tainted with sin. " 'Look not for Perfection in your relation,' " advised another. " 'God reserves that for another state where marriage is not needed.' "[8]

Certainly, not all colonial marriages were characterized by infelicity between husband and wife. Many were loving, supportive unions, yet too often we tend to think that most marriages of the past were idyllic and that only in our time have things fallen apart. Perhaps it is helpful to note with Professor David Brion Davis that "for over three centuries, ministers, moral philosophers, and their modern counterparts have been warning that children are becoming more contemptuous of authority, parents more irresponsible, wives more selfishly independent, [and] families more fragile and rootless."[9]

Such was particularly true as families moved from the colonial model to the "modern" American family in the years between the American Revolution and 1830. Under the influence of such Enlightenment philosophers as John Locke and Immanuel Kant, basic ideas governing families were undergoing radical transformation. Locke postulated that a child's character was not tainted at birth with original sin, as the Puritans had believed, but instead was created by the totality of the impressions and experiences inscribed on the blank slate of his or her mind. Parents thus no longer had to break their children's wills but instead were delegated by God to teach them by example; such nurture, not nature, determined a child's character. Kant stressed that each generation be allowed an education that encouraged an independence of mind. Also, several of the American revolutionaries extrapolated from their political philosophy to families. Thomas Paine declared in 1775 that only those marriages based on affection should be regarded as binding, stating that " 'no creature was ever intended to be miserable.' " Similarly, Princeton University president John Witherspoon worked for less stringent divorce laws, as did an anonymous pamphleteer from Philadelphia. Should not liberty, the latter argued, extend to " 'those united together in the worst bondage?' "[10]

The Revolution had altered the status of women, who for the first time began to assume a political role. The famous 1774 Edenton, North Carolina, declaration was drafted by fifty-one women who declared their adherence to resolutions against the British and defined their "duty" as supporting the " 'publick good.' " While the declaration was met with amusement by men, it, according to Mary Beth Norton, marked the first time American women had claimed a responsibility for public policy. Such actions slowly began to alter the traditional idea that even knowing about politics was beyond women's capacities. The culmination came in the awarding of the franchise in New Jersey to women and free blacks—not because of any liberal sentiments, but mainly because of an oversight in the drafting of the state constitution, which defined voters as " 'all free inhabitants' " without specifying gender or race. Women voted until 1807, when a bill was passed to restore " 'the safety, quiet, good order and dignity of the state.' "[11]

For most women, however, progress did not come from involvement in politics, but from what Linda Kerber has termed the idea of "republican motherhood." To many politicians and moralists, the proper rearing of citizens—i.e., sons—for the new republic was seen as one of the bulwarks of representative government, because the republican experiment rested on an educated electorate. Mothers could not properly instill republican virtues if they themselves were uneducated, so the curriculum for females was expanded from "ornamental" subjects to grammar, rhetoric, history, geography, mathematics, and science. The result was the first generation of educated American women.[12]

Bolstered by the ideas of the Enlightenment and the Revolution, the expansion of the frontier, the Industrial Revolution, which moved the locus of manufacturing from the household to the factory, and the increasing ethnic diversity of the cities, change was occurring in American families. Although it was slow and uneven, by the 1830s a different family from that of the colonial period can be discerned. Marriage was now based more upon affection and mutual respect between husband and wife, and the attention of parents was increasingly centered on rearing children, whose characters were formed under the tutelage of wise and virtuous parents. Further, the numbers of children born to families decreased throughout the century, while life expectancies rose during the latter decades of the 1800s, a phenomenon so significant that it has been termed the "demographic revolution." White women marrying in the seventeenth century could expect to bear an average of 7.4 children, while those marrying in the latter decades of the nineteenth century would bear only 2.8—a decline so momentous that most demographers see the only logical reason as the deliberate reduction of births through birth control.[13]

These alterations were part and parcel of the "cult of the home," which—according to the moralists and reformers who formulated the concept in response to the disorder they saw in nineteenth-century society—meant that the proper destiny of a middle-class home was to become a sacred sanctuary. In the home one could retreat from the battles of life into close emotional attachments with family members, who fortified each other for struggling with the world, which was seen as essentially corrupt. The world beyond the home lay in wait to entrap the unwary in the evils of crime, ruthless business practices, and disregard for individual dignity. Men in urban areas were seen as especially vulnerable to such enticements since their work now took them outside the home to confront the contamination of the world.[14]

To counteract the world's influence on their husbands, fathers, and brothers, women were enjoined to remain in the home, which was described as the last chance for the inculcation of moral values and, thus, the salvation of mankind, and to cultivate the characteristics of what one scholar has termed "true womanhood": purity, piety, submissiveness, and domesticity. Women were the spiritual guardians of the home, who, by their examples of virtue and piety, brought their husbands to God. The American Victorians had turned the Puritan idea of spirituality upside down: Milton's line in *Paradise Lost*— " 'he for God only, she for God in him' "—had accurately expressed the spiritual hierarchy accepted in the Puritan world, but for nineteenth-century Americans, women—not men— were the more naturally religious. As one Southerner counseled his daughter, "A woman never appears so *lovely* as when she is at her prayers." The nineteenth century had rejected the Puritans' basic suspicions of women's nature, based partly on the biblical story of Eve, as theology became more liberal. The assignment of the sexes to separate spheres reflected, then, both social and moral necessity and the happy fit, as the moralists

77

saw it, of each sex within the domain most "natural" to its capabilities. Each should thus be fulfilled and happy, with no need to encroach on the other's sphere.[15]

These assumptions regarding the separate spheres of the sexes, widely held by much of the middle- and upper-class population in the nineteenth century, were defined and explicated by authors of advice literature and marriage manuals. These moralists, mostly men of northeastern Protestant backgrounds, stressed gender as the determinant of role within the family. Such strictures limited full development for both men and women, who were taught to suppress, respectively, their emotions and their desire for authority. As one scholar has commented, both sexes found themselves "hemmed in by role restrictions" and labeled by society as "unmasculine" or "unfeminine" if they deviated from approved patterns of behavior for their sex.[16]

While contemporary scholars often see these proscriptions in negative terms, nineteenth-century Americans usually viewed them positively. Daniel Hundley commented in 1860 that the family was "God's school" to which the enlightenment and education of mankind had been entrusted through the ministrations of women. Assigned to the home "by right and by nature," women thereby ruled "the destinies of the world." Women's moral strength did not translate into intellectual, emotional, or physical sufficiency, however, and women were counseled to seek a good man to cling to. As one woman wrote her fiancé, "I shall look upon you as my Protector, as the pilot to steer my course through life's stormy way and as the one whose happiness must be my constant study." Another, who had survived the Civil War alone with her children in Vicksburg, the site of one of the major battles of the war, nevertheless described her daughter's fiancé as the "one to whom she has given the right to care for her."[17]

The dangers inherent in inculcating notions of helplessness in half a society's population were revealed when disaster struck. And strike it did. One-third of the 127 mid-nineteenth-century Southern marriages I studied lost a spouse before age fifty. Further, in 1850 nationwide life expectancies at birth for both men and women were only forty to forty-five years. Many women described themselves as "paralyzed" at any calamity that removed their husband from the household. They had been encouraged to remain girls emotionally, since men — fathers, brothers, or husbands — would take care of them and protect them from unhappiness in life. One Southern woman mourned that she was "so unfit for any of the duties I have to perform, *so unfit* for contact with the world: . . . I am not of a disposition to transact business with men, or to protect myself, and alas, now, I have no protector, or adviser." Another confided to her sister her "stubborn despair" and fear of life: "First he [death] took my dear greyhaired Father who had always been so dear and indulgent to me, but Charlie was left to me, and well did he fill the place of Father and husband to me. . . . It cannot be true he has left me to suffer and endure alone. He always would shield me from everything like trouble and annoyance, how can I walk the dark future alone and unassisted by his strong arm of protection. I have but one wish and that is to die."[18]

Not all women, of course, were so wounded. Many, after initial bouts of self-pity and fear, found themselves able to cope; others, crippled too painfully, never made the transition to self-sufficiency. Not all problems were confined to death of a husband or father, however. Living under this system was also a trial, because many women were far from satisfied with their lives as dependent children. Especially among the elite and the urban middle-class, many young girls had been plucked from their role as belle, for which they had been extensively trained, and transported into the foreign realm — for which they had little or no preparation — of wife, and inevitably, mother. The initial shock was compounded by expectations of perfectionism in personal attributes coupled with responsibility for the spiritual welfare of the home. Assigned such a weighty stewardship, many, quite naturally, fell short while suffering guilt for not properly fulfilling their role; others, less self-sacrificing, resented the simultaneous imposition of responsibility and a rhetoric that denied capability beyond a woman's sphere. One woman, depressed at her numerous obligations, invoked divine aid to become "a full grown woman!"[19]

Men also were required to fulfill exacting definitions of proper behavior for their sex. As mentioned earlier, men were assigned the economic realm, which usually took them outside the home for most of the day. Further, men were supposed to develop those characteristics compatible with the business world: assertiveness, strength, cunning, acquisitiveness, and endurance — traits that society now labels as masculine. As one scholar has observed, the result was a more authoritarian and distant, less nurturant figure than that of colonial times.[20]

The development of a domestic sacred sanctuary coincided with the growth of the so-called "cult of the child" during the nineteenth century. This marked a profound shift in attitudes toward childhood, as children were viewed as innocent and possessed of sensitive and impressionable natures more responsive to example and persuasion than to corporal punishment. Parents were enjoined by the veritable explosion in the numbers of child-rearing books to mold the child's will through love and reason so that the child would early develop a proper sense of self that made further correction unnecessary. Proper punishments were shaming the child, arousing guilt, or depriving the child of company or food so that he or she could meditate on the enormity of the deed and resolve not to repeat the sin.[21]

A favorite didactic story — used by many mothers of the period — concerned a little boy sent by the doctor to buy medicine for his critically ill mother. On the way the little boy's attention was distracted by a game of marbles, and he stopped to play. By the time he finally reached home, his mother had died. The doctor told him that medicine could have saved his mother and that he had killed her. One mother who used this story with her children reported them as being "very much affected." She was so pleased with the effect of her efforts that she requested her husband to purchase another volume of such morality tales.[22]

Women took their mothering responsibilities seriously because they had been counseled that the most effective method of guiding the child was through the force of parental example, particularly that of the mother, who was required to lead her children by piety and purity. The first six or seven years of life were crucial to a child's development, and these were precisely the years when mothers' influence was strongest. If mothers neglected their duty, they lost the best opportunity for molding the child, and the result was a detriment not only to the family but also to the nation, for mothers were responsible for producing disciplined citizens. As the moralists commented, what were women's rights in comparison to such a role and duty?[23]

Such ideas about the nature of mothering were new to the nineteenth century. While colonial mothers were technically at home with their children, they had little time for the hovering type of mothering demanded of their descendents by the nineteenth-century moralistic literature. The normal burden of domestic tasks in a colonial home meant that, in Laurel Thatcher Ulrich's words, "at any given moment everyone and no one might be watching the children." The results were often predictably disastrous. When Thomas Newall's son drowned, his mother testified that "the child was out of her sight no more than thirty minutes to an hour." Society did not blame the mother for what most in the twentieth century would consider flagrant neglect; she had done what she could, given her multitudinous responsibilities, and could not be faulted for the tragedy that had occurred.[24]

Nineteenth-century moralists also stressed the preservation of the innocence of childhood. School reformers sought to locate schools away from secular life to create "asylums for the preservation of childhood." Meanwhile, various "advice to youth" books appeared, advocating the necessity of an early religious conversion to form religious character at a young age. The great peril in the life of a child was leaving home — the sacred sanctuary — and the moralists wanted to be certain that the child was as prepared as possible to cope with the wickedness of the world.[25]

Despite the warnings of the moralists, however, changes were occurring among youth, partly on account of increasing urbanization. In cities, children often no longer contributed directly to family finances. Further, living near other families and children of their own age, young people formed strong peer bonds that competed for their allegiance to the family. The result, in the words of Kenneth Keniston, was a " 'discontinuity of age-groups' " separating family members. In response to the formation of a discernible "youth culture," the child-study movement was organized under the direction of G. Stanley Hall, who popularized the term and concept of adolescence. In his study on human development, Hall postulated the existence of an adolescent crisis marked by "storm and stress" as the youth was torn between conflicting impulses of hyperactivity and inertia, happiness and depression, selfishness and altruism, and sensitivity and cruelty. Hall's work marked a real break with the past, since from the available data it appears that the modern phenomenon of adolescence was not recognized, or probably even experienced, before the middle of the nineteenth century.[26]

Families in the nineteenth century experienced profound changes as their members were asked to conform to exacting standards of behavior that left little room for individual variation. Further, the family as an entity became sentimentalized and endowed with meaning as a redemptive force. For many, if home were denied, redemption was thought to be impossible. In popular culture, domestic novels, popular songs such as "My Old Kentucky Home," "Home Sweet Home," "Old Folks at Home," "Where Is My Wandering Boy Tonight?" and Currier and Ives prints all celebrated the virtues of the ideal family and home. Little mention was made of the increase in prostitution or the appearance in the family newspaper of patent medicine advertisements for relief of venereal diseases. Obviously, the "cult of the home" was not saving society nor all its family members, who were conflict-ridden — torn between "getting and spending" and the sacred sanctuary of the home.[27]

Further evidence that all was not well emerged in the increasing divorce rate, which paralleled growing life expectancies. As life expectancies began to rise in the last decades of the nineteenth century from the combination of the discovery of the germ theory of disease and the cleaning-up of municipal water systems, marital partners could expect to live together for greater periods of time; however, compensating for this development was the burgeoning divorce rate. In demographer Robert Wells' words, "Interestingly, the rise in divorce almost exactly balanced out improvements in life expectancy, so that the proportion of marriages being ended in any year was almost the same in 1970 as in 1890." Wells theorized that when death could "no longer be counted on to bring quick release [or relief]" from marriage, divorce became more socially acceptable.[28]

Families in the twentieth century have continued to contend with the burden of the advice of experts, who increasingly hearkened not to religious prescriptions about what constitutes the perfect family but to scientific data. Parents in the first decades of the century were counseled, as had been their nineteenth-century counterparts, that the most crucial variable in their child's development was their parenting skills; a mother was particularly liable, and if her child were ill-behaved, she was to blame. Parents were confronted with contradictory deterministic theories, each of which threatened parents with calamity to their child if they did not follow its precepts. But, which was right? The pop-Freudians argued that adult neurosis was the result of unresolved childhood mental conflict; the denial of an infant's instinctive needs was likely to injure his or her psyche permanently. Thus, one did not try to force a child to accomplish certain tasks, especially toilet training, too early.

The behaviorists following John B. Watson argued that such emphasis on the unconscious was folly, that one simply rewarded good behavior and punished the bad; the child, trained much like Pavlov's dog, would develop in any direction the parent chose. Further, in contrast to the Freudians, Watson's followers taught early and strict toilet training. Parents were caught in a bind, told that their children's fate hinged on their selection of and faithful adherence to the best system and that reliance on their own instincts or the methods used by their own parents could lead only to disaster. The good twentieth-century parent was the scientifically literate parent.[29]

Other areas of family relations also felt the weight of the advice of experts. Foremost in this group in the early twentieth century were the social feminists, that first generation of American college-educated women motivated by what Jane Addams termed the "subjective necessity" to do something useful, who founded settlement houses, worked for suffrage, and labored tirelessly for women's and children's protective labor legislation. Settlement work inevitably impressed upon them the dire conditions surrounding many poor urban families. Arguing that women's hours should be shortened to protect their health as mothers and that children should be in school, not in the factory, these reformers, including Addams, Lillian Wald, and Florence Kelley, sought restrictions on the number of hours women worked as well as legislation prohibiting the employment of children under fourteen in manufacturing, under sixteen in mining, and limiting older children's hours to forty-eight per week. A major turning point in the battle was the 1908 Supreme Court decision in *Muller v. Oregon*, which validated an Oregon law mandating a ten-hour day for women laundry workers. Argued by famed lawyer Louis D. Brandeis, who based his brief on research indicating that long hours damaged a woman's health for " 'a proper discharge of her maternal functions,' " the case was the first to utilize so-called "sociological jurisprudence," rather than being restricted only to points of law.[30]

Such arguments were increasingly used thereafter for the extension of protective legislation, which, ironically, was often opposed by those it was designed to benefit. Immigrant families, who had heretofore relied on the wages of their children to get by, were often adamantly against what they considered interference in their right to control their children's labor. Further, many radical feminists, who saw women first as individuals desiring to compete directly with men in the marketplace rather than as the weaker sex in need of protection, believed that women's protective legislation was inimical to their interests because it prohibited them from working as many hours as men. Such division among feminists came to a head in the 1920s when the social feminists vociferously opposed Alice Paul's equal rights amendment as destructive of everything they had erected to protect women over the past two decades. (This same division among women was revived in the debate over the ERA in the 1960s and 1970s and continues today in disputes about maternity leave. Are women primarily a sex in need of protection and special consideration because of their roles as mothers, or are women primarily individuals who should be treated equally with men and for whom special treatment may backfire because employers may be less inclined to hire or promote them? Accommodation between the camps is difficult precisely because one's answer inevitably reflects deeply held philosophical beliefs about the nature of women.)[31]

Such questions have gained increased saliency from the growing numbers of married women in the workforce. Before the turn of the century, few married women worked outside the home. By 1910, however, 15 percent of the female workforce was married; today, almost 60 percent of married women with husband present work outside the home. While the first generation of college-educated women generally had to choose between a family and a career (and, as a result, most stayed single), such has not been the case for succeeding generations. More than 80 percent of 1920s college graduates married, and most worked sometime in their lives, either before marriage or the birth of the first child. New realities called for new remedies. Smith College set up an institute to help women combine career and family, while Barnard College gave a six-month maternity leave, with pay, to any expectant woman faculty or staff member. In 1927 Smith's president, William A. Neilson, commented, " 'The outstanding problem confronting women is how to reconcile a normal life of marriage and motherhood with intellectual activity such as her college education had fitted her for.' "[32]

Such experiments were short-lived, however, as the Great Depression placed jobs at a premium and relegated feminism to the back row. Survival—a square meal and a roof over one's head—defined the social agenda. While the proportion of women in the labor force increased during the 1930s, women were concentrated in traditional women's jobs—service, sales, clerical positions—that reinforced the stereotype of "proper" female employment. Further, attitudes hardened against working married women. The president of the Massachusetts Women's Political Club referred to them as " 'deserters from their post of duty, the home.' " A 1937 Gallup poll revealed that 82 percent of respondents believed that wives with employed husbands should not work outside the home.[33]

The Second World War, however, turned a labor surplus into a massive labor shortage. As increasing numbers of men were drafted, the federal government mounted a propaganda campaign directed to women. Not only was it unpatriotic not to work, but husbands, fathers, and brothers might die if women didn't shoulder the load in the defense industry to keep the army supplied with ammunition and other war materiel. During the war, more than 6.5 million women, three-fourths of whom were married, responded to the call, entering normally male occupations that paid more and were more interesting than most traditional women's jobs. Yet, at the end of the war, a countervailing campaign was launched to bring women back to the home and to motivate women to aid the returning veterans' social adjustment by relinquishing their independence and adapting their needs and wants to those of men. While 3.25 million women left the labor force, another 2.75 million joined. Yet, most postwar jobs were in traditionally female occupations, and by April 1947, the prewar female employment structure had been replicated.[34]

The postwar period has been viewed as one of conservative consensus — the "baby boom," massive suburbanization (which Kenneth Jackson has termed the move to the "crabgrass frontier"), consumerism, and happy domesticity for women wearing a freshly-ironed dress and high heels in a perpetually clean kitchen — Ozzie and Harriet writ large. Beneath this new cult of domesticity, however, almost double the number of married women were working outside the home in 1960 than in 1940. Few paid attention to this major shift in women's work because most women still subscribed to and verbally upheld the domestic ideal despite their own behavior. Yet, there were other discontents — more than twenty-four thousand women responded to a 1960 *Redbook* article, "Why Young Mothers Feel Trapped," and Betty Friedan articulated "the problem that has no name."[35]

The women's movement of the 1960s and 1970s has, perhaps more than anything else, focused our attention on questions of the inevitability of sex-linked roles — to what extent is gender destiny? If gender does not define destiny, what does it mean, then, to be a woman? To be a man? And, how can men and women relate to each other without the security of carefully delimited roles? Such questions would have had little meaning for a Puritan woman, who believed not only that her biology determined her life course but that her gender assigned her an unchangeable status within the social hierarchy. In this area, we are in uncharted historical territory, and for many of us, it is profoundly uncomfortable precisely because of the ambiguity. As Peter Filene has commented, Dostoevsky's Grand Inquisitor "knew all too well [that] the price of freedom is more anxiety than most people wish to bear."[36] On the other hand, it is exciting for exactly the same reasons. We have the opportunity to try to solve problems that have vexed reformers for almost a century: how does one promote the *total* welfare of all members of the family? How can we structure the family so that no one's growth is limited to only certain prescribed areas? For many, the answers lie in increased devotion by *both* husbands and wives to family and home, to a sharing of domestic tasks and child rearing so that each partner can realize his or her potential in both the public and private spheres.

Historians are frequently asked what "lessons" about families can be drawn from the past. Although most historians avoid deriving "lessons," it might not be too hazardous to venture a few. First, from experiences in the past, we can say that families have proved remarkably adaptive to their surroundings, that what one person views as familial disintegration is seen by another observer as simply adaptation and change in family functions to meet the needs of new circumstances. Second, the nostalgia for the extended family is based on a myth as far as Western society is concerned. Most families in Western society and American history have always been nuclear in structure—husband, wife, and children.[37] Third, not until the latter part of the nineteenth century did increases in life expectancies allow the long-term perpetuation of marital unions for a majority of the people. Indeed, in the seventeenth and eighteenth centuries more marriages were prematurely ended by death than are now ended by divorce.[38] And, finally, there has not been a "golden age" of the family in American history: each era has had its share of problems and trials, yet the family has endured. Perhaps that is the "lesson" we receive from the past—that the family as an institution is remarkably resilient, and while its functions may change, the family continues to fill the most basic needs of love, support, aid, and encouragement to its members.

Did Grandmother Have a Happy Marriage?

Notes

1. Arthur Mann, Lecture for History 353, "Twentieth-Century American Social Movements," University of Chicago, 5 Jan. 1976.
2. William J. Goode, *World Revolution and Family Patterns* (New York: Free Press of Glencoe, 1963), p. 6.
3. Donald M. Scott and Bernard Wishy, eds., *America's Families: A Documentary History* (New York: Harper and Row, 1982), pp. 2–8; Edmund S. Morgan, *The Puritan Family: Religion and Domestic Relations in Seventeenth-Century New England* (New York: Harper and Row, 1966), pp. 65–86; John Demos, *A Little Commonwealth: Family Life in Plymouth Colony* (London: Oxford University Press, 1970), p. 131; Philip J. Greven, "Family Structure in Seventeenth-Century Andover, Massachusetts," *William and Mary Quarterly* 23 (1966): 238–40. See also Maris A. Vinovskis, "Angels' Heads and Weeping Willows: Death in Early America," in *Studies in American Historical Demography*, ed. Maris A. Vinovskis (New York: Academic Press, 1979), pp. 181–210.
4. Darrett B. Rutman and Anita H. Rutman, "Of Agues and Fevers: Malaria in the Early Chesapeake," *William and Mary Quarterly* 33 (1976): 31–60; H. Roy Merrens and George D. Terry, "Dying in Paradise: Malaria, Mortality, and the Perceptual Environment in Colonial South Carolina," *Journal of Southern History* 50 (November 1984): 542 and quotation, 549; Daniel Blake Smith, *Inside the Great House: Planter Family Life in Eighteenth-Century Chesapeake Society* (Ithaca: Cornell University Press, 1980), pp. 261–65; quotation from Fitzhugh, p. 261; Morgan, pp. 106–7.
5. Darrett B. Rutman and Anita H. Rutman, "Now-Wives and Sons-in-Law: Parental Death in a Seventeenth-Century Virginia County," in *The Chesapeake in the Seventeenth-Century*, ed. Thad Tate and David Ammerman (Chapel Hill: University of North Carolina Press, 1979), p. 156; Smith, p. 177.
6. Scott and Wishy, p. 3; Julia Cherry Spruill, *Women's Life and Labor in the Southern Colonies* (New York: W. W. Norton and Co., 1972), pp. 163–84; quotation, p. 180; for property laws, see pp. 340–66.
7. Morgan, p. 40.
8. Morgan, pp. 29–64; Winthrop quotation, p. 51; Oxenbridge and last quotation, p. 52.
9. David Brion Davis, "The American Family and Boundaries in Historical Perspective," in *The American Family: Dying or Developing*, ed. David Reiss and Howard A. Hoffman (New York: Plenum Press, 1979), p. 19.
10. For the effects of Enlightenment thought on American families, see Jay Fliegelman, *Prodigals and Pilgrims: The American Revolution against Patriarchal Authority, 1750–1800* (Cambridge: Cambridge University Press, 1982), pp. 1–6, 12–15, 123–54, and passim; quotations, pp. 124 and 125, respectively.

11. Mary Beth Norton, *Liberty's Daughters: The Revolutionary Experience of American Women, 1750–1800* (Boston/Toronto: Little, Brown and Co., 1980); pp. 161 and 193, respectively.

12. For a discussion of the idea of republican motherhood, see Linda K. Kerber, *Women of the Republic: Intellect and Ideology in Revolutionary America* (Chapel Hill: University of North Carolina Press, 1980; New York: W. W. Norton and Co., 1986).

13. Robert V. Wells, "Family History and Demographic Transition," in *The American Family in Social-Historical Perspective*, ed. Michael Gordon, 2d ed. (New York: St. Martin's Press, 1978); Robert V. Wells, *Revolutions in Americans' Lives: A Demographic Perspective on the History of Americans, Their Families, and Their Society* (Westport, Conn.: Greenwood Press, 1982).

14. For a discussion of what he terms the "emergence of the modern American family," see Carl N. Degler, *At Odds: Women and the Family in America from the Revolution to the Present* (New York: Oxford University Press, 1980), chap. 1; Wells, *Revolutions in Americans' Lives*, p. 92; term "sacred sanctuary" from James Wallace Milden, "The Sacred Sanctuary: Family Life in Nineteenth-Century America" (Ph.D. dissertation, University of Maryland, 1974); see also Kirk Jeffrey, Jr., "Family History: The Middle-Class American Family in the Urban Context, 1830–1870" (Ph.D. dissertation, Stanford University, 1972), pp. 86–88, and my study, "White Families in the Central South, 1850–1880" (Ph.D. dissertation, University of Chicago, 1983), chap. 4.

15. Barbara Welter, "The Cult of True Womanhood: 1820–1860," *American Quarterly* 18 (Summer 1966): 151–74; Milton, as quoted in Morgan, p. 20; C. S. Howe to his daughter Ellen Howe, 7 Sept. 1851, Chiliab Smith Howe Papers, Southern Historical Collection, University of North Carolina at Chapel Hill (hereafter abbreviated as SHC, UNC).

16. Ronald Walters, *Primers for Prudery: Sexual Advice to Victorian America* (Englewood Cliffs, N.J.: Prentice-Hall, 1974), pp. 11–12; quotation from Milden, pp. 106–7.

17. Daniel R. Hundley, *Social Relations in Our Southern States* (New York: Arno Press, 1973), p. 73; Frances Bestor to fiancé, James G. Robertson, 29 Oct. 1854, copied into her journal, pp. 56–57, Frances J. Robertson Diaries, Alabama Department of Archives and History; Diary of Mahala Roach, 5 Feb. 1874, SHC, UNC.

18. Southern mortality rate figure based on analysis of 127 marriages from Alabama, Mississippi, and Tennessee from 1850 to 1880 (Stovall, p. 72); for nationwide life expectancies, see Wells, p. 126; Diary of Octavia Otey, 17 June 1866, Wyche-Otey Papers, SHC, UNC; Mary Vaughan, probably to sister Louisa Clark Boddie, 22 Feb. 1863, Boddie Family Papers, Mississippi Department of Archives and History.

19. Diary of Lucilla Agnes (Gamble) McCorkle, entry of 1st Sabbath of June, 1847, SHC, UNC.

20. John Demos, "The American Family in Past Time," in *Family in Transition: Rethinking Marriage, Sexuality, Child Rearing, and Family Organization*, ed. Arlene S. Skolnick and Jerome H. Skolnick, 2d ed. (Boston: Little, Brown & Co., 1977), p. 70.

21. Robert Sunley, "Early Nineteenth-Century American Literature on Child Rearing," in *Childhood in Contemporary Cultures*, ed. Margaret Mead and Martha Wolfenstein (Chicago: University of Chicago Press, 1955); and Bernard Wishy, *The Child and the Republic: The Dawn of American Child Nurture* (Philadelphia: University of Pennsylvania Press, 1968).

22. Marion Henry to her husband, G. A. Henry, 7 Oct. 1850, Gustavus A. Henry Papers, SHC, UNC.

23. Wishy, p. 28.

24. Laurel Thatcher Ulrich, *Good Wives: Image and Reality in the Lives of Women in Northern New England, 1650–1750* (New York: Alfred A. Knopf, 1980 and 1982; New York: Oxford University Press, 1983), p. 157 (quotations), 158–159.

25. Joseph F. Kett, *Rites of Passage: Adolescence in America, 1790 to the Present* (New York: Basic Books, 1977), p. 122 (quotation); see also chaps. 8 and 9; John Demos and Virginia Demos, "Adolescence in Historical Perspective," *Journal of Marriage and the Family* 31 (November 1969): 632–38; Joseph F. Kett, "Adolescence and Youth in Nineteenth-Century America," *Journal of Interdisciplinary History* 2 (August 1971): 283–98.

26. Keniston, as quoted in Demos and Demos, "Adolescence in Historical Perspective," p. 637; for a discussion of Hall, see Kett, *Rites of Passage*, chap. 8.

27. Herbert Ross Brown, *The Sentimental Novel in America, 1789–1860* (Durham: Duke University Press, 1940); Scott and Wishy, pp. 271–89, 348–78.

28. Robert V. Wells, "Women's Lives Transformed: Demographic and Family Patterns in America, 1600–1970," in *Women of America: A History*, ed. Carol Ruth Berkin and Mary Beth Norton (Boston: Houghton Mifflin Co., 1979), p. 21.

29. Elizabeth M. R. Lomax, in collaboration with Jerome Kagan and Barbara G. Rosenkrantz, *Science and Patterns of Child Care* (San Francisco: W. H. Freeman and Co., 1978), chaps. 3 and 4.

30. Brandeis, as quoted in Lois Scharf, *To Work and to Wed: Female Employment, Feminism, and the Great Depression* (Westport, Conn.: Greenwood Press, 1980), p. 12. For a discussion of this first generation of college-educated women and social feminism, see Ellen Condliffe

Lagemann, *A Generation of Women: Education in the Lives of Progressive Reformers* (Cambridge: Harvard University Press, 1979); William L. O'Neill, *Everyone Was Brave: The Rise and Fall of Feminism in America* (Chicago: Quadrangle Books, 1969); Peter G. Filene, *Him/Her/Self: Sex Roles in Modern America,* 2d ed. (Baltimore: Johns Hopkins University Press, 1986), chaps. 1, 2, and 5; Degler, chap. 16.

31. William O'Neill, "Feminism as a Radical Ideology," in *Dissent: Explorations in the History of American Radicalism,* ed. Alfred E. Young (De Kalb, Ill.: Northern Illinois University Press, 1968), pp. 275–300; Degler, pp. 402–4.

32. Neilson, as quoted in Degler, p. 413; see also Filene, chap. 5 and table on female labor force participation for 1890–1980, p. 237.

33. Quoted in Filene, p. 150; see also his chap. 6; Degler, pp. 413–16; Ruth Milkman, "Women's Work and the Economic Crisis: Some Lessons from the Great Depression," in *A Heritage of Her Own: Toward a New Social History of American Women,* ed., with an introduction, by Nancy F. Cott and Elizabeth H. Pleck (New York: Simon and Schuster, 1979).

34. Degler, chap. 17; Filene, pp. 161–65; Maureen Honey, *Creating Rosie the Riveter: Class, Gender, and Propaganda during World War II* (Amherst: University of Massachusetts Press, 1984), chap. 1; see also Karen Anderson, *Wartime Women: Sex Roles, Family Relations, and the Status of Women during World War II* (Westport, Conn.: Greenwood Press, 1981).

35. Filene, chap. 6; Betty Friedan, *The Feminine Mystique* (New York: W. W. Norton, 1963), p. 15.

36. Filene, p. 232.

37. Peter Laslett, "Size and Structure of the Household in England over Three Centuries," *Population Studies* 23 (July 1969): 199–223, and his *Household and Family in Past Time* (Cambridge: Cambridge University Press, 1972).

38. Scott and Wishy, p. 3.

Previously published in *Family Perspective* 23, 2 (1989): 133–48. Reprinted with permission.

Equal Partners: Two Versions

MARTI S. AND DENNIS L. LYTHGOE
ELLA H. AND WILFORD M. FARNSWORTH, JR.

Introduction by Marie Cornwall

American society has changed tremendously over the past thirty years, and women's lives are changing too. Marriage patterns, birth rates, divorce rates, labor force participation — all the indicators of the status of family life and women's lives have changed.[1] The data indicate that women marry later, have fewer children, are more likely to divorce and to remarry, and are more likely to work for pay. Such dramatic social change is a two-edged sword for women. On the one hand, women have more opportunities — more education (women received half of all bachelors and masters degrees awarded in 1987),[2] better pay (in 1979 women who worked full time earned only sixty-three cents for every dollar earned by men — in 1989 women earned seventy-two cents for every dollar),[3] and the majority of married women are not totally dependent on their husband's income.[4] But we also live in a time when women head half the families living in poverty, a social phenomenon known as the "feminization of poverty."[5] Social change affects women's lives in another way as well. The expanded opportunities of our modern world mean that many women have more choice, more decision points in their lives. Because of that, women's lives are more diverse. Unfortunately, many women are not yet comfortable with the diversity represented by their lives. Many have become embattled in arguments about which life choice, which contribution to the community, is best.

Two very different perspectives on achieving an equal partnership in marriage are presented in the following pages. Marti and Dennis Lythgoe describe a marriage partnership that attempts to equalize responsibilities across all categories: child care, income earning, household chores, and so forth. Ella and

Bill Farnsworth describe a marriage partnership that achieves equality by each partner recognizing and supporting the work of the other. It is, by comparison, very traditional; but from the point of view of both partners, it is also equal.

There are actually many social factors which dictate the shape of these marriages. Marti and Dennis represent a younger generation. Their choices were shaped by the changing society of their time (new definitions of gender roles, new occupational opportunities for women) and by a college professor's flexible time schedule and modest salary. Because of Dennis's willingness to share household responsibilities, Marti was able to pursue a writing and editing career. She has helped write grammar school textbooks for D. C. Heath and Houghton-Mifflin and now works part-time as a technical writer. Because of Marti's financial contribution to the family, Dennis was able to pursue his own writing projects. His book, *A Marriage of Equals*,[6] reflects not only his efforts to create an equal partnership with Marti but several years' experience as a bishop counseling with couples. Marti and Dennis have been married for twenty-five years and are the parents of five children.

Ella and Bill Farnsworth have been married forty years. They are the parents of three children and the grandparents of eight. Their choices were shaped by the dynamics of an international business career. Besides being a senior executive at Citicorp/Citibank, Bill was head of a large, overseas bank. Ella's marriage partnership took on corporate dimensions. Bill's professional work required her contributions in the banking community and her willingness to adjust to geographic mobility in an international arena. The belief that men advance in corporate careers by their own merits is simply untrue. Their wives play an essential role.[7] Bill's professional work provided a comfortable income and resources that freed Ella to make important contributions in the community. She received the BYU Alumni Association Distinguished Service Award in 1990 for her service in the many communities in which she has lived.

Marti and Dennis and Ella and Bill offer their ideas on achieving an equal partnership in marriage. We hope that readers will not feel they must emulate either version but will recognize the creative, healthy diversity they represent.

Dennis Lythgoe

According to a *USA Today* survey, women in their twenties want love and romance but also want to be respected for their brains and talent. Men's wants are simpler. They want a beautiful and sexy woman.[8] I think that to a large measure these survey results truly reflect our society. To some extent they fit me as a young man playing the dating game — except that I was also progressive enough at the time to want a companion who was smart and stimulating. I was lucky enough to find such a person in Marti.

Although my parents' marriage was traditional, my background was extraordinary in that I had an assertive, high-achieving older sister who went to college, earned two college degrees, taught at the university level, and wrote books. So it was natural for me to want a woman with some of those dynamic qualities. I was not unlike Henry Blackwell in the nineteenth century whose high-powered sister, Elizabeth Blackwell, eventually became the first female physician in the United States. Henry was brought up to respect women intellectually, even though nineteenth-century America did not promote high re-

Dennis L. Lythgoe is a columnist for the Salt Lake City Deseret News *and adjunct professor of history at the University of Utah. For twenty years he was a professor at Bridgewater State College in Massachusetts, where he specialized in American Western and political history and served as chair of the department of history. He received his doctoral degree from the University of Utah. He has written four books,* including A Marriage of Equals, The Sensitive Leader, *and coauthored with Marti,* You're a Mormon Now: A Handbook for New Latter-day Saints. *He has served in the Church as a high councilor and as a bishop.*

gard for women. Henry met and finally married Lucy Stone, but only after a long, arduous courtship.

Lucy had been raised by an insensitive, authoritarian father who seemed to teach her, she thought, that marriage was not a good thing. And so she had determined to avoid it altogether. That is why it took Henry Blackwell so long to convince her — five years. When they finally married, in 1855, they read a joint protest, prepared together, against "such of the present laws of marriage as refused to recognize the wife as an independent, rational being while they confer upon the husband an injurious and un-natural superiority, investing him with legal powers which no honorable man would exercise and which no man should possess."[9]

It was the first marriage of equals. Yet, a month after their marriage, Lucy asked Henry's permission to attend a convention in Saratoga, New York. His response was, "Ask Lucy Stone."[10] Clearly their joint protest was only a first step toward escaping cultural assumptions about marriage. Nevertheless, their relationship was exceptionally enriching, and as the years went by, it blossomed into deep affection.

Our marriage strongly resembles their model, even though it began in a much more traditional way. Far from collaborating on a joint protest, we fell easily into traditional patterns. In the early days of our marriage, Marti did all the cooking and all the domestic work. I did very little, believe me. I did not seek for the equality of sharing domestic responsibilities.

The first impetus to change was a dynamic woman in Boston named Lela Coons. We listened to her speak one day about how she had saved a certain balance in her marriage by getting one afternoon a week to herself. Her husband had agreed to give her one afternoon a week. He would come home and she would do whatever she wanted from 3:00 P.M. on into the evening. It was wonderful. She could prepare a Sunday School lesson, or go shopping, or whatever else interested her. Marti and I looked at each other and thought, "Wow, that sounds progressive," and we did it. Now, looking back on it, it seems like tokenism — but it was a start.

Our next step was inspired by Marti's going away for a weekend. She was gone from Thursday evening until Sunday afternoon — not a very long time — but it seemed like an eternity to me. By the end of the second day, I was exhausted. I can still clearly remember lying in bed, looking at the ceiling with glazed eyes, wondering how I could be so tired after such a short time. Then I wondered how tired Marti must be every day. After thinking about this through that night, I decided to present her with an experimental idea. Why not share the load 50/50? She was barely in the door when I made this proposal. She was stunned, but interestingly enough, she accepted immediately. Over the next few days we planned the details, resulting in a sharing arrangement with respect to cooking, laundry, cleaning, and parental responsibilities.

After only three weeks of this, Marti received an attractive job offer, which would involve work in the afternoons. It was a job she wanted to take. That brought us to a crossroads because my upbringing had taught me that only the man should earn the living. It hurt my ego to think that I might need help to support my family. So we thought it through. It was clearly sensible in an economic sense: we lived in a very high cost-of-living area in Boston; my salary as a college professor was moderate. Besides the economic benefit, it was something Marti really wanted to do.

We decided to try it. As a professor, I found it possible to teach and counsel students in the mornings and then come home afternoons to spend the rest of the day preparing, researching, and writing. I managed this task in a strange way. Like a city editor of a newspaper, I would set up shop on the kitchen table, where I could be available to everyone: I could meet the children when they came home from school, listen to their day, and occasionally make afternoon snacks. It was a very hectic way to live, but I liked it. It was an opportunity for me to become better acquainted with my own children.

Since then we have discovered that almost 60 percent of married women in America are employed,[11] many for economic reasons. We have also learned the percentages are the same for Latter-day Saint women.[12] The average employed wife spends an average of 26 hours a week on housework, while the average husband spends 36 minutes.[13] Moreover, 87 percent of employed women desperately want their husbands to share the load.[14] It seems evident that any marriage with that kind of pressure will suffer eventually.

Marti and I have been very happy in our sharing arrangement. She handled the children's music lessons, planted the garden, did the taxes, cleaned the kitchen floor, did repairs and mechanical assembly, sewing, and cutting hair. I did the vacuuming, the laundry, took the cars to the garage, plowed the garden and helped weed it, took care of the lawn, paid the bills, and wrote to our missionary son. (That is, until he informed us that he was the only missionary he knew who received letters from his father only; so then we alternated.) We took turns cleaning bathrooms, cooking, helping the kids with their homework, and ironing. Neither of us washed windows.

Sharing the load this way has made me a more productive person domestically. It has eased Marti's fatigue considerably and given us a lot more time for each other. It has taught our children that men and women should spend equal time acting as parents. And it has given me a much appreciated opportunity to nurture my own children, a role I believe our society doesn't stress enough. Fathering and the need for the father to try to be close to his children is not highly valued.

Marti and I also share every decision we make. I have known many couples who have suffered as a result of one of them assuming sole control over the finances. If the family slips into financial trouble, it comes as a total shock to the other. Marti and I never make a major purchase without consulting each other. We also share our thoughts and plans about our professional work, and we share our problems and satisfaction in church work.

Sharing in marriage is an inherently controversial topic among men. As a bishop doing marriage counseling, I often brought up the possibility of sharing to the men who were in the bishop's office. I never suggested my own 50/50 arrangement but only a fraction of the load to ease the wife's burden. In most cases, these men were not anxious to hear such suggestions. In fact, they were worried that a comfortable status quo was being invaded. When I wrote articles about sharing, both in Boston and Salt Lake City newspapers, I received some angry responses from men — even from colleagues who did not appreciate my introducing this concept to their wives. So I realize that women do not find it easy to convince men that this is a good idea — but in my opinion it is eminently worth doing.

When we moved from Boston to Salt Lake, only eight months ago, our relationship received a new test. As part of a midlife crisis, I changed careers from college professor to newspaper columnist with the *Deseret News*, requiring a total change in life-style. I was now away from home much more than before — the way most husbands are. I would arrive home excited to share everything that happened to me during the day. Since then I have seen a *New Yorker* cartoon depicting a man standing at a microphone under a spotlight, in what appears to be a nightclub, with one woman watching him. He says, "And that was my day at the office! Thanks, Alice. You've been a great audience." That was me.

Even though we were still committed to a marriage of equals, our sharing technique almost immediately began crumbling. Instantly I had become a clone of the stereotyped executive who not only spends long days at work but brings it home with him. In large measure I was out of touch with what was happening in the home, particularly the first several weeks.

It took a lunch with Marti in a downtown Salt Lake City restaurant for me to see the light. We met for what I thought was a harmless romantic lunch, but Marti had another agenda. She brought up — in a very sensitive, diplomatic way as she always does — what she thought was a developing problem. I realized by the end of the lunch that I had developed tunnel vision. Preoccupied with my new job, I wasn't even worrying about how things had changed at home.

I pledged to do better. We reworked our domestic load, realistically considering how many hours I was out of the home now. What we worked out entailed a little less than my share in Massachusetts but a lot more than I had been doing in Utah. Mostly we changed cooking arrangements because I was so unpredictable in the hour I returned home. Now I only cook on Saturday morning and Saturday evening. Otherwise, it remains pretty close to 50/50.

I am pleased that we saved our equal partnership. Our relationship is stronger for having weathered a career change crisis, and I understand better than before the mentality of the typical male who works such long hours that he thinks he cannot share the domestic load. I would still encourage that man to remember the statement of former Senator Paul Tsongas from Massachusetts. Senator Tsongas left the United States Senate to spend more time with his family. In the press release he said, "No one on his deathbed ever said 'I wish I had spent more time with my business!' "

Marti Lythgoe

Marriage is a continuing adventure. The desire to make that adventure an equal partnership is a challenge for many couples. Dennis and I didn't just one day decide that we wanted

Marti Sorensen Lythgoe, homemaker and part-time technical writer, received a degree in elementary education from the University of Utah. While living in Massachusetts, she worked as an editor and a writer of elementary- and secondary-school textbooks. She also served on the board of Exponent II. *She has published in* Exponent II *and* This People, *in addition to the book she coauthored with Dennis. Her Church service includes four years as Gospel Doctrine teacher and three years as stake Young Women president. She and Dennis are the parents of five children.*

to have a marriage of equals and then live happily ever after. We did decide very early in our relationship that communication was vital to our happiness, and we have tried to talk out anything that bothered us. I discovered one thing that had to be talked out during our "moving to Utah" adjustment period. I was bothered not so much by doing more of the housework but by my expectation that Dennis would be doing the same domestic things he had done in Massachusetts, and he wasn't, and he wasn't even feeling guilty about it!

I think unmet expectations make a lot of women unhappy. And I think that most men don't even know what those expectations are. We think that our husbands will notice how hard we're working and just naturally pitch in and help out.

When I was first married, I expected that devoting all my time to my husband, children, and house would make me happy. Consequently, I gave up doing most of the things that had made me happy before I got married, things like reading, writing, having time for myself, and physical exercise. I didn't realize what I was doing to myself until suddenly I went an entire week without sleep and broke out in hives. When the doctor told me that the problem was depression and stress, I started looking at my life to see what might be missing.

Now, my husband had not made me give up those things. His greatest wish was for me to be happy. As soon as I was able to articulate what it was that I wanted to do, he was willing to help me do it. Of course, neither of us gets to do all of the things we want to; there are lots of compromises. But from that time forward, things started to get better for both of us, because when I was happy, Dennis was happier, too.

Over the years I have learned that there are things that I and other women need to do to make possible an equal partnership. One is to talk and act in ways that show we believe we are equal to our husbands. Lucy Stone asked her husband's permission to go to the conference, thereby giving him the right to assume that she needed his permission. It is one thing to plan together, and quite another to give our husbands authority that they didn't ask for. How many of you have said or heard another woman say, "I'm so lucky that my husband *lets* me do things like this"?

Many of us say things like, "Thanks for helping me with the dishes tonight, honey," giving our husbands permission to help us on a one-time basis. We *could* say something like, "This really gets done fast when we work together. Now I have time to go on that walk with you." What we want is to have our husbands feel that household chores are their responsibility too and that sharing them will benefit both of us.

We need to consult with our husbands before we say such things as, "My husband would never go along with that," or "My husband always wants me to do such and such." Our only assumption should be that because our husbands love us, they want to make us happy. Propose plans, express desires; don't assume and second-guess yourselves out of happy changes in your relationships. Don't assume your husband knows how you feel.

We need to communicate to our husbands by what we do that we think we are just as important as they are. When we encourage him to go to the gym while we feel that we can't take the time, or can find no one to tend the children while we exercise, what are we saying to him? Or if we make sure that he has quiet time to relax and read the paper while we never do, what message are we sending?

Dennis and I made some small changes in how we do things that have made a big difference. It took me five children to figure out that the person who sat by the youngest child at dinner—me, naturally—seldom got to enjoy the meal. We started taking turns sitting by the baby. My morale at dinner time soared, and Dennis became more involved with the children without taking time away from anything else.

After several long drives across the country, I finally figured out that the person sitting in the driver's seat got to look at the scenery and listen to the radio, while the person sitting in the passenger seat got to keep the kids from killing each other, pass out snacks, and change all the diapers. Dennis, of course, felt noble for doing all of the driving. When we started taking equal turns, the trips became less wearing on both of us.

And how much can you look forward to an evening out when you have to spend the entire afternoon calling every teenager you know looking for a baby-sitter? Reading an article entitled "He Got the Sitter" helped Dennis to understand that if he really wanted to give me a break and get me "away from it all," taking the responsibility for finding a baby-sitter now and then really helped.

When I went back to work part-time, I had my good days and my bad days, just like any man on the job. But when I vented my feelings about my bad days, Dennis would say something like, "Well, if it's so hard on you, maybe you should quit." I pointed out to him that when he complained about his job, I did not urge him to quit. All I wanted was a little sympathy and an opportunity to talk things out. Husbands sometimes inadvertently put us in an unequal position.

Of course, Dennis is also the same man who one Sunday left the ward where he was bishop and came home to take care of our sick child so that I could go to church and teach my Gospel Doctrine class. That told me, more than any words ever could, that he considered my church job just as important as his.

How did Dennis and I develop such a great partnership when we started out with a very traditional and unequal arrangement? There were definitely things that I did that made a difference. You might want to try some of them. Try going away for a weekend. Leave your husband a list of all the things that need to be done. But don't cook meals ahead or do other things that would make it too easy for him. Dennis has already told you how one such weekend affected him and our relationship.

Decide what it is that you would do with your time if you only had more of it. Until you know, there won't be much motivation for things to change. One of the first things I knew

I needed time for was to prepare my Sunday School lesson in peace and quiet. Once it was determined that I needed some quiet time to think and be inspired, we were able to work out a two-hour block of time where I could be uninterrupted by children.

After about the fifth time I sat down with the instructions for some "assembly required" gift and painstakingly told Dennis every step to take to put it together, we decided that chores should be divided on the basis of who does what best. I started putting things together, and he started making chocolate chip cookies. I do the taxes, and he does the laundry. A great way to encourage husbands to do more around the house is to list and divide chores according to interests and abilities.

All of us need a good reason to change what seems to be a comfortable situation. Dennis and I have discovered some really good reasons why men should want to become more involved in domestic duties and parenting. If you can discuss some of these reasons with your husband, change might be less painful.

Dennis has a wife who is less tired, physically and emotionally, because of all he does to help. I have more time to spend with him and more energy to do things that he would like me to do.

Our children adore Dennis and go to him with both problems and good news. He influences them more than an absentee father would. If anything should happen to me, Dennis knows how to cook, clean, and do the wash. And the children can no longer use the excuse, "Well, Dad doesn't have to do it." We are all responsible for making messes, and we're all responsible for cleaning them up.

Some women have a hard time giving their husbands free reign in the kitchen or in the laundry room. They find that, when husbands do more around the house, there are certain things women have to give up. Dennis's method of doing the laundry is to dump all of the clean clothes in a basket and then shout, "Everybody come and get your laundry." I have to give up clothes folded neatly in drawers and accept the "wrinkled look" on our children's play clothes, but I *don't* have to do the laundry. It's an acceptable trade-off based on the truth that sharing chores works best when each has his and her own responsibilities. Dennis does not help me with what remains *my* job. That way we each have the satisfaction of doing things in our own way and when it is convenient for us. Dennis often does the laundry in the evenings while he's unwinding from a long day.

Through it all we have tried to put our relationship first. We have been very fortunate that each of us was willing to change and let the other grow. We realize that change can be threatening and that a request for change needs to be accompanied by reassurances of love and commitment. On the other hand, we have decided that it is far kinder to communicate dissatisfaction than let little, easily changed things grow into an immovable mountain.

Bill Farnsworth

That eminent authority Bill Cosby once said of equality in marriage, "If any man truly believes that he is the boss of his house, then let him do this: pick up the phone, call a wallpaper store, order new wallpaper for one of the rooms in his house, and then put it on. He would have a longer life expectancy sprinkling arsenic on his eggs."[15] Despite Cosby's point of view, I firmly believe that an equal partnership is the only way two people can have a truly happy marriage. It doesn't come easily. It takes hard work, understanding, respect, unselfishness, love,

Wilford M. (Bill) Farnsworth is a banker, recently retired after serving nearly forty years with Citicorp/Citibank and as CEO of the Grindlays Bank Group in London. Together with his wife, he presided over the Puerto Rico-San Juan mission and is currently serving the Church as a regional representative. He graduated from Brigham Young University in 1947 and pursued graduate work at Rutgers and at Harvard.

pride in each other, and a willingness to support each other in agreed-upon goals. It takes dedication, communication, patience and time, and in our view it helps enormously, as in the gospel, to have an eternal perspective.

Now it helps when you have a companion like mine. All I have to do is try hard to fulfill my part and live up to her example. Even before our marriage, we started off right. Immediately following World War II, I returned to Brigham Young University to complete my senior year after four years' service in the United States Navy. That year I met Ella, and it wasn't long before we realized that we wanted to share our lives. By spring we were formally engaged. I had accepted a job offer in San Francisco, and our wedding plans were in process. One evening I came home to find a letter, a shocking one given my plans. It was a letter from my bishop telling me to report in Salt Lake City to a member of the Quorum of the Twelve to be interviewed for a mission. That was totally unexpected. In more than five years I had not been home for more than a few days at a time; I had had no interview with my bishop. My plans were made. I thought that four years in the service had preempted a mission, at least for the time being. I was too old. I had my degree, I had a job, and I was about to be married. Yet deep down I had always known that I would serve a mission. I confess, though, that at that moment I felt none too kindly toward that bishop.

The next morning after breakfast, without comment, I handed the letter to Ella. I'll never forget her reaction; it changed our lives. She opened and read the letter, paused a moment, and then simply said, "Bill, I always wanted to marry a returned missionary." Together we made a decision, and I did go on a mission. That decision was reflective of our life together: major decisions would always be joint decisions.

Three years later I returned from my mission to marry within the week, setting, I imagine, a record for shortest elapsed time from release to the altar. On the way home, I had stopped in New York where CitiBank had offered me a job in their overseas division. The San Francisco offer with a major accounting firm was also still available, so we had a major decision to make. The Citibank offer was attractive but involved an overseas life. Again we made this important decision together. We decided to give overseas living a chance.

Interestingly enough, Ella's patriarchal blessing had told her that she would "help build the waste places of Zion." We haven't yet figured out just where those "waste places" are, but wherever they are, we've been there. Time after time, as my work has moved us all around the world, Ella has packed up, left family, home, and newfound friends, and uncomplainingly moved. And life wasn't easy overseas, particularly in those days. I remember our first assignment to Montevideo, Uruguay, where I gained immense respect for this woman with whom I was so deeply in love. Ella spoke no Spanish, had no friends; I was working long hours. She could have stayed in our small apartment and wept and worried all day, but she didn't. I would come home in the evenings to find her excited. She would leave the apartment early in the morning and visit every museum and every place of interest she could find. She probably visited every shop—not to buy anything, because we didn't have two nickels to our name—but to learn. When I came home, she was excited to share with me, and we both benefitted from her self-education expeditions.

Two weeks after we arrived, she gave in Sunday School her first two-and-a-half-minute talk in Spanish. A few months later, she was called to be the very first district Relief Society president ever to serve in that country. Some years later while living in Rio de Janeiro, I gained even more respect for this wonderful woman. Most wives of American businessmen there spent their lives playing bridge or golfing; Ella didn't. She became deeply involved in the community. She volunteered as a "pink lady" at the hospital. When an Episcopalian minister opened a clinic in one of the worst slums *(favelas)* in Rio, she began working with him. She became involved in so many things that she had no time to feel lonely or bored. While the

women at bridge spent their lives complaining about the fore-
gone conveniences and opportunities at home in the United
States that were not available in Brazil, Ella was out accomplishing.

As my responsibilities in the bank increased, Ella's support
was generous and unflagging as we were called upon to entertain
customers and government officials. She became almost an
institution in bank circles as a role model for what a senior
bank officer's wife should be. She was active in church and in
the community. During many of those years, I traveled a great
deal overseas for the bank, and Ella often accompanied me.
On those travels she visited with the wives of our bank executives, often learning of and helping to solve problems that
I never even knew existed.

During those years, she fulfilled her Church responsibilities, working in the Relief Society where she served for more
than twenty-two years as stake or district Relief Society president in three stakes, four districts, and six countries. She was
and is an outstanding Church leader. She and her co-workers
performed miracles as they transformed sometimes dormant
organizations into dynamic, fully functioning Relief Societies.
During many of those years, even while I enjoyed success in
my work, it was humbling to go to church and there be known
as Sister Farnsworth's husband. I loved that.

Meanwhile I too served as a branch president and in the
stake presidency, and her support for me was steady and unbounded. In addition, she was an unbelievable mother to our
children. She loved them, played with them, worked with them,
laughed with and at them, inspired and drove them, and taught
them how to work. I can't resist one story. We were in a new
country and I, with a new job working long hours, had also
just been called as branch president. In Sunday School the
week before Mother's Day, one of the teachers asked the children what they did to help their mothers. After they excitedly
told what they did to help, the teacher asked, "Now what does
your daddy do to help her?" All the children but one raised

their hands, and one after another enthusiastically told how their daddies helped at home—washing the dishes, sweeping the floor, mowing the lawn. All had something to tell—all, that is, save one: my son. He was absolutely quiet. Finally, after all the children had had a turn, the teacher prodded my son, "Marty, surely your daddy does something to help?" Brow furrowed, he thought and thought—then suddenly a smile brightened his face: "He brings home the mail!" When she prodded him a little bit more—"Surely, Marty, your daddy does something else?"—he remembered one last thing: "Oh yes, he brings home the money." Well, the teacher—and several others—made certain I heard that story, and I tried to be a little more thoughtful of Ella at home.

Finally, in the later years of our life, we received the totally unanticipated call to serve as mission president in Puerto Rico. That was different from any call either of us had ever received before. Indeed, there is no other call quite like it in all the Church. It was a call to the two of us, and it proved to be one of the most glorious experiences of our lives. The two of us worked side by side, twenty-four hours a day, seven days a week, 365 days a year in the Lord's work—together. And I emphasize *together.* We were constant companions during that period and were truly partners. I can't even conceive of accepting a call such as that without someone like my wife at my side. Yes, I was the mission president, but she was my principal confidante and counselor. She had an office right by mine, and at my request she quickly and efficiently took charge of the health of the missionaries. In a tropical climate, maintaining health is a very difficult and serious undertaking. Overnight, she became an expert on tropical diseases from dengue fever to depression and on that most persistent, difficult, and troubling problem of missionaries: ingrown toenails.

She talked with the missionaries, listened to them, inspired them, prescribed for them, and then sent them back to work. There is no background quite like what one gets in Relief Society. Can you even imagine the wealth of ideas, creativity, and assistance she brought to the planning of zone conferences? Her creativity was such that I and my assistants invariably sought her thoughts and suggestions as we prepared our zone conference talks. Her influence was remarkable — indispensable! She participated in our planning sessions. The missionaries loved her, loved her talks, loved her motherly advice, and were buoyed up by the excitement and joy she showed at their success in baptisms. She inspired and lifted me when I was down or discouraged, shared my sorrows, and rejoiced with me as our missionaries honored their priesthood and their calls. For the first time in our lives, we were in all ways together. She was not the stake Relief Society president, and I was not the bishop or stake president. When we attended church, we were both called to the stand and identified as the mission presidents, President and Sister Farnsworth. I was not known as the stake Relief Society president's husband, and she was not known as the bishop's wife.

In conclusion, a life and a job like mine did not allow us to share household responsibilities, but I think mutual respect, mutual and shared decisions and responsibilities, also permit an equal partnership, an equal marriage. And I do know that only where there is mutual respect, love, and shared decision-making can there be true happiness.

Ella Farnsworth

Until recently I had never asked myself, is there really equality in our marriage? I had never worried about it before, yet as I have analyzed and dissected our marriage, I find ours

Ella Hull Farnsworth, together with her husband, spent nearly thirty years living and traveling in every corner of the world. An indefatigable worker, she served not only in the communities where she lived but in the Church as a stake or district Relief Society president for more than twenty years in three stakes, four districts, and six countries. She attended Idaho State University and Brigham Young University, where she received her degree in elementary education in 1948. She and Bill are the parents of three children.

is an equal partnership, however different it may be from that of our friends, the Lythgoes. Our marriage certainly hasn't been like the Donna Reed television sitcom with that beautifully neat house and the constant smiles and their ever-sweet relationship with those disgustingly well-behaved children. We have had our bumps and our share of ups and downs, from the frustrations of rearing children to our constant moves from one country to another, as well as the constant challenges of daily living. But our marriage has endured for forty years, and it has become stronger and richer with each passing year.

Our relationship is founded on mutual respect, mutual consideration, and common agreement on goals. We have tried hard to recognize each other's needs and be considerate. Not that it was that way in the beginning; we have worked hard at it for forty years. As we were about to be married, my father gave us some very wise counsel: "Marriage is wonderful but it is not always rosy. You have to work together, pull together as a team. And if you are truly going to have a happy marriage, each partner must be willing to give at least 90 percent." We took this advice to heart and committed to it. Often one of us would exceed that percentage, but we have not kept score. As I have listened to some of the marital problems that others have confided to me, I have wondered at times if there is too much time spent on scorekeeping—too much time deliberating whether you are giving enough or whether he is giving enough or whether he is taking more than you are.

The other evening we had dinner with one of our returned Puerto Rican missionaries who is married. When I referred to their common goals, he noted that he had his goals but she didn't have any for herself, nor did they have marriage goals. I was concerned. Goals are very important. When we were first married, these were some of the goals we set for ourselves: we determined to seek a happy marriage and an eternal family, putting the Lord first; we also wanted to learn, grow, and develop continuously together and yet each in our own way; we committed to be aware of and meet each other's needs;

111

we agreed to make joint decisions; and last but not least, we determined to have fun in our marriage.

Goals are important. In a marriage, couples need *both* common and individual goals. When I married Bill, I knew I was marrying a talented man who was ambitious. He was energetic. He had a big motor and wanted to grow and make his way in the world. That was fine with me. I too was energetic and wanted to learn and grow and make my way in the world. Early in life I made a commitment to myself that I was going to serve the Lord and that I was also going to contribute to the community in which I lived. Bill respected these commitments and did his best to help me achieve them.

One reward of a rich marriage is knowing you are the most important person in the world to your partner. That ensures emotional security and establishes trust. While the children were young, Bill traveled a great deal, sometimes for weeks at a time. Unlike Donna Reed, I felt quite put-upon at times, especially when other bank wives reminded me that our husbands were traveling to exotic places, staying in great hotels while we were at home drudging away washing floors, diapers, and dishes plus attending to small children. There were times when I felt so sorry for myself that I let that short-term agony almost obscure our long-range goals.

Shortly after Bill began traveling, however, a chance remark from one of his colleagues helped me appreciate something I had been forgetting. He said, "Ella, I have never seen anything like Bill. If we finish our work a little bit early, Bill checks the plane schedules and if he can find a night flight, he will fly all night to get home to you and the family. The rest of us will play a round of tennis or a round of golf and then take a comfortable flight the next day. What goes?" And it was true. Bill often arrived home at some unearthly hour. He frequently told us he would much rather be home with us than anywhere else, and he proved it. Our daughter Deney says, "Sure, Dad was gone a lot, but he let us know that he would rather be home with us. We knew that we were number one." This knowledge often proved a great comfort in his absence. And we were not twiddling our thumbs waiting for him to return. In fact, I must admit that sometimes after he returned from these trips, it would take a while to get our team back on track. It was difficult for me sometimes to give up those decision-making responsibilities that I had shouldered so long during his absence.

One thing I especially appreciated was that when Bill was home, he was home. He was home for me and the children, not shut up in a library with his work. He was there to work with us, and he was not averse to picking up a broom or a vacuum. I didn't have to ask him to do it. He did it.

When our children were in early-morning seminary, Bill, who was commuting into New York at 6:30 A.M., assumed the task of getting them up and fixing them breakfast. Those breakfasts did not add to his reputation as a cook. Our daughter describes the fried eggs as still cackling when they were served to her. But more important than the cackling eggs, she remembers the love and concern that her dad always showed to her. Then he would catch the train, and I would drive the children to seminary.

Good communications and joint decisions bring a closer union as each partner makes an honest effort to see and fulfill the other's needs. We knew when we chose an overseas career that we would have a transient life. We discussed those transfers every time they came. At one point, our three children were either married or serving on missions. We had lived in Germany almost a year when Bill received an offer to head up the bank operations in Southeast Asia. He was excited when he told me about it, but I said, "Bill, I don't want to go; I don't want to leave Germany. We just arrived. I love it here. I love the proximity to all the exciting places in Europe. No, I don't want to go." Bill was taken aback. Obviously, we were on different wavelengths. But he paused and then he said in his determined way, "All right, we won't go." Knowing him the way I did, I knew that was the end of the discussion. Once again, as has been the pattern in our life, my happiness was more important to him than anything else, even a career opportunity.

As I thought about this matter the rest of that day, however, I began questioning my own determination to stay in Germany. This move would be an opportunity for him, and it would undoubtedly be enriching for the two of us. So the next day I said, "Let's discuss this transfer." And so we did. We fasted and prayed about it, and the Lord, Bill, and I decided to go. It turned out to be one of the most satisfying experiences of our lives, but we would not have been so happy if the two of us had not made that decision together, each concerned for the happiness and welfare of the other. Both of us had to work at it.

Each time I was called to be part of a stake Relief Society or became heavily involved in community projects and community boards, I always talked to Bill about it first. Not because I had to. I didn't have to get permission from him, but I respected his opinions. And I needed his support if I were going to invest the time. He always said, "I will give you one hundred percent support." And he never stinted on that promise.

In New Jersey I was stake Relief Society president. Before leadership meetings or Relief Society activities, Bill and the children would be slaving away making posters, typing, putting programs together, peeling potatoes, or whatever else needed to be done. At one stake conference when the Relief Society board was sustained, our son Craig whispered, "Mom, don't you think that Dad and the rest of us ought to be sustained on the stake Relief Society board? We sure put a lot of work into that stake board."

Bill's pledge of support was never just lip service. At all the functions, if he were at home, he would quietly assist in any way that he could. He would load my car, then drive his own car to the church and help me unload before driving back home. When the function was over he would be back to load the car again, to clean up, and to put tables and chairs away.

One of my counselors in the stake Relief Society in Los Angeles described our relationship thus: "Ella always knows when to put on her Georgio perfume and kiss the clients, and Bill knows when to put the tables and chairs away."

Of course, Bill did more than put tables and chairs away. He fed my self-esteem by constantly encouraging me and complimenting me on the things I did well. In his eyes, I did everything well. We all need our self-esteem fed and lifted, especially by those we love. If I were to point to one major problem that troubles many marriages, it would be a lack of mutual respect. Many women have talked to me about marriage problems. Too often the complaint is that their husbands belittle the things they do, the things that are important to them. Sometimes husbands and wives feel their mate constantly criticizes everything they do, their choices, their behavior or habits, their clothes, even what they say. There is nothing more important in a partnership than mutual respect.

In England when I was serving as stake Relief Society president, Bill was the chief executive of a large British overseas bank with major networks around the world. We traveled a great deal together for the bank, but Bill never conveyed the impression that his commitments preempted mine. Before scheduling any trip, he would sit down with me, look at my calendar, and whenever possible schedule his and our trips around a Relief Society or community event for which I was responsible. My commitments and plans were important to me, and therefore they became important to him. As our son Marty said, "Dad didn't do this because he's such a nice guy, but because he has respect for you. Respect for your contributions, for your commitments, and for your work." Respect is a key to marital equality and happiness.

Bill set an example not only to our children but also to the husbands of Relief Society board members. When we were in England again, the sisters could not believe their eyes when they saw Bill Farnsworth doing dishes, cleaning up, and hanging little crepe-paper roses for decorations. I dare say many

Englishmen would rather die than dip their hands in dishwater; yet the sisters saw Bill, who in their eyes was a high-powered executive and wealthy bank president, regularly up to his elbows in dishwater after a ward or stake function.

A happy marriage is a partnership. It grows as each partner accepts more responsibility; it changes as his or her circumstances change. Our circumstances have recently changed. We are now adjusting to our return from a glorious mission. We have moved to an area where we have never lived before, and Bill has retired. We are working out the challenges these changes have brought into our lives. I am grateful for the happy marriage that we have had, grateful that it has grown stronger and richer over the years, and I truly can say that I have never felt that we did not have an equal partnership in our marriage.

Marti Lythgoe

Let me add a few words in summary for the four of us. Clearly an equal partnership means different things to different people. No two marriages are exactly alike. What each individual couple needs to be happy varies from marriage to marriage. What each individual in a marriage needs to feel valued and content varies from person to person. There are, however, some basic similarities in what is required to make marriage partners feel like equals. Mutual respect for each other's talents and abilities is certainly necessary. A willingness to discuss major family decisions and make compromises is essential. Understanding and empathy for your partner's role plays a large part in whatever sharing goes on, whether it is household chores or sharing of emotions. Making your partner happy will make you happier too.

In short, the kind of equality that we all want is the feeling that our spouse considers us of equal importance and deserving of the very best that he or she has to offer.

Notes

1. Suzanne M. Bianchi and Daphne Spain, *American Women in Transition* (New York: Russell Sage Foundation, 1986).
2. Virginia Sapiro, *Women in American Society*, 2d ed. (Mountain View, Calif.: Mayfield Publishing Co., 1990), p. 21.
3. United States Department of Labor, Bureau of Statistics, "News," 27 Oct. 1989.
4. Annemette Sorensen and Sara McLanahan, "Married Women's Economic Dependency, 1940–1980," *American Journal of Sociology* 93 (November 1987): 659–87.
5. Janice Peterson, "The Feminization of Poverty," *Journal of Economic Issues* 21 (March 1987): 329–37.
6. Dennis Lythgoe, *A Marriage of Equals* (Salt Lake City, Utah: Deseret Book, 1985).
7. Rosabeth Moss Kanter felt the role of wives was so important to understanding corporate cultures that she included a whole chapter on the contributions of wives in her groundbreaking book *Men and Women of the Corporation* (New York: Basic Books, 1977). See also Martha A. Fowlkes, "The Myth of Merit and Male Professional Careers," *Families and Work*, ed. Naomi Gerstel and Marriet Engel Gross (Philadelphia: Temple Press, 1987), pp. 347–60.
8. Kim Painter, "What Women Want Most: Intimacy," *USA Today*, 14 Oct. 1986.
9. Leslie Wheeler, "Lucy Stone, Wife of Henry Blackwell," *American History Illustrated* (December 1981): 41.
10. Ibid., pp. 39–45. Lucy Stone is the first woman known to have retained her maiden name after marriage. Women who afterwards followed in her footsteps were derisively referred to as "LucyStoners."
11. U.S. Department of Labor, "Employment in Perspective: Women in the Labor Force," Report 786, First Quarter 1990.
12. Kristen L. Goodman and Tim B. Heaton, "LDS Church Members in U.S. and Canada: A Demographic Profile," *AMCAP Journal* 12 (1986): 88–107.
13. Carol Tavris, "Marriage Isn't a Fifty/Fifty Affair," *Reader's Digest*, July 1984, p. 134; condensed from *Woman's Day*, 6 Mar. 1984.
14. Martha Lear, "How Many Choices Do Women *Really* Have?" *Woman's Day*, 11 Nov. 1986, p. 111.
15. Bill Cosby, *Love and Marriage* (New York: Doubleday, 1989), p. 106.

Children: Assembly Required, Instructions Not Included

CAMILLE COLLETT DELONG

As a marriage and family therapist with three children of my own, I have yet to see or hear of a baby arriving with instructions pinned or stamped on it. Each child is so individual that on occasion I feel a little lost, even though as a professional I am supposed to know all the answers. One of my main concerns in child-rearing is to promote self-esteem.

As we seek to build self-esteem in our children and grandchildren, we must also attend to the child that lives within us. Self-esteem concerns that child within us as well as the children that are part of our lives.

Let me explain. Last year I was talking to my brother-in-law, who works for a ski patrol, about avalanches. I asked him, "What is the first thing you do in an avalanche?" He told me to take a guess.

"Swim," I said.

"No."

"Dig a pocket for air," I guessed next.

"That's pretty good," he said. "Then what?"

"Dig for the surface!"

"Yes," he said, "but there is one essential step that you have left out. One of the first things you must do when you are covered with snow in an avalanche is spit."

"Oh come on," I laughed, incredulous. "Spit?!"

Camille Collett DeLong is a marriage and family therapist in private practice in Provo, Utah. She teaches courses at the Brigham Young University Marriott School of Management on creativity in business and balance in private and professional life. She and her husband, Tom, are the parents of three daughters.

But he was dead serious. "How do you know which direction you are digging in?" he explained. "We have found people who were digging down into the mountain who were buried only a foot underneath the surface. Totally disoriented! You need to spit to know which way to dig."

So if you are like me, there are avalanche times—times when I need to spit because I'm not sure of the direction I am headed. Many of you have specific questions, specific problems. Some of you may be feeling buried under. Although I can't provide specific answers to your specific situations, I hope to provide information and general guidelines that will help you determine which way is up and which way is down. One of those guidelines is to attend to the child within you.

All of us have a child within us: a healthy, playful part of any adult personality. For some of us, however, the child within may be frozen by unresolved childhood conflicts and negative memories. You may have a child within who never got enough acceptance or enough love, or a child within who learned to be ashamed of part of herself. Sometimes in an attempt to survive, the child within will have placed the hurt and shamed feelings, along with the parts of herself discovered to be unacceptable, out of her adult conscious awareness. They subsequently remain forever frozen at the age when that part of the self was rejected. As we grow, the adult self often adopts the same critical and rejecting stance towards those unaccepted feelings and parts as our parents held. When that occurs, we generally suffer from low self-esteem and may engage in critical and judgmental internal mind chatter. Sometimes that internal voice of judgment is heard in our own voice, sometimes the voice of one or both of our parents, or sometimes the voice of a person in our early life who was particularly critical and shaming of us.

The first step of healing is to allow the adult part of ourselves to recognize the internal voice of judgment, to actually hear the words and recognize the voice that is speaking. Second, the adult self must replace the negative messages with heartfelt loving, encouraging, and supportive statements. When that happens, our child within can slowly heal.

One way I have found to attend to my child within and to counteract the effects of my voice of judgment is to live by a set of four guideline statements that I have developed for myself. These statements help me know if I am digging toward the mountain or toward the air.

The first is, "I am committed to silencing my voice of judgment." The second is, "I am committed to my own growth and to nourishing myself." The third is, "I am committed to speaking the truth from my heart." The fourth is, "I am committed to being accountable."

Let me share a few stories about the child within me that is growing up along with my children. About a month ago, it became abundantly clear to me that a family member — a man forty years of age — needed to be in a substance-abuse program. I have been very close to him for the last five years, working with him, believing in him, loving him, being angry with him, all those things that people go through who have a loved one in trouble of this sort. Often over the past five years I had sensed the innocent, delightful child within him struggling to be free of his immensely critical, internal voice of judgment; however, when his voice of judgment would win out over self-love, as it regularly did, his adult self would douse the pain with drugs and alcohol. Unable to break the cycle, his life was finally so out of control that suicide began looking to him like the only alternative. At that point, I realized that there was nothing more that I on my own could do for him. So I mobilized several other family members and together we confronted him, insisting that he go to the hospital.

To my surprise, his situation was so miserable that he was actually relieved to have us demand, "You have to go into treatment. There is no other choice." I began thinking, "Why didn't I say this to him five years ago? I'm a professional. I should have known better." Can you hear my voice of judgment speaking out here?

Over the next few days, I continued berating myself with I-should-have-known-betters: pummeling myself with questions such as, "Why didn't I do this earlier? Why did I believe this person so long? Why didn't I do the hard thing five years ago and save us all of this grief?" Finally I began to notice the emotional bruises and realized, "I have let go of my guideline." I was digging down towards the mountain and not up towards the surface. "I am committed to silencing my voice of judgment," I reminded myself—but simply realizing what I had been doing was not enough. I had to deliberately commit time and effort toward silencing that voice of judgment. I talked to some people, I prayed about it, and I was eventually able to let it go.

Silencing the voice of judgment is one of the principles that I am determined to live by. Not only does it help my self-concept but it spills over to my children. I call this benefit the trickle-down effect. Their anxiety over the situation—which they were well aware of—died down as I was able to silence the voice of judgment in myself. I saw a direct correlation in my children's faces and their behavior.

The second personal guideline that I live by—"I'm committed to my own growth and to nourishing myself"—also benefits my family, for obviously I cannot give what I don't have. If I am withering inside, how can I nourish my children? This truth was brought home to me after we spent a year in Boston in 1986. While there, I had an absolutely wonderful time, growing, learning, finding aspects of myself that I had never known existed. But when I came back to Utah at the end of that lovely year, I felt like a part of me had died and was left in Boston. Clearly, I needed to make some major changes in my life in Utah to provide myself with similar opportunities for growth and intellectual stimulation. At first, however, rather than address the problem, I ignored it.

I should know better, right? Knowing better has been my profession for twenty years. But what finally made me realize I was digging the wrong way was watching my twelve-year-old daughter. The lights were going off in her too. She started losing some of her bounce and her spunk. My distress was spilling over on her. So I decided that this had to stop, the buck stops here: I sought some counseling. I changed my living situation, I changed my working situation, and I did some fine-tuning in my marriage. In the next month or so, after I had done my work, my daughter's lights came back on, because mine did. The trickle-down effect had worked again. When my spirits revived and my life took on energy and excitement again, so did hers. At one point, after I had expressed to her my sorrow that she had had to live with me while I was in such pain, she hugged me and said, "Don't worry, Mom, we can grow up together." She's right, of course. There is definitely a twelve-year-old child in me, a companion to her. So I'm committed to my growth and nourishing myself.

A third guideline statement — one that is important to me, yet always a struggle — is to live and speak from my heart rather than from my intellect, my head, or my image. For instance, two weeks ago when I was driving home from somewhere with my daughter, my twelve-year-old again, she had a very exciting book along that she was reading. At one point she said, "Mom, I've got to read this to you." She related a very touching story about a black girl in the South who had been able to forgive a neighbor who had killed her father. As she was reading it to me, I found myself being very, very stirred emotionally and noticed my immediate reaction was to cut off my emotion, to cut off my tears, to stop myself from feeling it so intensely.

As I was driving down the road fighting my impulse to cry as my daughter was still reading, I suddenly thought, "What am I doing? This daughter, who is one of the lights of my life, whom I have such a soul connection with — I'm hiding my emotions from her. I'm hiding from her. I'm hiding how her story and her passion about this story is affecting me." Once I realized what I was doing, I was able to say, "I'm going to go with my heart." And so I let the tears roll, still driving my car. I didn't pull over; I simply let the tears, the feelings, well up as I drove. And then I expressed to my daughter how much it meant to me to have her read it to me and my deep delight that this particular story meant so much to her. I just let the tears come and the words from my heart pour out. I was able to do it because I remembered my vision statement which is, "I'm committed to speaking the truth from my heart." Sometimes I forget it, but when I remember, it points me back to the surface. Again, I know which way is down and which way is up.

My fourth guideline statement is, "I am committed to being accountable." Last week my two older daughters took me aside and said, "Mom, we need to talk to you about something." I said, "Okay, what?" They were upset about Joanna, our youngest daughter who is almost seven. "You are really letting Joanna get away with everything," they said. "She doesn't have to clean her room; we have to clean our room. She doesn't have to do the dishes; we have to do the dishes. You make excuses for her. You say she is too young, or this, or that, or the other. And she is the very best one at getting out of work of any of us three kids—and Mom, you need to change this because, frankly, she is just not being accountable."

We use that word in our home, *accountable*. I felt the defenses coming to my lips, "Yes, but she is only seven. I used to do this for you," and so on. But I stopped and I acknowledged to myself, "You know, they are right. Because she is the noisiest of the three, plus the one who can beat me in a verbal battle, I give up and give in to her sometimes." Joanna wasn't learning to be accountable because I wasn't being accountable. Being accountable means being responsible for myself and my decisions, plus requiring accountability from those I have responsibility for. I was teaching Joanna to evade responsibility by arguing with me. So I worked on finding ways to help Joanna and me be accountable—without criticism or judgment but also without simply caving in and doing it for her.

Because being accountable is such an important guideline

for me, at night when I go to bed I try as often as possible to spend a moment to reflect on the day, to evaluate how I have been, and reflect back on my guidelines: have I lived them or have I not? Then I have some idea whether I'm digging toward the mountain or toward the surface. Of course, I don't ever score absolutely perfect, but that's all right because, remember, the first guideline is, silence the voice of judgment. What matters is not perfection but heading in the right direction.

Self-Esteem in Children: Grandmothers Can Help, Too

MICHAELENE P. GRASSLI

A "Peanuts" comic strip shows Sally standing before the class, announcing, "For show and tell today, I have something unique. I'm not going to tell about a pet or show you a toy or a book or anything like that. Instead I'm going to tell you all about someone I consider quite fascinating." The last frame shows her with a big smile on her face, her arms spread wide, proudly proclaiming, "Myself!"[1]

Five-year-old Sara sitting on the floor looking at herself in a mirror said to her mother, "Mom, I adore me!"

All children come into the world with a little seed of self-esteem deep inside. Whether or not they will grow up feeling good about themselves depends upon others' nurturing that little seed of self-esteem. What impressions does a baby receive from the mother as she handles him or her? When she changes a diaper, does she talk and play with the baby or is she screwing up her face in disgust?

What impression does a growing child receive from the world around him? Does the neighbor think ten-year-old Andy is a pain in the neck or a fascinating living thing? I often wonder how Dennis the Menace can continue feeling okay about himself with a neighbor like Mr. Wilson. The Church, the school,

Michaelene P. Grassli has served as General President of the Primary since April 1988. Active in local school affairs, she is a member of the National Cub Scouts of America and a recipient of the Silver Buffalo award. Sister Grassli also serves on the board of directors of the Primary Children's Medical Center. She attended Brigham Young University as a home economics major. She and her husband, Leonard, are the parents of three children.

and the community all leave their mark. It needs to be the mark of love.

Children's sensitivities are keen, even from their earliest moments. Four-year-old Mandy was standing outside on a rather crisp day with her little face turned upward to the sun, her eyes closed. When her grandmother walked out and saw her, Mandy said, "Oh, Grandma, the sun is giving me a hug!" In a cold world, that warm-hug feeling is what love can create.

Many valuable sources of information on self-esteem are available to us, ranging from the theoretical to the practical, from the academic to the home-grown. We can help children feel as Sally in the cartoon did—that *she* was the most interesting thing she could think of for show and tell. As I listen to others and read about how to develop self-esteem in children, however, I could feel very guilty! "Why didn't I do that when my children were young?" I might ask myself. Or "I should have done it this way instead of that way." About parental guilt, let me just say, in summary: it is useless to berate ourselves for the things we wish we had done. We do the best we can and go on. The beauty of the gospel is that people can change. Our children can change, and we can change! So if we have been doing things that destroy our children's self-esteem or don't do enough to build it, we can learn new, positive ways to influence children. And sometimes we can have a second chance with another generation. Let me tell you how grandmothers can influence a child's self-esteem.

I have been thinking about the grandmothers I have known. I had a grandmother and a gramma. *Grandmother* was formal and proper. *Gramma* was casual and informal. Grandmother taught me that there should be a place for everything and everything in its place, a phrase which comes into my mind without fail every time I clean house. She held good manners in high regard. Her gifts to me were books—scriptures, a book of poetry. She was a lady, and she expected me to be a lady. She promoted the virtues in me. She didn't like our swimming down her stairs. Oh, they were marvelous stairs! Softly carpeted, wide and gently sloping, Grandmother's stairs were not like the steep steps down to our basement. It was so fun to swim down head first, but she didn't like that much nor did she like noisy running through the house. But because she cared about my character development, I knew she loved me very much and that I was important to her.

Now my *Gramma*, on the other hand, knew what children liked and let us do it. She had little chairs and a table and little dishes just our size that we could eat on. That made us feel significant. She always had goodies in her cupboard. There was always fudge at Gramma's house, and if there wasn't, she would say, "Let's make some."

Gramma was an artist and taught us how to water color. She had an eye for elegance and beauty. I remember her kneeling on the grass to show us the faces on the pansies, pointing out how the colors ran into one another as though they were watercolored on wet paper. She showed us how rose petals curve around one another.

I celebrated my eighth birthday at Gramma's house. I don't remember any other birthday cakes in my life, but I remember the one she made for me that year. It was white angel food cake with pink frosting, and in the center hole of the cake she had placed a slender glass vase with beautiful pink roses in it. I remember thinking it was the most beautiful cake in the world.

Gramma's house was clean, but there were art supplies all over, books piled on the floor to read, and a dog to play with. *Grandmother's* house was not only clean but tidy. Thanksgiving dinner at her house was crystal, linen, china, and best dress.

From both my *Grandmother,* whom I loved, respected, and wanted to emulate, and my *Gramma,* whom I adored and had fun with, I was bestowed with great gifts—all precious to me. *I* was launched into grandmotherhood four years ago and now am blessed with two little sweethearts. And I want to be for them a little bit *grandmother* and a little bit *gramma.*

Anyone can grandparent, even if you don't have children

or grandchildren of your own. I have a friend who grand-mothers her nieces and nephews. A single friend has even been honored by children's being named after her because of her nurturing nature.

Another "Peanuts" cartoon shows Linus with his blanket, sucking his thumb, saying to Charlie Brown, "I think the world is much better than it was, say, five years ago." Charlie Brown, outraged, turns to him and yells, "How can you say that? Don't you ever read the papers? Don't you ever listen to the radio? How can you stand there and tell me this is a better world?" Then Linus turns to Charlie Brown and says, "Because I'm in it now!"

How do grandmothers make children feel that the world is a better place because they are in it? My Gramma and Grand-mother did it. Dr. Victor B. Cline, psychologist and author of *How to Make Your Child a Winner*, defines self-esteem in a way that I find very understandable and useful. In summary, he teaches that self-esteem consists of four component feelings about oneself:

1. Acceptance (People like me)
2. Competence (I can do things)
3. Virtue (I am a good person)
4. Power (I can control my life)[2]

Grandmothers are able to bring these feelings of acceptance, competence, virtue, and power into the lives of their grand-children. Let me tell you of some instances.

Grandmothers can be a sympathetic sounding board. Cynthia remembers how her grandmother helped her work through times when she and her mother were not seeing eye-to-eye. "When I was a little girl, my grandmother and I enjoyed lots of pretend games. My grandmother pretended to be Mrs. Brown, and I pretended to be Mrs. Green. If ever there were a problem at my house, I couldn't talk about my mother and the problem, but I could say things about Mrs. Green's mother. Mrs. Brown listened with great patience and understanding and always said just exactly what I needed to hear to make everything all right again."[3]

In another instance, Kathy, now a grown woman, recalls spending afternoons at her grandparents' home as a child. Sometimes she would hide under the table. Grandmother would enter the room asking, "Where's Kathy? Oh, didn't she come today? I'm so disappointed. It's always a lot more fun when Kathy's here." She knew Kathy was there but always played this game. She might exclaim, "Oh, how I wish Kathy were here! I was looking forward to talking with her. I like it so much when she's here. She's such a wonderful girl. I surely hope she will be here tomorrow." On and on she would go until Kathy would at length reveal herself amid shouts of delight from Grandmother. Kathy says she kept this routine going for years, even when she was so big her legs stuck out from under the table. She loved every word as she overheard Grandmother telling Grandfather how much she enjoyed Kathy and what a darling little girl she was. Kathy looks back on those times as perhaps the central self-esteem building experiences of her life.[4]

One overlooked power a grandparent has is the ability to help a grandchild develop what Victor Cline labels a sense or feeling of virtue. Some children may be more "difficult" than others for their parents and teachers. These children especially will benefit from a grandparent who recognizes their special worth. Jason and Eric were two such children. These two on a visit with their grandmother came home from Primary. All the children in Primary that day had made bookmarks for their scriptures. They were to describe themselves or draw something about themselves on their bookmark. Jason's showed a picture of sunshine and flowers and a drawing of a little boy with a smiling face. On Eric's bookmark were these words, written in black crayon: "Eric is a bad boy." Seeing that bookmark stabbed like a knife into the pit of their grandmother's stomach, and she determined to do something to change that little boy's image of himself. She recognized that self-esteem is rooted in the concepts of the gospel and that her little grandson was not being taught his true worth. Eric's parents were divorced and struggling with their own testimonies. The gospel was paramount in the grandmother's life, and she knew the influence it could have on his self-esteem. She read Bible and Book of Mormon stories to Eric. She took him to Church. She spent time with him. She arranged fun things for him to do, so that he knew that she cared about him. She knew that if Eric loved her, he would love what she loved. He would come to know, as she knew, that he was a precious child of God.

Another grandmother friend of mine understands her grandchildren. She lets them put food coloring in their bath water and play with shaving cream on the tile while they are bathing. She feeds them breakfast in bed. She writes them lots of letters even when they live right in town just a few blocks away. She always puts tiny foil hearts in the letters, and they collect and save all the hearts. Those sparkly hearts say to her grandchildren, "Nanna loves me."

She also helps them feel good about themselves by encouraging them to do good things for others. They do Christmas projects together. Last year they planned a Christmas surprise for a needy family. The children all worked with their grandmother to make, sort, and wrap things, and then one evening they all went together to deliver their gifts on the doorstep, ring the bell, and run.

Grandparents can also be audiences for their grandchildren's fledgling skills and talents. One grandmother of my acquaintance allows her grandchildren to play her grand piano if they've learned a new piece when they come to see her. She pays for violin lessons for a talented little grandson whose family can't afford that luxury.

These grandmothers have enough of the child in them to know what children need. These grandmothers have surrounded children with *acceptance*, have given them opportunities to develop *competence*, have taught *virtue*, and have shown children they have *power* over their lives.

When we parents, grandparents, friends, and teachers who have the power to love children exercise that love as He who loves most has done, then we touch their lives as He would have us do. When we are with children, a caring look, the warmth of our voices, the gentleness of our touch, the kindness of our actions will leave love marks on their hearts and souls. We then will have helped give them an edge in life, an advantage — self-esteem that turns problems into opportunities, heartache into understanding, and disappointments into courage.

Notes

1. Charles Schultz, "Peanuts," syndicated comic strip.
2. Victor B. Cline, *How to Make Your Child a Winner* (New York: Walker and Company, 1980), pp. 23–24.
3. Daryl V. Hoole, "Just for Grandmothers," unpublished manuscript in possession of author.
4. Ibid.

WOMEN AND EVERYDAY LIFE

"For that which ye do send out shall return unto you again, and be restored"
— Alma 41:15

Not one of my distresses has seemed to lie outside Christ's consciousness or power. When I have done as he has instructed, especially in keeping my mind firm, my reaching has reached his.
— M. Catherine Thomas

The LDS Superwoman:
Methods, Myths, and Myopia

JANET GRIFFIN LEE

Somewhere out there is a woman who one morning last fall bottled about sixty quarts of fruit and in the afternoon practiced the violin, all while paying strict attention to her twin babies. There is also someone out there who got up at 4:30 this morning to jog and read the scriptures before baking ten loaves of bread, cleaning the kitchen, and arriving at this conference on time. There is probably someone else who made her seven daughters new dresses for Easter, completing them the day after Valentine's Day so that she would have time to recover the living room furniture in between her responsibilities as Relief Society president. There are undoubtedly single parents out there who run circles around all the rest of us. And lots of someones who are unmarried and without children who think that to keep up they need to speed around the track four times faster than anyone else.

I prefer to believe, however, that most women are somewhat like I am: you are desperately trying — given your talents, your abilities, and your time — to do as good a job as you know how to do with your home, your family, and your life. Even so, do you ever worry that perhaps you are lagging behind

Janet Griffin Lee holds a bachelor's degree in elementary education and human development and family relations. Specializing in kindergarten through third grades, she has twice developed reading curriculum and phonics programs that have been adopted by the districts in which she has taught. She has served the Church on various stake boards, as Young Women president, and as a teacher. She and her husband, Rex E. Lee, are the parents of seven children and the grandparents of three.

while others press ahead? I want to open for you briefly four windows into my life that may help you deal with these feelings, maybe even challenge them.

The first window opens to a day in kindergarten. I am five years old, and I am sitting next to my very best friend, Margaret. The teacher, Mrs. Kane, tells us to draw "a pretty picture." Margaret takes out her box of forty-eight Crayola crayons and begins designing a beautiful swing set with flowers and trees and children. With my box of eight, fat, school-issue crayons, I draw the only object of art I know how to: a flower with little petals around it that my brother has taught me. I place next to my five-petaled, standard-red flower a little brown house. I glance over at Margaret's desktop. Immediately, I can see that Margaret's picture is a lot better than mine. My heart sinks a little. At the end of the coloring period, an endless ten minutes with only eight colors to choose from, Mrs. Kane holds up Margaret's picture for everyone to admire. I know now that I am in terrible trouble in kindergarten. Even though I have not yet heard of the superwoman image, I am already comparing myself to someone else; I feel inferior.

I went home that day and told my mother that I needed a box of forty-eight Crayola crayons like Margaret's so that I could have silver and gold and so that I could make a pretty picture like hers. My mother indulged me. She could tell how important this was. It didn't take me long, however, to see that although the number of crayons in my box had increased and my art work had improved somewhat, my pictures still did not look like Margaret's. But I did not give up. Margaret continued to draw beautiful pictures, and sometimes she would bring them to my house and we would tape them up on my playhouse wall. After she left, I would get out my box of forty-eight crayons and try to copy her pictures. Gradually my drawing did improve.

I remained diligent. I never quit trying to improve, but even at age five, it eventually became apparent to me that my graphic, artistic skills were never going to equal Margaret's.

My mother, being a very bright and observant mother, enrolled me in dancing lessons. Soon, as I applauded Margaret's coloring, she clapped when I danced. That seemed a fine trade-off. And I really did learn something about life in kindergarten that year. The problem reappeared in junior high school when a new friend learned to dance better than I, but that is another story for another day.

Instead, let me open the next window in time to a Relief Society miniclass where we are learning counted cross-stitch, something that as a young, married mother I thought would be fun and easy to learn. At first I am enthusiastic, but as my fingers struggle—for I am neither nimble nor quick—I begin to panic. For reassurance, I glance over at the other ladies. They are chatting, easily weaving in and out, making their work look beautiful. I feel an overwhelming urge to change my baby's diaper, even though she is sleeping peacefully in her basket beside my chair. In the bathroom, I change her dry diaper, debating whether or not to go back. Finally, I stuff the cross-stitch into my purse, convincing myself that I will finish it another time, and I go home very discouraged. In fact, all the way home I chastise myself with gloomy thoughts: "This takes so much patience. I have no patience. Patience is a godly virtue, and I have none."

No longer full of kindergarten confidence, I did not persist with that project. It is probably still in a drawer somewhere. But I did persist in feeling downcast and in drawing negative conclusions about my character. "I have no patience," I told myself, certain I had discovered a deep, eternal flaw.

A few days later, while visiting my mother-in-law, I struggled through the usual bedtime routine of a very resistant, typically stubborn two-year-old. I finally got him bathed, dressed, and into bed. When I returned to the living room, my mother-in-law shook her head and remarked with obvious sincerity, "I wish I had your patience."

I simply glowed inside. "I really do have patience after all," I thought. "If someone saw patience in me, maybe some element of this godlike virtue does reside deep within. Maybe godlike traits could be manifest in other ways than counted cross-stitch." A happy conjunction of events had taught me another important lesson, which I have since applied on many occasions.

The next window opens to a time in 1981 shortly after our family moved to Washington, D.C., so that Rex could serve as the United States solicitor general. At that time, it becomes financially necessary for me to take a full-time job outside the home. We have a large family of seven children, ages eighteen to two. I don't want my family to feel in any way penalized because I am a working mother, and so I proceed to do what many of you are doing or have done. I continue both my stake and ward jobs. I accompany my husband to the Supreme Court and participate in social events. I take care of my home with the help of my children and husband but no outside help. I continue to try to jog and exercise regularly. I even try to read daily, sometimes between the hours of two and three in the morning. When possible, I spend individual time with each child. I am that determined not to let anything slide or to compromise in any way. I am, of course, exhausted. The lesson I must learn is so clear. And finally the time comes when some adjustments have to be made. Surprisingly, life becomes easier and happier again for all of us.

The last window I will open into my past is a glimpse into a more recent time—only three years ago, during a period of critical illness in my husband's life. We are many miles from home and away from our children. My husband remains in a hospital room for more than five months, and I spend much of my time there with him. The longings that we feel during his long hospital stay are in some ways surprising. During this period of prolonged inactivity, we don't remember with particular longing our days of being busy—the days when we have felt the thrill of going the extra mile or of accomplishing more than we thought possible in a day.

Instead, as Rex lies inactive, isolated from work, family,

and friends, our thoughts turn to the simple pleasures of life. We long for a walk in the spring sunshine. We yearn for a visit, even in the wee morning hours, with a teenager sharing his joys or her aspirations. We wish we could sit in a sacrament meeting among friends and neighbors, singing a well-loved hymn and feeling the sweet sense of community and shared hopes with all those around. We recall with longing such high points in our life as watching the evening news together after the children are in bed. Simple pleasures. I even remember thinking one day, "I wish I could go home and scrub the tile and the grout in my bathroom." Again, simple accomplishments, simple pleasures.

Perhaps we misunderstand the scriptures that admonish us to "Be ye therefore perfect." Do we think that perfection needs to be attained immediately—in fact, right now? We set off at a relentless, impossible pace. Do we expect to arrive at perfection in this life? Maybe tomorrow, if we hurry? At one point in my life, a dear friend shared this enlightening thought with me: "Becoming perfect is an eternal process, not an earthly accomplishment."

The same friend also suggested that I evaluate myself on a continuum rather than in absolutes. So each day I evaluate myself—something I can't seem to help doing. I concentrate on what I accomplished, focusing on one single aspect in my life where I am making progress. I rate myself with a seven or an eight or maybe even a ten, depending on what I accomplished that day. Once I have done that, I then ignore the fact that the wonderful meal I was going to prepare was replaced by Campbell's soup and toast. I stop thinking about how I missed my five-mile run in the morning and concentrate on the time I spent with a dear friend. In essence, this plan allows me to feel good about myself, to value what's good in my life and not to focus on all the worthwhile things I did not quite get to . . . yet—whether they be counted cross-stitch, or PTA meetings, or even visiting a neighbor in the hospital.

I find that dealing with the superwoman image gets harder,

not easier, as we advance in years. When I was in my twenties and had three young preschoolers at home, I actually had the audacity one day to identify it in my journal as "a perfect day." Not just a ten, but perfect! Let me briefly summarize that day for you. The major event was spending the afternoon at the park, pushing my children on the swings, and then having an early picnic with another family. That evening, we were joined by my tired husband. Hungry again, we were delighted that he had brought a bag full of fifteen-cent hamburgers. No drinks. (We were really saving money in those days; we would drink from the water fountain.) While we watched the sun go down, the baby fell asleep in her walker while our other two children played on the swings. We felt life was perfect.

I wonder whether I finished the laundry that day. Most likely, I did. But I'm sure I didn't jog — I didn't even know yet that I was supposed to. I probably didn't even bake bread. But that was a perfect day. Even rating myself on a continuum was superfluous. May we all have many such days, full of loving relationships and simple pleasures.

Learning Points of Faith

JAYNE B. MALAN

To believe is one thing, but to know the reality of God and to grow up with that knowledge is a blessing. At times I haven't understood God's timing or why something bad had to happen, but I've never had occasion to question his love for me. I was taught at an early age to "pray always, and be believing, and all things shall work together for [my] good." (D&C 90:24.) I believed it. As a result, I grew up in a happy, uncomplaining atmosphere filled with love and selfless service. My parents went to church; my brothers and sisters and I all went to church along with them. I can remember, however, not liking general conference—the long hours of being quiet and sitting still, the hard benches, the talks that went on and on and on—but I loved Primary, except for the time they wanted me to lie down on the floor and let an elephant step over me. It was circus day, and the children were all dressed up as clowns and animals and dancing girls. I was a dancing girl—a little ballerina dressed in blue who happened to be the smallest child in Primary. Two of the biggest boys were wearing an elephant costume. All elephants, real or not, are big and heavy and dark to a three-year-old.

Jayne Broadbent Malan is first counselor in the Young Women General Presidency, having previously served on the Relief Society, Young Women, APMIA, and YWMIA general boards and as a Lambda Delta Sigma national officer. She received a degree in drama from the University of Utah and has been a free-lance writer and producer with Bonneville Media Communications and Brigham Young University. In addition to writing children's shows, she has been involved with many Church-related productions. She and her husband, Terry, are the parents of two children and the grandparents of six.

141

I've come a long way since Primary, and I'm not afraid of elephants at church anymore, although I've had a few mammoths of one sort and another to face over the years.

I don't remember when I began liking general conference or when I discovered for myself that the gospel of Jesus Christ is true and that I have a personal responsibility concerning it. Some people can identify specific "turning points" in their conversion process. Mine are more like "learning points" that built faith.

One time when I was a little girl, I was hiding in a dark corner behind the door in my mother's bedroom because my feelings were hurt. Being the youngest in a family of nine, I often suffered from emotional nicks and scrapes. I could hear my brothers and sisters talking and laughing in the kitchen, and I remember thinking, "How can they be so happy when I'm so miserable? Don't they know?" I wanted them to come so that I could send them away. "Why don't they come and see how miserable I am?" I thought. I waited and waited. It was lonely. It was dark. It was not fun at all sulking in my gloomy corner behind Mother's bedroom door, but I didn't know how to come out without losing face. Finally, I pushed the door open a little and the dark dissolved. With the light, my mood changed. In a few moments I was happily involved with the family again, and I don't think they'd even missed me.

At a very young age I learned from this experience the truth of Mormon's prophecy that "he that is happy shall be happy still; and he that is unhappy shall be unhappy still" (Mormon 9:14), and, more importantly, the crucial message that the choice is up to me. This was a lesson I needed to learn.

The lesson paid off many years later when I was a new General Board member and part of a committee responsible for a production to be held in the Tabernacle. It was my time to shine. (I think they call this attitude pride.) I could even imagine my name in lights across the organ pipes, "Script written by Jayne Malan." We worked on the project day and night for months—fasting and praying, writing and rewriting. I put off vacations with my family and put my very heart and soul into the project. With the script finally finished, we were making last-minute plans to go into production when those in charge called our committee together and told us that the program had been canceled. I tried hard to be brave, but I couldn't hold back the tears. The more experienced committee members looked at me with sad eyes and long faces. I didn't want their pity. All I wanted to do was to get out of there and hide in a dark corner. My feelings were hurt. Many desperate and pleading prayers for understanding followed.

The next few days were difficult. In addition to feelings of failure and inadequacy, I struggled with anger and frustration over the time, the energy, the creative thought that had gone into a project never to be produced. Concerned about the time and effort of the other men and women on the committee as well, I prayed for understanding, for peace of mind. Gradually, with prayerful pondering, the realization came that the work I had been called to do was not *my* work and for *my* glory, but it was *his* work and for *his* glory, to help "bring to pass the immortality and eternal life of man." (Moses 1:39.) I also realized that his work would go forth according to *his* will and not *mine*. These were "learning points," dearly come by.

I then had a choice, to hide and stay unhappy or to come up with a plan to cheer things up. So, when the committee met again the following week, I suggested a plan. The committee agreed. We invited our spouses and a few close friends to a funeral. We dressed in black, sang sad songs, and buried the script in a planter box on the dining room table where we laughed a lot and feasted on good food and the memories we shared.

Then there was the Wednesday I was to meet with Elder Vaughn Featherstone to be set apart for the new Young Women General Board. Under normal circumstances that would have been the most exciting day of my life. But the timing seemed wrong. I had already served for six years on the general level, and the past year, in particular, had been extremely demanding. I was tired. I was especially tired of giving my total time and energy to the Church. As the day approached, the possibility of having more time for my family and doing more non-Church related things became more and more enticing. I thought, "Don't I have a choice? Don't I have anything to say about what I do with my life?" With the adversary's help, I began to review everything that I had ever done wrong in my life. Soon I felt unworthy to serve at all. Being deeply troubled, I prayed for direction or peace of mind but didn't find either. When Wednesday came, things were no better, so I went to the temple. Afterwards, there was still time before my appointment, so I wandered over to the Temple Square Visitors' Center and idly looked at the paintings of Christ. Winding my way upstairs, past the Joseph Smith diorama, I studied a painting on the north wall. I don't remember the painting, but the words above it said, "Ye have not chosen me, but I have chosen you." (John 15:16.) The answer was there, and I knew.

When I met with Elder Featherstone, I poured out my heart to him and after praying for guidance in my behalf, he placed his hands on my head and set me apart as a member of the Young Women General Board. We both knew that there was yet a time and season remaining that I should serve. This knowledge became another "learning point of faith" to build upon.

I guess the most difficult "learning point," the one that tested and yet strengthened my faith the most, was when our beautiful young daughter began to make choices that led her away from us and away from the influence of those in the Church who cared about her. It happened so quietly. One step at a time, one day at a time, she drifted away. The story is old, but it was so agonizingly new to us, so very difficult to handle. When I realized what was happening, it was already too late. She had built a wall of defense that we couldn't penetrate.

I felt guilty and frustrated. Over and over I asked myself, "Have I done too much? Was I too busy doing things I thought were important rather than tuning in to her needs?" I played the "What If" game. What if we hadn't let her go to the party? What if we had encouraged her to change schools when she had suggested it? What if...so many things. Then I began thinking about the neighbors and her aunts and uncles and cousins. What would they think if they knew what she was doing? And my being a member of the General Board didn't help at all. What would board members think? What kind of an example was I setting as I traveled throughout the Church talking about loving young women unconditionally when I was having trouble loving my own? Yes, I knew she was free to choose, but I wanted her to choose *my* way!

We found that tears and prayers and counseling and pleading didn't help. I was angry at her and at myself for not being able to deal with the problem. Finally, one night—a long, sleepless night—I realized that if this child belonged to anyone else but me, and she appeared at my doorstep asking for acceptance, I would take her in my arms and love her—love her unconditionally! Why couldn't I do that for my own child? I was again at a "learning point." And I had to cast off pride again. Once I set aside my pride, I could open my heart to her and love her anyway, even though I couldn't accept the choices she was making. Relations began to improve between us.

After a time she married a young man who would also be classified as "less active." They moved out of state with the intention of escaping the Church and remaining comfortably lost from the Zion flock. I prayed that someone would find my lamb and bring her back. Loving family members who lived near them contacted and worked with a wise bishop who could sense that this couple, now with a little daughter, were really searching for a way back. The Church resources were brought into action.

Caring home teachers were called to watch over them. Faithful visiting teachers befriended her. Primary leaders carefully tutored her when she accepted a call into Primary service. And then came the bright and beautiful day my daughter and her husband entered the temple of the Lord and with two precious children were united as an eternal family. Another "learning point." I learned to never, never, never give up, and also to allow others to help carry burdens too heavy for one to carry alone. It's all part of the gospel plan: "Bear ye one another's burdens and so fulfill the law of Christ." (Galatians 6:2.)

I have also learned that the adversary is real. Very real! He will do all in his power to stop, or make less effective, work that has the potential of bringing lambs to the fold. I have learned, by experience, to prepare myself spiritually to combat this problem, to "trust in the Lord with all [my] heart" (Proverbs 3:5), and believe that through him there is power that makes all things possible. The power of God, the architect of the "grand design," is available to us through prayer, through priesthood blessings, and through faith unwavering.

I know this is so. I saw clouds part long enough to shoot the final footage for the first Young Women satellite broadcast. I saw "a girl in prayer," "an open book of scriptures," and "temple spires" become Personal Progress symbols for young women. I saw a young woman standing on a hilltop, her hair and her dress blowing in the wind, become the Young Womanhood medallion. His purposes will be fulfilled despite the pride and sometimes limited understanding of his servants. Yes, I've come a long way since Primary. And although I know there will be more learning points and more elephants to face, both in and out of the Church, I'm not afraid. I know the reality of God.

Fear, I Embrace You

LOUISE PLUMMER

All my life I have been a dreamer. In my first dream, I wanted to be the queen of Holland's daughter. Not the oldest one, Beatrix, who is now herself the queen and who always reminded me of a plump squirrel with nuts stored solidly in its cheeks. Nor did I want to be the youngest daughter, the one with cross-eyes—I forget her name. I wanted to be Katerina, the second daughter, who was my age and fair and lovely as a princess ought to be. She wore her hair parted on the left side with a generous white taffeta bow on the right. In fact, all her clothes were white: white socks with white shoes, white dresses with white lace trim. She was clean enough to be translated.

I looked like the immigrant girl that I was. I wore Buster Brown oxfords with brown laces and cable-knit knee socks.

When this dream was used up, I replaced it with another dream. I dreamed of a family: a mother named Sally, a father named Jim, and a beautiful eight-year-old girl, who was me, only her blonde hair was naturally curly and her name was Betsy, not Louise. Not surprisingly, the family of my dream

Louise Plummer has written two novels, The Romantic Obsessions and Humiliations of Annie Sehlmeier *(Delacorte Press, 1987) and* My Name is Sus5an Smith. The 5 is Silent *(in press). She has also published stories and articles with* Young Miss, Lake Street Review, New Era, *and* Ensign. *She received her master's degree from the University of Minnesota and teaches critical and creative writing at Brigham Young University. She has served in all the auxiliaries, has taught seminary, and currently serves as second counselor in the Provo Oak Hills Stake Relief Society. She and her husband, Tom, are the parents of four boys.*

dressed in white and never got dirty. Their world was the perfectly sunny world of the impressionists. Betsy wore a taffeta ribbon in her hair and walked between her parents holding their hands when they weren't all three riding in their white Packard convertible with the shiny chrome bumpers.

In reality, when I was eight years old, I was the oldest of five children, and I still wore Buster Brown oxfords with the brown laces and the cable-knit knee socks. My father drove a 1936 Ford sedan.

In seventh grade I dreamed that I dressed every day in the same dance outfit: a short black taffeta skirt and a white silk blouse with enormous butterfly sleeves and black patent leather tap shoes. I tap-danced my way into the heart of every other seventh grader and became the most popular girl at Hamilton School because I was a star.

In reality, I had plenty of friends, but I wasn't the most popular girl in school. Diana Mitchell was. I wore Joyce shoe imitations from Baker's. In junior high school, I wanted to be an actress. In high school, I wanted to be an artist or a writer. All my life I have dreamed dreams of being transformed into someone as popular as Diana Mitchell, beautiful as Grace Kelly, talented as Georgia O'Keefe, and smart as Margaret Mead. I wanted to soar like some mythical bird with gauzy wings and spell my name — Louise — with my white breath across the sky while ordinary mortals stared at me in awe, calling my name, pleading for my autograph from the sidewalk below.

These dreams were my vision of a creative life. For me, being a creative person means to make a mark in the world. It is "the act of making something new, whether a symphony, a novel, an improved layout for a supermarket, [or] a new and unexpected casserole dish."[1] My question is, what keeps us from making our mark?

One of my favorite stories from Greek mythology is the story of the boy, Icarus. He and his father, Daedalus, were held prisoners inside a labyrinth on the island of Crete by King Minos. In order to escape, Daedalus devised a pair of wings for himself and a pair for Icarus. He fastened them to his own shoulders and those of the boy, using wax as the binding material. Then both triumphantly flew away. Swiftly they skimmed through the air, and closer and closer they came to the mainland. But Icarus, flushed with excitement and exhilaration, soared even higher toward the sun — despite the warnings of his father. At last, he flew so high that the heat of the sun melted the wax, and off dropped the wings. The lad plunged downward into the sea and was drowned.[2]

Artists and poets frequently allude to this Icarus myth. Brueghel, in his painting *The Fall of Icarus*, shows a tiny pair of white legs protruding from the ocean just short of the coastline in the lower right corner of the canvas. Most poets focus on the failure of Icarus — his fall from the sky. Anne Sexton, however, in her poem, "To a Friend Whose Work Has Come to Triumph," focuses on the exhilaration of the flight and not the fall. She writes:

> Consider Icarus, pasting those sticky wings on,
> testing that strange little tug at his shoulder blade,
> and think of that first flawless moment over the lawn
> of the labyrinth. Think of the difference it made!
> There below are the trees, as awkward as camels;
> and here are the shocked starlings pumping past
> and think of innocent Icarus who is doing quite well:
> larger than a sail, over the fog and the blast
> of the plushy ocean, he goes. Admire his wings!
> Feel the fire at his neck and see how casually
> he glances up and is caught, wondrously tunneling
> into that hot eye. Who cares that he fell back to the sea?
> See him acclaiming the sun and come plunging down
> while his sensible daddy goes straight into town.[3]

Most of Sexton's poem concentrates not only on the thrill of the flight but on its success: "See him acclaiming the sun," she writes. She is not, it seems to me, applauding the safe, "sensible daddy."

Flight, in literature, is often a figurative expression of

149

creativity. The paradox is that the flight is both exhilarating and life-threatening. The metaphor also holds true in real life. There is always the danger in creating anything (taking flight) that like Icarus, we could fall from the sky and die. It is this paradox in my own life that I want to explore.

I used to say to my mother, "I'm going to marry a rich man. I want to travel all over Europe. I'm going to be an actress. I want to be an artist. I want to live in New York City. I want to be a writer. I'm going to be famous some day."

My mother's reply was "Pff." Just a little explosion of air through the lips. "Pff." It meant a myriad of things like, "You're crazy. Don't get your hopes up. Life is harder than you can imagine. Things don't work out so simply. No one I know is an artist, a writer, or an actress. No one I know married a rich man. What you want may not be possible. Pff. Pff."

I don't blame my mother. It was her job, I now realize, to be sensible, to steer me away from that brilliant sun before my wax melted.

My own sons have dreams, and they are not my dreams. To tell you the truth, I want every one of them to be English professors. That would make me happy. After high school, my second son, Ed, signed up with BYU's Air Force ROTC and was allowed to join student pilots in those little planes the size of cars and fly above Provo. The first time he did that, he flew by our balcony and had the pilot tip the wings of the plane at us. That was friendly, and I liked it. I liked Ed's enthusiasm too, but then he began talking about flying F-16s and stalls and barrel rolls. Like Daedalus, I began to see the danger. From then on, it made me cringe when Ed, in his most exuberant, unique voice, would say, "I'm gonna fly F-16s. It's gonna be so cool. I'm gonna be Top Gun."

And even though I've fought this attitude all my life, I say "Pff" — because that creative dream he has for himself, his own expression of self, is not one that I know — is not one that seems possible to me. It scares me, just like my dreams scared my mother. I'm afraid that boy's going to melt his wax and fall into Utah Lake.

I repeat my question: What keeps us from making our mark in the world? I think it is fear. Fear that stems from repeated warnings we have received from loving, well-meaning, "sensible daddies and mommies" who want to keep us safe and who are themselves afraid. In Shakespeare's *Hamlet*, Laertes warns his sister, Ophelia, against Hamlet's advances with this dictum: "Be wary, then, best safety lies in fear." (I, iii, 43.)

Here I am faced with that paradox again of taking risks that lead to creative expression versus safety. In my son's case, the risks are real. He could, like Icarus, literally fall out of the sky and die, but he claims the flight is worth the risk. I have come to realize that for most of the rest of us, becoming the self we dream of being, the self who can make a joyful mark on the world, means taking a risk that only *feels* life-threatening. It only *feels* like we're falling out of the sky. The risk is not death but disapproval from family and friends. The risk is becoming the butt of the joke. Failure and humiliation are the real risks, and humiliation feels as scary as drowning.

I know that from my own experience. From my adolescent journals two tasks emerge again and again: drawing and writing were my work. But I became afraid of that work.

When I was nineteen years old and attending the University of Utah, I changed my major about as often as I changed my underwear. One day, I was an art major. I took Basic Drawing in the barracks on the east side of campus. I sat in front of an easel with a large sketch pad, a piece of charcoal that stained my fingers, and a gummy eraser that I could knead into a ball. I drew cylinders and globes lit from various angles. I drew the back of a sculptured male figure, shading the muscles. Whereas in high school I had received A's in art, at the university, my drawings and my notebook received B-pluses. This didn't bother me. I knew the competition would be stiffer at the university, and I was satisfied for the time being with the B-pluses. Logically, I should have received a B-plus in the class;

however, my ability to draw was only part of the grade. I was also tested twice, in a midterm and a final exam, where I was to identify the drawings of famous artists.

My art professor told us we could study the drawings in the Art Library. I went into that library just once, searching for books containing the drawings of the masters, but I didn't know how to find them. I couldn't see a card catalog, and I suppose now that if I had, I wouldn't have known what to look for. There was a librarian behind the desk, but she was busy with other people. Besides, there was an efficient, brusque air about her that intimidated me. I was afraid that when I approached her, she would say, "Pff." So I did not ask for help, and because I didn't ask for help, I received a C in Basic Drawing—a grade of C for a subject that I had always excelled in before. The professor, in an end-of-the-class interview, told me I had a flair for fashion illustration, but I needed to apply myself more. I got a C in art because I was too afraid to take a risk and ask a librarian for help.

The next day I changed my major to English. The first class I took was Introduction to Literature. The professor was a slim, grayish man who wore only black turtleneck sweaters and who sat cross-legged upon the desk in front of the room like an aging Hamlet. I thought he was part of the beat generation, sardonic, cynical, and witty in an arrogant sort of way. He spoke about literature with an eastern accent. Sometimes he smoked in class. For all of these reasons, I loved him. Naturally, I wanted to please him, but that was not to be. I had to write a paper on Ford Maddox Ford's novel, *The Good Soldier*. I read the book on a train to San Francisco during the Thanksgiving holiday. I was clueless as to what the book was about. On Sunday night, coming back from San Francisco, I was still clueless—and in that state, I wrote the paper. After the papers were handed in, my professor began telling us about *The Good Soldier*. I was astonished to hear that the first-person narrator was a *naive narrator*, a term I had never heard in my life, and that his view of what was going on around him was a *distortion*.

I knew then that I had missed the whole point, and sure enough, when the papers were returned, I had received a C-minus, which was exactly what I deserved. There was no chance for revision. I felt humiliated. All that reading and writing I had done through childhood, through adolescence, was not good enough to save me in this class. I was too scared and too proud to ask the professor for help. He might, after all, say "Pff." The next day I changed my major to child development.

I did not return to English literature until I was thirty years old with two babies and was thoroughly fed up with child developing. I took a class on the short story. My husband sat up with me the night before a three-page paper was due on Hawthorne's "My Kinsman, Major Molineux." He practically moved the pencil while I hyperventilated. Not only did I get an A, but the professor read it aloud in class. So now I knew that my husband could write a good paper. Then I discovered the library—finally. When I was clueless about a text, I went to the library and borrowed others' ideas freely. I never again received a grade below A-minus. By the time I reached graduate school, I had learned how to write a paper by myself.

Because of my chronic fear, I am a classic late bloomer. I finished my undergraduate degree when I was thirty-seven years old. I wanted desperately to go to graduate school, but I almost didn't, because I was too afraid to ask three professors for letters of recommendation. I was afraid they wouldn't remember me, that they would give me vague looks and say, "Pff." Finally, a supportive friend, recognizing both my desire and my fear, said she would meet me at the library on a Thursday night and that I was to report to her that I had asked for the letters. I did it. All three professors remembered me. No one laughed. I got into graduate school, and because I did, other dreams came true. I write, I teach, I even tap-dance. Because I finally got the nerve to ask for three letters, I got a whole new life. (Although I am still waiting for all those white dresses to arrive.)

I am now forty-seven years old, and I am still afraid, but

I've learned that to limit myself to safe activities because I'm too afraid to ask questions, or too afraid to take a class, or too afraid to ask for letters of recommendation, or to apply for a job, or to give a talk or teach a lesson—to limit myself out of fear is more like drowning in the ocean than confronting the fear itself. For me, it led to depression. Fear does not kill; it only gives you diarrhea. I have come to think of diarrhea as a friend who helps me lose weight. The really big fear makes me gag, or worse, throw up. I have lived through that too, and again, it's good for weight control. Fear, I have come to realize, is my companion for life, and I embrace her. Fear has become the force that drives my creative energy.

Finally, I find that when I am living the life I want to live, I can allow others to live theirs. I don't need to control or manipulate them into fulfilling some dream that I can't fulfill for myself. I can live with Ed zooming through the sky, piloting his F-16. He really doesn't have to be an English professor for me. I don't know if I can live with my younger son, Charles, though. He tests me sorely. "What do you want me to be when I grow up?" he asked me one day. I should have known it was a trap.

Generous spirited, I said, "I want you to be what you want to be."

"Well, then," he said, his eyes flashing at me, "I want to be a hit man."

Notes

1. S. I. Hayakawa, *Through the Communication Barrier: On Speaking, Listening, and Understanding*, ed. Arthur Chandler (New York: Harper & Row, 1979), p. 106.
2. Edith Hamilton, *Mythology* (Boston: Little, Brown and Co., 1942), p. 193.
3. Anne Sexton, *The Complete Poems* (Boston: Houghton Mifflin Co., 1981), p. 53.

"My Hands Are Martha's Hands"

HELEN CANDLAND STARK

My mind zeroes in on a small framed print, sitting for many
years on my desk. It is a reproduction of Jan Vermeer's painting
of Jesus in the house of Mary and Martha. It is one of only
forty paintings the seventeenth-century Dutch artist produced
in his short lifetime.

For me, it is an icon, a religious picture with symbolic
meaning. For me, it represents two competing life forces in
the lives of other women as well as in my own.

I was surprised to realize that Mary and Martha's story is
told only in the book of Luke and that it comprises only four
verses. Bible translations that I compared tell the story essentially in the same way:

"Now as they went on their way, he entered a village; and
a woman named Martha received him into her house. And she
had a sister called Mary, who sat at the Lord's feet and listened
to his teaching. But Martha was distracted with much serving;
and she went to him and said, 'Lord, do you not care that my
sister has left me to serve alone? Tell her then to help me.'
But the Lord answered her, 'Martha, Martha, you are anxious
and troubled about many things; one thing is needful. Mary
has chosen the good portion which shall not be taken away
from her.' " (Revised Standard Version, Luke 10:38–42.)

*Born 18 September 1901, Helen Candland Stark has lived through
almost all of the twentieth century. Her experiences have been varied:
pioneer, scholar (M. A., 1936), teacher of English and dramatics in
high school and college, actress, wife (Henry M. Stark, DuPont
chemist), mother, and writer. She is compiling a collection of her
verse to be titled* Knots in the Grain.

Does one consciously choose to be Mary or Martha? Are genes or the environment determining factors? I don't know.

I do know that for most of my eighty-eight years I have been Martha.

My life falls into three eras — life before marriage, married years, and postretirement years when we moved from Delaware back to Utah. For most of my life I bought the whole Mormon Martha package. I lived it, lock, stock, and barrel. But from earliest memory, I also knew a Mary tug. Here are some particulars:

Life on our ranch in Sanpete County was rugged pioneer stuff. I was the eldest of nine with my next sister ten years younger. Our menfolk came in late for supper, after which dishwater had to be heated on a coal range and the dishes washed under a kerosene lamp.

Once in a fit of adolescent self-pity, I wrote:

> The canyon breeze comes floating down
> A perfume-laden stream.
> The tired housewife only knows
> Its time to skim the cream.

Of course, someone quickly pointed out how lucky I was to have cream to skim.

Once, after a long, hard day at a treadle sewing machine, turning a bolt of outing flannel into winter pajamas for my five brothers, I was so tired I began to weep. My mother took me for a walk along the dusty country road. She said nothing, but her hand on my arm communicated, without words, "This is the way it is, Helen. This is the way it is."

I was an accepting participant in the way it was. And I did not, with conscious intent, dig in my heels for time of my own. But two limits I insisted upon. Sunday afternoons on the ranch were to be mine. I spent those hours putting together a newsletter, complete with columns, for two absent friends.

And I would not darn. If I managed, purposely, to complete an assigned task early, my mother was wont to say, "Good,

Helen. Now you have time for a little darning." No way. The basket of hose for eleven people was bottomless.

But Martha chores were evidence of a good woman, so when I married belatedly and gratefully, I was determined to be the best wife known to man. That meant that I would never just open a can of beans. I would do tedious and intricate things to them.

My husband, a gardener at heart and raised in the same pioneer tradition, thought that was just fine. For his own part, he lavished loving attention on vegetable patch and fruit trees. He was justifiably baffled, therefore, when one day I came up with a verse I titled "Green-eyed Dirge," with apologies to Joyce Kilmer:

> Alas, that I can never be
> As lovely as a garden pea.
> The bulby beet, the carrot svelte,
> Can both be tucked behind a belt.
> The parsnip knows its proper place
> Upon a plate beneath the face.
> I was not even made to wear
> A nest of parsley in my hair.
> And I have cravings wild. I talk.
> Not so, the docile celery stalk.
> With bugs I am not overrun
> To challenge sprayer and spray gun.
> If I am nicked by careless prod
> I do not meekly kiss the sod.
> No charms, alack, my love will heed
> Unless they have been grown from seed.

Still I wore my Martha role like a halo. If someone fell heir to a lug of kumquat plums, I was the expert to call. If our homeless branch in Delaware needed dinner space for eighty-five people, I could cope. In the struggle of our small LDS group to earn money for a chapel, our family raised and sold corn, raspberries, apples, and squash. I operated a bread route. With a laden basket, once a week one of the children delivered loaves to the neighbors. A student who brought his fiancée to call said, "I want you to meet the woman who bakes the best bread in Delaware."

But my specialty lay in salvaging borderline produce. Seventeen split cantaloupes in the morning became seventeen jars of cantaloupe butter by night. The celery crop that froze one night became quarts of puree for soup. A blender and assorted ingredients turned overripe corn into pudding. Eastern guests got the grand tour of the house and gawked at the row on row of bottled produce.

Perhaps I am carrying this too far, because my Mary side continued to ruffle the waters. What came out was verse. For others of you, it might well be music, painting, or dance, to name but a few Mary outlets.

At this juncture, I planned to share a few of those Ah-moments when I felt the Spirit break through. Instead I now want to make a small end run. That series of words —*poetry, music, painting, dance* —prompts a new line of thought about the Martha role.

In the third period in my life, when after retiring we moved back to Utah from Delaware, I inexplicably bought *new* bottles for canning. The culture prodded. My inner backlash was an essay for *Exponent II*, "The Good Woman Syndrome, or, When Is Enough, Enough?"[1] The *Era* had previously printed an article about cookies.[2] They were identified as a woman's "medals of honor." Apparently one whipped up a different recipe every day, for seven recipes were included.

My "Good Woman Syndrome" is almost a cliché statement about the role of females in my generation. My own rebellion in the 1970s I now explain as an early stirring of the women's movement, which prompted many of us to question our totally domestic script. Maybe, after all, we had been merely drudges doing chore work.

But the new enlightenment, while sorely needed, was not necessarily benign. Glad to abandon their aprons and even their children if urged, a new work force in tailored suits

asserted itself into the market place. Before long, few house-
holds could function without two paychecks.

Implications for society have been widely explored. Are
gender roles now more evenly divided? Do many of the new
outside jobs offer restrictions similar to the old homebound
ones? Are women less tired? And particularly, are they freer
to touch life at many points?

This last question leads me back to Martha and Mary. Martha
roles in *whatever guise* are essentially outer-oriented. Mary
turns within for creative inspiration from feeling and from
intuition. Hence, it seems to me, Mary is more truly feminine.

These ideas are all subject to argument. My thesis is that
Mary-ness arises in the central core of the individual. It is not
a persona that can be put on or taken off. It is a given.

Now please try to visualize with me some small Mary epi-
phanies. My poem called "Marriage Portion" tells of our
pioneer heritage of hard work:

> You muscle down defeat.
> By labor, deserts blossom as the rose;
> Weariness choked off yields shining wheat.

The last couplet summarizes:

> Roses from deserts are a brilliant yield
> If we prize, too, the lilies of the field.

Here are three short nature poems. The first describes an
experience with snow. The mother is an archetypal figure who
speaks the one-line refrain of each quatrain. The daughter
begins:

NIGHT SNOW

> My mother and I will walk in the snow:
> This is an hour to keep.
> Drifts mount high on the tulip beds.
> "As snow, so falleth sleep."

159

Gone is the moon and gone are the stars.
The sky is foam tonight.
We tread on meadows of mother-of-pearl.
   "Snow filleth our hands with light."

The wire harshness of leafless bush
Is soft as a mourning dove.
Beautiful, gracious, transfigured world.
   "So sayeth all who love."

Quietly, patiently falls the snow,
Cool and sweet to the face.
We have not striven. The gift is given.
   "As snow so cometh Grace."

Next is a sonnet about autumn. My husband and I were visiting in the Vermont woods. He went off exploring, and I used my quiet time to write!

AUTUMN IN VERMONT

How shall I make myself one with this time?
Let go, let go, even your scarlet treasure,
Maple despoiled. Knee deep in gold. I measure
Leaves' profusion — know they melt to lymn
With amber dust the fern's first leaf in spring.
In the cone's cup the blood-root makes its bed.
The bare fingers of birch so whitely dead,
Point to the pulse of each transmuted thing.

Now I am drunk with color, now at last
Submerged in peace. I turn for one more look
To hope the floating oak leaf on the brook
Returns, swirls into consciousness, to cast
In some dark hour its secret on my shore.
Oh, baby hemlock trees, be spirit's store.

Our house in Salem overlooked a little lake. Here is a Japanese haiku about a transient moment:

> Come!
> Over the dark water
> A soaring rainbow —
> Too late. It is gone.

Now I am eighty-eight years old. Jesus said, Mary has chosen that good portion *which shall not be taken from her.*

My Martha accomplishments have been taken from me. The prom dresses have vanished along with sumptuous dinner parties. Now I write a haiku about aging:

> Hush!
> In the dark center
> DNA unravels
> Its intricate spirals.

All those years of domestic chores. Were they worth it? I was never consciously trying to influence my world. But yes, it did help my struggling branch in Delaware to have a home base. The woman with the kumquats happily managed. In our Wilmington Ward Cookbook, my Zuni bread is considered a minor classic.

And what do my children say who grew up within this framework? They say they are grateful. They say they may have kicked sometimes against a way of life that made finishing chores a condition for going out to play. But they learned responsibility to the family, to work efficiently so as to have private time, to develop skills especially useful for their marriages. We had two kinds of work: help work and money work. Raspberries had to be picked; that was help work. But polishing the silver could be money work. Order and efficiency are Martha gifts.

But I am just now gathering up my verses. Would a photocopy of them be a welcome present to my children? I see my son sharing an Ah-moment with his little daughter, and I hope so.

That brings me to my last poem. Martha is speaking.

MARTHA AND THE WAY

My sister, when our Lord was gone,
Brought me a drink fresh from the well.
I said, "O worthless one." I struck
The cup of water so it fell.

She laid her fingers on my arm.
I threw them off. I would not stay.
The heavy house is quiet now.
She sought my Lord and went away.

My hands are Martha's hands, alert,
Skillful, strong, and swift to hurt;
But, ah, my soul, could I surprise
The look of Mary in my eyes!

Before I had compared the story in the various translations, I remembered—wrongly, as it turned out—that Jesus had said "Mary has chosen the *better* part." I thought, if there is a better part, then there must be a good part as well as a best part. And that is the way I still ponder that verse in my heart.

You notice that Jesus chided Martha with great tenderness. "Martha, Martha." The repetition of the name endears it. He loved Martha as well.

Not *either* good or better, not even *both* good *and* better, but something greater than both transcends toward wholeness. We enrich ourselves, and we bless each other. That is the reward of the creative blending of roles that I wish I could pass along, especially to you young women. All of us are "cumbered by much serving," as the King James Version so wisely puts it. (Luke 10:42.) It behooves us, therefore, to heed those quiet promptings to "sit at the Lord's feet and listen."

162

Notes

1. Helen Candland Stark, "The Good Woman Syndrome, or, When Is Enough, Enough?" *Exponent II* (Winter, 1976), p. 16; reprinted in *Dialogue* (Fall 1990):34–8.
2. Florence B. Pinnock, "A Mother Ten Feet Tall," *Improvement Era*, May 1968, pp. 68–69.

Changing the World through Changing Ourselves

MEG WHEATLEY

For most of us, the following scene is part of our everyday experience: other people at home, or work, or church have annoyed us. We become angry. As our anger grows, so does our clarity about their failings. Our head fills up with words and advice about what *their* problem is and how to correct it. We keep wondering why they're so blind to the reality of what *they* are doing or who they are. "Why can't they see . . ." or "If only they . . ." become common phrases to start many of our sentences. And yet for all our clarity and conviction about what is wrong with *them,* how often does our analysis lead to the changes we desire for them?

To put it more simply: how many of us have tried to change another person, and how many of us have succeeded? Given that most of the time we have *not* succeeded in changing others, it's curious how dearly we hold onto the notion that trying to change other people is a useful expenditure of our energy and attention, or that trying to change others is the way to resolve the things in our own life that disturb us.

Several years ago I encountered a different approach to changing my world. After years of testing it out, I know it works,

Meg Wheatley is an associate professor of management at Brigham Young University, where she teaches ethics and organization design. She received her doctorate from Harvard University and has been a consultant to corporations for sixteen years. She has published numerous articles on the effects of large organizations on individual behavior, approaches to organizational change, and women's career issues. She is married to Nello-John Pesci. They have a combined family of seven children.

but it is not something I embrace gracefully. The approach is contained in the simple realization that the only person we are ever capable of changing is ourselves. Yet we all play powerful roles in helping one another change. How can we support one another in these changes without being able to change anyone but ourselves? There are two key roles that we play for one another. The first is that we all enter one another's lives as friends — not necessarily as a *friendly* person but as one who is concerned with another's growth. Second, we serve as mirrors to one another, reflecting back what angers us about ourselves. These are difficult roles for us to accept, but my experience suggests that they are valid and that as we see others in the light of those roles, we grow, our world changes, and we find more peace.

On the surface, the notion that everyone who enters our lives enters as a friend seems to be an incredibly Pollyannish idea, given the numbers of people who not only bother us but openly seem to be trying to deceive or even abuse us. The "friends" I am speaking of, however, originate at the eternal level. They are souls who are concerned with our growth and development, because they understand the importance of our growth to their own and because they love us as an expression of God. And we, at the eternal level, play a similar role in their lives from the same basis of understanding about who we truly are. That is a definition of friends as God might express it. At least, it takes an eternal perspective even to hope that the person who is berating you, tricking you, or generally making you feel terrible has your interests in mind!

Several experiences have confirmed for me the value of this perspective, but one of the most dramatic occurred several years ago during a consulting project in Texas. This project had become particularly difficult — I felt constantly watched and evaluated and did not have a comfortable relationship with the client. Early in the project, we had given a presentation that did not go well. Now we were at the end of the project, ready to give another presentation to the original group of executives plus others. My client was nervous about the presentation to his "big bosses" and so were we. I'd spent a lot of time mentally defending myself against this group of executives—I was sure that they were narrow-minded, petty, and distinctly unvisionary. I prepared the presentation, all the while arguing with them in my mind, criticizing them, anticipating their criticisms of me—the kind of exhausting mental chatter we all get into when we're feeling defensive.

While I was preparing for this "attack" I encountered a reading that said, "Everyone comes into your life as a friend, to teach you something you have asked to learn." As I pondered that idea, an image came to me very forcibly. In the image, I was delivering the presentation to these corporate executives when, for an instant, I saw behind their faces and perceived them as radiant and smiling. They were welcoming me, saying they were there to help me and urging me to be more than I thought I could be in this setting. This mental picture made it much easier to go into the presentation, and as I looked out on the group of gray-suited, gray-haired men, I sensed a different dynamic working between us. Since that experience, I've had many opportunities to encounter my enemies as friends. It is not an easy process, but simply by making the effort to assume that everyone who comes into my life is there to forward my greater purpose has had a liberating effect on many of my relationships.

A second principle explains why the "friend doctrine" works. This principle is firmly embedded in the psychological construct of projection, which states that whatever we don't love or value in ourselves, we try to get rid of. We project it outside of ourselves and attach the trait to someone else. We then get angry with that someone else for exhibiting the traits that we dislike so much in ourselves. Said very simply, people act as mirrors to us, reflecting back to us things about ourselves we don't love. What angers us in other people are aspects of our *own* behavior that we dislike.

To really believe and work with the concept of the-other-as-mirror can literally transform our lives. It means that every time we get angry with another person and begin listing our grievances against that person, we consciously stop that mental activity and instead ask ourselves, "What is this person reflecting back to me? What is this person doing that is really bothersome, and *when do I do the same thing?*"

Let me describe the process in more detail, because to live this way takes some effort and a lot of courage. As an example, suppose that every time you set up an activity with a friend, she is always late. Frequently, after waiting for her for twenty or thirty minutes, you find yourself angry, almost unable to be civil to her when she finally arrives. You may be so angry that you are unable to voice your annoyance to her. Instead, it becomes a sore point between you.

In this case the other person clearly is behaving inconsiderately. By all standards, she and her lateness really *should* be the object of change, not you. But there is another issue in this situation, and that is your anger. Anger is something that divides us from sisterly and brotherly love and, I assume, anger is an emotion we would prefer to have less of in our lives. (Please note that I do not mean *repressing* anger that is already there; I mean letting the emotion develop less frequently so that it never has to be dealt with.) In our example, there are two things to resolve with your friend — her lateness and your anger. If you were not angry, you could more easily call attention to her behavior and ask her to recognize its consequences on you. The anger, however, prevents you from discussing the issue for fear of damaging the relationship. You cannot envision a way to talk about it without threatening her.

The distinction between the two issues is an important one. The first issue is that someone is doing something inconsiderate and that person needs to know it. The second issue is that the anger you feel blocks you from finding a peaceable resolution to the problem. I emphasize this point because I am *not* advocating that in focusing on changing only ourselves we

167

become doormats for other people to walk on or that we justify letting people do whatever they please. The intent of this approach is to find ways to make the world more delightful for each of us, not to make us smiling zombies who accept anything from anybody and call our behavior unconditional love. But how do we become more effective in creating a world that supports and enriches us? One way is to be able to have conversations with others that are not tainted by the emotion of anger. The second is to be constantly growing in love toward who you are.

Understanding that others function as mirrors to us is a way both to dissolve anger and to get more in touch with those aspects of ourselves that we don't value and would do better to change. A story will illustrate this point. A few years ago, I was working in a consulting firm where my closest associate was another woman. One afternoon, I took a phone call from a potential client, not realizing that my associate had wanted that specific client. She became very angry with me for "grabbing" a client away from her. I in turn felt very angry at her anger, feeling she was unjustified in her emotions. I could see that she felt very competitive toward me, and I became increasingly critical of her competitiveness over the next few days. Nor did my anger abate—instead, I felt more and more justified in my criticisms. It took about a week before I had the nerve to ask myself if she was mirroring something back to me, some attribute in myself that I didn't love. I hotly denied it to myself, but the question remained, and in my calmer moments I began to see that her competitiveness mirrored my own need to achieve and do better than she did. Her competitive streak was nothing compared to mine! My intense reaction to her behavior became a means for me to identify areas within myself that I didn't like and wanted to change.

More recently, I found myself angry at two students who had cut one of my classes. I spent an evening thinking of witty and biting things to say, of chastising notes to send, of how I could punish them for their disrespect. The next morning, when my anger had subsided, I again called them into mind to see what they could possibly be mirroring to me about myself. This process took some time, because their surface behavior — cutting class — was not something I did. As I probed what exactly about their behavior was bothering me, I realized that their casual attitude toward my class was very similar to the casual attitude I was taking toward myself. What I was really angry at was that I was not taking myself seriously, and these two students had reflected that attitude back to me. They still shouldn't have cut class, but once I was clear on the source of my anger, I could talk to them about their behavior in a constructive manner, and, more importantly, I could focus on my own issues with my work.

Thinking about this mirroring role requires us to take three steps, which must be separate. Step 1 is simply to notice when you're angry at someone and realize that there is an opportunity for self-insight.

Step 2 needs to wait until you have calmed down. It does no good to reflect about anything while you're still caught up in the emotion of anger. But after the anger dissipates — whether it's an hour, a week, or a year — ask yourself, "What is this person doing *specifically* that bothers me so much?" Identifying it may take some time, because often the surface behavior is not what is tapping into your anger. Look for the attitudes or behaviors behind the surface behavior. Probe deeper and deeper until you feel you've reached the essential behavior that is troubling you. What irked me, in the last instance I described, was not simply having students cut class but the underlying attitude that what I had to offer them was not all that important.

Step 3 is to ask, "When do I do the same thing, or its opposite?" Asking whether you do the same thing or its opposite is very important. For example, someone who is late may anger you either because you're also sometimes late or because you're never late. In either case, time is a big issue for you, so big that it makes you get angry at others. The last step is, then, the step toward insight and change. If you're never late, you may want to ask yourself why you've made timeliness so important that it interferes with your relationships with others (because you now get angry at someone who is late). Or, if being late is something you do, you may want to change that behavior.

When you concentrate on fixing the things in yourself that you don't love, you are able to discuss more calmly and openly with people the aspects of their behavior you find inconsiderate, problematic, or demeaning. And you are able to do so from a position of self-love that gives you both clarity and strength.

People come into our lives as mirrors and as friends to help us grow. All growth, I believe, is a process of learning to love ourselves more and more, of realizing our essential goodness and holiness. A spiritual teacher of mine once said, "Teach only love, for that is what you are." It made me wonder how often I truly encounter myself as love. Not as someone who is nice, not as someone who is kind, not as someone who is a model Relief Society woman. How often do I experience myself as an offspring of the Divine? If God is love, so am I, so are you, so are we all — but how often do we really appreciate ourselves for being evidence of divine love here on earth?

We all know the scripture "Be ye therefore perfect, even as your Father which is in heaven is perfect." (Matthew 5:48; 3 Nephi 12:48.) It is common practice to interpret this passage as an admonition or a prescription of how we should be. But recently, I've been struck that it is a *description* of our true state. As children of a perfect Father, our essential natures are also perfect. The process of our lives is a moving toward an awareness of our essential, divine nature. *We* lose sight of our divine nature — *we* cloud it up with mistakes and guilt — but I earnestly believe that the Father never loses sight of our essential divine nature. Through all his struggles and temptations, Christ never forgot who he was. I believe that he was trying to show us our own essential goodness as well, to call us to

170

remembrance of our own divine natures. Jesus was a model of what it means to keep in mind one's eternal identity and to act from one's divine power. He never lost sight of who he was. Our forgetfulness of our divinity causes us much grief and, I believe, saddens our Father as well.

So for us, as children of our Father, the journey of discovery is to look into ourselves, to notice what we don't love or value in ourselves and to move inward into the divine, eternal self that we all are. Clearly that is not an easy task. Most of us are scared to look within ourselves, because we are convinced that what's in there is garbage—a combination of dark, ugly traits and behaviors overlaid with a thick layer of guilt. We become scared of our internal places and avoid going within. To disguise those rotten cores, we go outward, and we try to be loving and kind and good, but we seldom look within to experience the light that shines there.

We constantly tell ourselves how bad we are. I see it in my students all the time. They are so quick to notice what's wrong in themselves, so eager to feel guilty, and so unable to praise themselves for work well done, fearing it will be egotistical. Sometimes I have an image of the Father looking at us as we look at our own children when they are filled with doubts or when they tell themselves how bad or how insufficient they are. He is filled with sadness that we don't realize how essentially beautiful we are, how powerful we are, how little reason there is to be finding fault. A friend of mine once pointed out to me that we are all first-generation divine offspring, straight from our Heavenly parents. There is nothing between us and God, except all the junk we throw in.

Each of us needs to be more in touch with our divine origin. Each of us needs to let the radiance that is within us shine forth. Each of us needs to recognize the other as the offspring of the Divine. Each of us needs to realize that all the power we desire is already within us—that we don't need to create it: we merely need to clear the way for it to come forth.

We need to allow ourselves to be powerful and trust in our powers as Jesus trusted in his.

The techniques I have outlined are one means of getting closer to an appreciation of ourselves as divine offspring. To recognize everyone as similarly divine is to realize that they can do us no harm — that they come into our lives for purposes that were created in another sphere. Every one of us is an agent of God to every other person, moving with purpose through our lives. Those who anger us the most can teach us an essential lesson, to have us reckon with some aspect of ourselves that we don't love. Their role as a mirror is a means for us to clear out some of the clutter that stands between us and recognizing our own essential goodness.

The process of changing ourselves is never easy, but it becomes easier as we stop berating ourselves for our failings and instead think of the process as digging deep into ourselves to rediscover our essential goodness. And a very strange and wonderful thing happens as we change ourselves. Others who were bothering us either change themselves, or they move away. That is a very important concept to remember: in the process of changing ourselves, we seem to attract to us those who will support the changes and repel from us those who would drag us backwards. As we remember more of our divine goodness, we find that the people around us exhibit more of their divine goodness. Those who are unable to manifest their goodness move out of our range.

The process of changing the world, then, is opening up ourselves to who we really are, getting rid of the interior garbage that we have accumulated in our lives, and remembering ourselves as first-generation offspring of the divine. The task is one of remembering our essential goodness, not creating it or seeking it but remembering and allowing it to come forth. That is a much easier task than thinking that somewhere out there some day in the future we'll be good. The task of remembering who we really are takes us inside to a lovely place, if we will but trust that it exists within us. And it is a task for which we have all committed our support to one another, even though we don't always interpret one another's actions as support.

These simple techniques bring me closer to remembering who I am and afford me a way to recognize the support we obtain from everyone who enters our lives. As I become more conscious of the things I do that I don't love, I have the capacity to change them and thus move closer to the love that I am. As I love and nurture myself, I move more and more to my divine center. And by doing that, I change the world around me.

Loving Wisely:
Codependency and Inner Spiritual Strength

MARYBETH RAYNES

Loving wisely means loving others in ways that not only credit and count them but also credit and count ourselves. For the sake of definition, let me categorize *loving* into three types: some loving is easy, some loving is hard, and some loving is loving too much.

Loving is easy when we are attracted to the other person or we find our own needs met easily in the relationship. Loving is also easy at times when we find our dreams or expectations being fulfilled, as is the case when we fall in love with the "right" person or that person falls in love with us. When our dreams of having children are fulfilled in a healthy baby, love comes easily. When our dreams of having a close friend come true, love comes easily. Love seems to just happen.

Loving is hard even with those people we care deeply about when the relationship has become a struggle and our love or commitment holds us long beyond our wanting to be there. Sometimes the struggle pulls the best from us. A marital or friendship difference that seems irreconcilable, a child who always opposes our wishes, year after year of taking care of a chronically ill child or parent — all are examples of loving when loving is hard, giving of ourselves even though it involves sacrifice. Most sermons about service mention the difficulty, yet ultimate worth, of this type of love.

Marybeth Raynes is a marriage and family therapist in private practice in Salt Lake City. She received her master's degree in social work from the University of Utah and is a licensed clinical social worker. She is a regular presenter at workshops and lectures on women's issues. She is the mother of three children.

Loving when it is hard, however, needs to be distinguished from another type of loving, which benefits neither party: loving too much. That may seem a paradox at first. Can there be too much love in the world? Is it possible to feel too much love for another person? Loving too much, however, actually implies nothing about the level of feeling in a relationship but measures instead the effort we invest in meeting another person's needs in a loving relationship. Let me give you an example. The husband of one of my clients had open heart surgery. Afterwards, his healing did not progress in the way the doctors predicted. Over the months not only did he not get well but he became depressed. Besides performing all her daily tasks, my client began investing more and more energy in providing emotional support. Finally, exhausted, she said, "No matter how much I love him, it doesn't seem to make a difference."

Research about many seriously ill patients, particularly heart-transplant patients, indicates that if you help them too much, they do not get well. The same is true for a child who is helped far too much or far too long. She or he never grows up. We can love too much by not allowing the other person to carry his or her own burdens in a loving relationship.

I first became aware of the idea of codependency, or loving too much, almost twenty-five years ago. Reed Bradford, a professor of mine at Brigham Young University, made a comment in class which I still remember very clearly, "You are never really loving someone if you are letting that person use you." In other words, if you let someone infringe upon you and if you don't stand up for yourself, you are hindering that other person's emotional development. This principle applies broadly, from sexual relations to decision-making to household chores.

A few years later, I heard Arlene Skolnick, a writer and researcher in marriage and family relationships, cleverly voice one of the reasons women fall into self-effacing patterns of behavior. I am vowing to someday cross-stitch her insight for display on my dining room wall: "Housework is absolutely necessary, socially devalued, and invisible when well done."

When we do things too well, or when we do more than a fair or equitable share of the work in a relationship—be it household or emotional responsibilities—we become invisible to those around us. Two years ago my doctors mandated that I stay in bed for the recovery period after an operation. My oldest daughter had just received her driver's license and was eager to be off with friends one of the first weekends after my surgery. I told her I needed her at home to run errands since no one else could drive. She insisted, "I really want to go," and reassured me, "You will be fine." I emphasized, "I really need you here." She replied, "But, Mother, you're always strong; you'll do fine." I realized then that this was not simply headstrong, self-absorbed teen behavior. Rather, I had taken care of my own needs so well for so long that she could not see or believe that my request for help was based on real need. I was Mother, invincible and therefore invisible.

Sometimes competence becomes overcompetence or, to use Harriet Goldhor Lerner's term, "overfunctioning." Such overfunctioning is less than responsible because it encourages others to underfunction. I highly recommend Lerner's *The Dance of Anger* and *The Dance of Intimacy*, both written specifically for women, because she explains with great clarity and in detail how to achieve a balance of responsibility in intimate, loving relationships.[1] One unfortunate tendency in current concerns about women's issues is that discussions often become polarized. We hear either that we must give unselfishly all the time or else that we must be only standing up for our own needs and not attending to those of others. Dr. Lerner explains why you *should* and how you *can* give to the other and stand up for yourself at the same time.

Another way to recognize codependence is as a reassertion of childhood behavior patterns. To children the world at first consists exclusively of up-down relationships. We depend upon parents who are more competent, hopefully, than we are. They are up; we are down. We go to Sunday School and the teacher is up and we are down. So the relationships we first experience are ones in which the "up" person gets his or her way more often than the "down" person, and that is as it should be — or so we are told.

Then a magical thing happens in our early elementary school years. At that time most of us make a friend. And as you may remember, it never works to one-up your friend, because your friend will leave or stop liking you. Most of all, your friend won't put up with it. Of course, you may find a too compliant friend who will go along with whatever you want. Or alternately, you may be the insecure one, always giving in. If so, you will have recreated the up-down relationships of early childhood and will not enter the world of equal friendship.

Up-down relationships facilitate learning some basic life skills. We learn how to obey, how to do dishes and make our beds, how to do arithmetic, and so on. But up-down relationships don't work when we seek out friends nor when we become adults. As adults, we need relationships where the needs and preferences of both are regarded as equally important. What we often fail to notice in our zeal and commitment to loving is that by giving too much, we sometimes inadvertently create an up-down relationship. We become so focused on others' needs and so thoroughly competent that our own wants or needs become invisible, even to ourselves. We are scarcely aware of having needs of our own, separate from our responsibilities and concerns about others. A joke I heard several years ago describes this state of codependence wonderfully. Imagine you are drowning in a lake. As you are sinking under the water, someone else's life passes before your eyes!

Codependence, then, means that both people are dependent in a relationship, even the ostensibly competent, responsible one: one will generally be overfunctioning while the other is underfunctioning. Our society currently identifies alcoholics and addicts as underfunctioning. Those individuals who, for one reason or another, couldn't "get it together" were in my childhood simply labeled "lazy." The overfunctioning person, on the other hand, seems to be able to do everything well — or at least exhaust herself in the effort. And in spite of exhaustion, she does not feel she has done well enough! Another maxim that I will someday cross-stitch for a wall-hanging is "Not everything worth doing is worth doing well."[2]

I want to credit the heart and soul of wanting to give and to love. It is the very glue of life. But I also want to state very clearly that loving effort has to have limits, or we expend all our energy and have little left to create or keep our life's meaning intact. In fact, you can be overfunctioning and underresponsible. You can do too much and not allow enough space for another person to grow, like a top-heavy tree that has grown too broadly and widely. Such a tree allows no sunshine to reach its neighboring trees, and yet it also lacks a root system deep enough to support its own overextended foliage.

Before talking about roots, about developing inner spiritual strength, let me first point out that although *codependency* is a family therapy term now in vogue, the concept has been around for more than thirty years, alternatively labeled as enmeshment, triangulation, and collusion. The newer term, however, has achieved an almost fad status as a new disorder of relationships which women, as usual, need to fix. As Harriet Lerner points out, blaming women for what is wrong in relationships has been in vogue for millennia. And that practice will probably continue, because blaming women makes money, sells self-help books, sends us to support groups, and keeps us working on ourselves.

I don't disagree with working on ourselves, but let's not embrace negative labels. Not all people in out-of-balance relationships are automatically diseased or addicted. To assume so keeps us in a one-down, dysfunctional, and unloving position. We need a label for the process of achieving balance that does not pigeonhole us as sick or dysfunctional human beings. If instead of asking, "Am I loving too much?" or "Am I codependent?" we ask, "Am I loving wisely?" I think we might see that we are already doing well. Labeling a relationship diseased if something is discovered out of balance reminds me of the tactics that used to be a common practice in standards- or chastity-night talks on sexual transgression. I recall graphically described — sometimes demonstrated — analogies of nails pounded into boards, squashed twinkies, crumpled roses, chewed gum, licked butter, frosting scraped off the cake. All were images of unrepairable harm. I firmly believe that no matter what happens to us in life, whether it happens to us involuntarily through abuse or violence, or whether we create it by being abusive or violent ourselves, we are not beings who are irreparably harmed. We are beings who can grow beyond our mistakes. I'm not excusing error or abuse; I'm simply saying that we are not beings who are irreparably harmed nor are those who are in relationships with us. Our mistakes and even serious misdeeds do not have to reverberate forever in our lives or in theirs. That is the message of the Atonement.

Using the term "loving wisely" helps us see even our out-of-balance efforts more kindly and credit all our expressions of love. Even very young children are remarkably compassionate and loving at times. I recall my son at about age five looking at my mother one day and suddenly announcing, "Grandma, I will never let anyone put you in a nursing home." Even though he could never fulfill such a promise, love was his intent, as is ours.

So how do we develop mature ways of loving? First of all, our loving wisely needs to include loving *ourselves* wisely. We cannot remain centered while loving others without going inside first — developing our roots. We must find our inner strength by defining clearly who we are and what our life's purpose is.

How do we go inward? How do we find inner clarity and strength? A useful conceptual model is to envision our larger self as a circle consisting of many subselves that manage different parts of our lives. There may be, for instance, a part that manages how we behave when we are treated unjustly, a part that becomes angry or wants to stand up for just causes. One part feels the sadness in our life, another part responds to joyful events, and still another part struggles with moral or spiritual issues. One part may handle childcare beautifully and simply loves children, while yet another part would, in truth, rather not have had any children—especially during that half hour or so every night when we can't get them into bed or the crying won't stop. All are real, valid, necessary parts of the whole self.

The difficulty of knowing how to love wisely—when to give and when not to give, when to stand up for our needs or desires and when to allow another to have his or her needs met instead—is that many of those inner parts of the self are, you might say, not on the same committee. Indeed, according to another conceptual model, those subselves are not even the same age. Inner conflict arises when one part of the self is at odds with another part. The part that loves children, for instance, may feel ashamed of the part that looks forward to freedom from childcare responsibilities.

Just as siblings have rivalries, so do these parts with different ages and different agendas conflict, wanting different needs met. So, the part of our self that enjoys nice clothes, for instance, may chafe when the frugal parent part of our self ignores that need and yet will splurge on new school outfits for the children. An angry statement to a child such as "After all I've done for you, how can you . . . " may be fueled less by the child's misbehavior than by a resentful backlash from a part of the self that has been consistently denied over the years. Or perhaps at some point we do invest our resources on something for ourselves alone, only to have the giving-to-others part of our self feel miserably guilty about it.

These conflicts are inevitable. Even when all the parts of our self are accepted as valid members to be coordinated in decision-making, we will experience conflict. Nevertheless, some inner peace and clarity come from simply realizing that many situations in life have no good solutions, no ideal outcomes. Sometimes we face two positive yet conflicting choices, sometimes the choices are both negative, and sometimes the situation is even more muddled than that. Often we must make the best of what is not an ideal situation. Idealists and perfectionists frustrate themselves by believing that the right choice will ensure that things will turn out exactly right or that the correct choice in any given situation should be clear. My experience is that the more you look into a situation, the more complicated it becomes and that nothing is crystal clear on many, many issues of loving. So when making a very difficult choice, let yourself feel that you are okay — that you have made a good effort and that at times your effort is as important as the outcome. Many before us have given their lives to solving the puzzle of a ravaging disease or violent conflict and died long before a satisfactory outcome was reached.

What is the solution, then, to having parts of our self in conflict? Beyond seeking to know and credit all the parts of our self, I believe that finally to achieve inner clarity and strength we must go even farther inward to find the part of our self that is deeper, wiser, and more spiritually connected. We then can make easy or difficult choices, small or larger and radical changes, with a lot more ease than when we are confused or split between inner and outer messages about what we should be doing. Anger, grief, hostility, and other negative emotions can be transformed into energy contributing to our spiritual wholeness when those feelings are no longer split off or repressed. The gospel suggests that we will experience *all* of the human condition on our way to greater spirituality. The scripture "the Son of Man hath descended below them all" suggests to me that he willingly let in every emotion and experience to be suffered with his love. (D&C 122:8; see also D&C 88:6.) Each part of our self, regardless of its feelings, memories, or skills, has a positive function in our life. Our sadness, for instance, when we are less preoccupied with our own losses, can help us develop greater compassion for the grief of others. This part of our self may then more effectively reach out to heal the wounded of the world.

A workshop I attended several years ago included some discussion on the concept of an inner adviser or guide. The workshop leaders acknowledged that there may exist an inner part of our conscious selves that is wiser than our more superficial consciousness. That inner, wiser part seems to know who we are, why we are here, and what is best for us. Rather than build or create clarity, then, the essential task for therapists would be to help clients find and unlayer that wiser part of themselves. The notion of an inner guide is much the same as the gospel idea that the light of Christ is in everyone, that there is some center of our being, or consciousness, that knows the answers (or where to find them) to the guiding, central questions of our lives. Even though our inner self may be covered over by abuse or by our being in circumstances that are not true to us, the inner guide is still there and can be unlayered. This part can help all parts of ourselves gradually to join and be at peace on the same committee as we make difficult choices, resolve conflicts, and love more wisely.

How do you find that part of yourself? In the Church many methods are taught. We emphasize ways of going inward, such as prayer, pondering, and listening to the Spirit. Several other guidelines and techniques are also available from other sources, not linked to any particular religious doctrine, including meditation and exercises in guided imagery. Throughout the United States in the last few years some modes of therapy have devoted considerable attention to meditation and relaxation techniques as routes to inner strength or fulfillment. If you allow quietness to occur again and again, over time you will become more centered, more focused. Most people who practice these techniques with any regularity can sense a real difference in their lives within two to four months. Rather than using one of the popular meditation or relaxation techniques, you may prefer to use an hour a day to sit quietly reading or listening to music. Some people are also able to use exercise time in a way that helps them remain focused within. So if you are a person who lives at times with a lot of tension or worry or, like the majority of women in the world, depression, these techniques may be very helpful in your quest to move inside and to learn to love yourself and others more wisely. I recall my grandmother as a busy, competent woman but one who always communicated an impression of peacefulness. She had a calmness on the inside even when she was angry. Possessing a centered quality, whether in facing a major dilemma or the daily exigencies of life, is something that comes from repeatedly reaching into the inner calm or deeper sense of direction within you.

In conclusion, let me suggest some general guidelines that can help us know when we are loving wisely. First, assess the balance of struggle versus joy in your life or in a relationship. If there is too much struggle and too little joy, you are out of balance. Probably you are giving too much—but you may be giving too little and be without joy for that reason. If you find in making day-to-day decisions that everyone else's needs come before your own and you allow only ten minutes for yourself during the day—perhaps to wash your face and comb your hair—that's not enough.

Reflect on the last month and gauge how you have spent your time. How much was joyful and fulfilling, even if it was hard? How much was just a struggle with little or no fulfillment? How much was spent on you and how much on others? I fully believe that the service we do for others brings us joy. That is my own experience in life. I love being a therapist and being involved in other people's lives. But I also believe that we must spend time on ourselves.

If you are allowing very little, please find ways to create more time for yourself. You may find that idea acutely uncomfortable at first. One client of mine agreed to spend one hour a day on herself, talking to no one, being with no one, and doing something pleasurable. For the first two days she sat in a chair and felt frightened. Then she tried to take a walk and felt lonely. She could think of nothing pleasurable to do. Over a week's time some things finally occurred to her. She started to take regular walks; she began to read. But at first she found it overwhelming to spend even an hour totally on herself.

Another technique for assessing how wisely you love or how well you balance relationships is to ask some trusted friends for feedback. Question them about how they see you; ask them for some helpful criticism. "Am I giving too much in this relationship?" "Am I being too rescuing or too controlling with my children?" "Am I failing to do something that would help?" If you fear hearing something painful, caution your friend, "This may hurt me, so would you please say it slowly?" One difference between rats and humans is that in a maze, once the rat discovers a blind alley, it does not go down that blind alley a second time. Humans, however, will continue indefinitely going down the same blind alley, especially if the entry to that alley is labeled, "This is the way it *should* be." If you have taken the same route fifteen times, that is probably enough. The difficulty may be something minor, such as a slight edge to your tone of voice. Or it may be major, such as your being the only one who ever initiates trying to solve a problem. We all have blind spots; others may help us pinpoint what we are not seeing.

Finally, recognize that change is a slow process. Value the choices you have made thus far, even in the process of changing. Whenever I have tried to integrate a new concept into my life, particularly a complex one such as codependency, it has always taken me about three or four years to grasp it well enough to change my behavior significantly. Even the simpler ideas elude me for months. I am unable to simply throw all my old ways of behaving out of my repertoire. Nor is that a bad thing. We *should* maintain our patterns of loving until we can adopt ones that are better. We should not automatically assume that we are all wrong and attempt to abandon long-term habits of loving. Those of us who struggle with weight

184

cannot suddenly stop eating the way we have always eaten. It takes a long period of retraining combined with understanding how to do things differently. So even if you recognize some pattern as codependent or out-of-balance in your relationship and wish to change it, retain that behavior as you include new ways of relating and the old ways will gradually be replaced. In that way you can love yourself in the process of trying to love more wisely.

Notes

1. Harriet Goldhor Lerner, *The Dance of Anger* (New York: Harper & Row, 1985); *The Dance of Intimacy* (New York: Harper & Row, 1989).
2. Sheldon Kopp, *What Took You So Long? An Assortment of Life's Everyday Ironies* (Palo Alto, Calif.: Science and Behavior Books, 1979), n.p. [26].

When Our Reaching Reaches His

M. CATHERINE THOMAS

I am an adult child of an alcoholic father. My father has since given up alcohol, but what I experienced in my childhood family seemed to color every aspect of my life. I came out of that home with many confused and uncomfortable emotions, but I didn't know until I was about forty how my childhood experience had affected—and was continuing to affect—the emotional and spiritual quality of my life.

When I was nineteen, I joined the Church. Much of my healing began at that time. But though my conversion was real, and I came to have real spiritual experience, some of my emotions continued to be at odds with gospel teachings, and I didn't know what to do about them. As a young mother, I felt that I was only barely keeping my anger and overall distress from leaking out. I had to struggle too much to be cheerful at home. Inside I was unaccountably angry, I was guilty, I was driven, and I was afraid. On the outside I was tense with my children. I was irritable and controlling. Sometimes I was also loving and patient, felt the Spirit of the Lord, and did parenting things well, but not as consistently as I needed to.

I have observed that if we don't learn consistent and mature love in our childhood homes, we have to struggle to learn it

M. Catherine Thomas received her doctoral degree from Brigham Young University in early Christian history and is an assistant professor of ancient scripture in Religious Education at BYU. She and her husband, Gordon K. Thomas of the BYU English Department, are the parents of six children. She served as Relief Society president of the BYU Second Stake before assuming teaching responsibilities with her husband on the London Study Abroad (Summer-Fall 1990) and the Jerusalem Study Abroad (Winter-Spring 1991) programs.

when we become marriage partners and parents. We may spin our spiritual wheels trying to make up for childhood's personal losses, looking for compensation in the wrong places and finding it very elusive. But of course the significance of spiritual rebirth through Jesus Christ is that we can mature spiritually and make up for those deprivations, in perhaps unexpected ways, through our Savior.

In those days I carried the big three sick emotions: Fear, Guilt, Anger. After I'd spent some nineteen years in motherhood, my children seemed to me like enemies, I was a workaholic, I was exhausted, I thought I didn't love my husband or anybody, and I had no idea where to go for help or even what help I needed. I was functioning, but my emotions were very brittle. I felt deeply hungry.

About one o'clock one morning when I was waiting for my teenager to come in way past the agreed-upon hour, for the ninety-ninth time, I found myself in my upstairs study, sobbing. I cried out from the bottom of my soul for deliverance from my indefinable distress. I heard the words very clearly, "Go home." The next morning I made arrangements to fly back to Ohio, to my parents' home, where my father had just finished an intensive rehabilitation program for recovering alcoholics. That drying-out process had gone on before, but this time there was a new development. The program reached out to help all the members of the alcoholic's family, because all members of such a family are sick and need help until they know who they are, why they feel as they do, and what to do about it.

Thus began the second great healing period for me. My life started to come together in a new harmony after I attended an orientation program for children of alcoholics. I read books on being an alcoholic child, I talked to alcoholics and other adult children of alcoholics, and I didn't stop praying.

Something I have learned since is that many people who did not come out of alcoholic families nevertheless suffer from the same kinds of distress I did. Apparently it doesn't matter what the manifest problem is in the child's family, but in a home where a child is emotionally deprived for whatever reason, that child will take some emotional confusion into adult life.

Children from families with emotional problems are often addicted to stimulation. Steady living is difficult for them and perceived as boring. This adult-child is always looking for a high—if not a chemical or substance high, then an emotional high through seeking ego satisfactions, or even stirring up trouble among loved ones. Therefore, she is restless and always trying to change her life. She is very me-centered, finding it difficult to keep a steady commitment to others and to maintain real interest in their well-being. This adult-child is always taking her own emotional temperature, asking herself if she is happy and fulfilled. The answer is usually no, because she doesn't know what happiness is. When the Savior told us that we would find our lives if we would lose them for his sake, he meant that it would help us to deflect our consciousness from ourselves to him and to those the Lord has given us to love and nurture. That is not to say that we shouldn't seek to do fulfilling things but that preoccupation with our own needs is a dead end. The purpose of life, I have found, is not that everything and everyone (especially my children and my husband) should satisfy me but that *I* could grow. I could enlarge my patience and my tolerance, deepen my humility, and heighten my sensitivity to the Spirit of God. I could recognize and activate the divine power in me to nurture happiness and emotional security in those around me. My preoccupation with my own distress had actually created abuse for my family. I appreciate so much the way my family relationships improved as I got better.

In my early days my mental sonar seemed to operate relentlessly, searching out certain types of thoughts to dwell on, such as self-debasement, despair, anger, feeling unwell, self-pity. I did not then see the relationship between this mental sinning and my unsatisfying life. I was looking for a magic wand, even a priesthood wand, to solve everything right now.

But there are no instant cure-alls. There is only the work that goes into repentance, the spiritual exertion that develops the new habits which soon bear the fruit of peace. (See Alma 33:33; D&C 6:36.)

I learned that I had to take responsibility for my own thought patterns: they were a key. I began to use what I found was a powerful agency to interrupt the thoughts that led me into emotional trouble. That is, I found new ways to deal briefly with bad thoughts or memories, to give to the Lord what hurt too much to carry around, to humble myself more deeply when I felt so below standard. I found I could interrupt critical thoughts about my children and my husband and replace them deliberately with mental images of oneness. I practiced a lot of forgiveness. I learned to let go of things that hurt me. I learned that the Lord would cause things that were important to come together right for me. I could quit manipulating events and stop trying to control people. (See Romans 8:28; D&C 90:24.)

Recovering alcoholics recognize what they call "stinking" thinking. If they want to get well and understand what the Lord's rest is, they have to repent of bad mental habits: fear, self-pity, self-condemnation, bad memories, unforgiveness, certain kinds of fantasizing. I found I did not have this power fully in myself to reshape and heal my mind, but Christ did.

I learned that my spiritual superficiality had been betraying me. On the outside I was going to church, teaching, paying tithing, and so on, but inside, I was allowing mental sinning. I learned that the real work of living the gospel begins in the microdots of the mind, in planting mental virtue deeply, in keeping my mind firm. (Alma 57:27; Jacob 3:1–2.) What we sow in our minds and actions, we reap in our emotions. So, we cease searching for that elusive self-fulfillment and consciously, deliberately, give to others what we, ourselves, hunger for most. "For that which ye do send out shall return unto you again, and be restored." (Alma 41:15.)

Essentially, I have described here my discovery of Jesus

Christ. Not one of my distresses has been outside his consciousness or power. When I have done as he has instructed, especially in keeping my mind firm, my reaching has reached his.

WOMEN'S LIVES:
OTHER TIMES, OTHER PLACES

If we are to "see life steadily and see it whole," we must not focus exclusively on the conspicuous wielders of power, but rather we must explore the contribution of all segments of society in shaping values.

— Catherine Corman Parry

Women's Traces: The Words They Left Behind

CAROL CORNWALL MADSEN

In 1888, remembering a long-ago childhood in New Salem, Massachusetts, Emmeline B. Wells, editor of the *Woman's Exponent*, a Mormon woman's paper in Salt Lake City, recalled some of her thoughts on a sunny spring afternoon fifty years earlier, when she had rummaged through letters and other papers stored in the garret of her New England home. "A light had dawned upon me in that out of the way place," she wrote. "I had found out that women sometimes put their thoughts upon paper, and I conceived the idea of making rhymes, or jingles . . . and, in time, even a book."[1]

That was quite a revelation for the young Emmeline, for women did little public writing before the nineteenth century. In fact, many women did no writing at all, never having had opportunity to learn. Indeed, until the middle of the nineteenth century when women's literacy rate rose dramatically to eighty-seven percent, no more than half the population of American women at any one time could read or write, and few dared to

Carol Cornwall Madsen is an associate professor of history and senior research historian with the Joseph Fielding Smith Institute for Church History at Brigham Young University. She has served as associate director of the Women's Research Institute at BYU. She received her Ph.D. in history from the University of Utah and has coauthored Sisters and Little Saints: One Hundred Years of Primary *and coedited* A Heritage of Faith *and* As Women of Faith, *collections of speeches given at BYU women's conferences. She is working on a biography of Emmeline B. Wells, suffragist, editor, and fifth General President of the Relief Society. She has served as Relief Society president in her ward. She and her husband, Gordon A. Madsen, are the parents of six children.*

put their writings before the public.[2] With the upswing in literacy, however, along with the invention of a steam-powered press which revolutionized printing, came a dramatic explosion of public writing by women. As novelists, poets, and journalists, women found writing a legitimate form of public expression—as long as their topics were properly "womanly"—and at mid-century, women's novels dominated the literary market.[3] As with popular fiction today, few of these literary works survived their own time; however, contemporary historians, along with literary critics, are reevaluating them for what they tell us about how women thought, felt, and lived in the past.[4]

Literacy skills changed the lives of far more women than those few whose names became household words as popular novelists. Women in a variety of circumstances could now preserve their experiences and thoughts in a written record of their lives. Writers of personal literature—journals, diaries, letters, poetry—"have a higher priority than fame," one critic observed. It is "the pleasure of self-inquiry, the desire to validate their lives through vivid accounts."[5] Moreover, "vernacular literature," the jottings of ordinary people who write to learn more about themselves and the world in which they live, has become a major source in the study of women's history.

Recent interest in women's personal writings reflects a renaissance of interest in women's lives, a benefit of the woman's movement and the rise of feminism. Traditionally, women have been poorly represented as either subjects of history or authors of literature. To retrieve the female side of the human experience as well as to claim a literary form long ignored, historians and literary critics are evaluating autobiographical writing by women in all its forms—diaries, journals, reminiscences, letters, as well as the more formal autobiographies—for woman's experience can be discovered in few other documents.

Historians have found that these gendered narratives describe a woman's world separate and distinct from the dominant male world, replete with its own values, symbols,

and language. Women ministered at the primal points of life —
birth, marriage, sickness, and death — performing female rituals
bequeathed from generation to generation. The prevailing view
of women as more sensitive, religious, and refined than men
together with a well-defined division of tasks between men
and women (except under the exigencies of frontier life) contributed to the creation of two gender-defined social spheres.
Women themselves reinforced and valued that distinction.[6] The
vivid private accounts of life from a woman's perspective have
become the tools by which historians can "read women's culture," a term used to designate a rich and singularly female
world.[7]

The earliest extant diaries written in English, dating from
the sixteenth and seventeenth centuries, indicate that women
kept diaries then as a form of "spiritual bookkeeping."[8] Some
women kept these religious records of their own volition;
others followed clerical counsel to do so. Puritans, for instance,
were admonished to record their responses to their Bible
reading or to the sermons they heard in order to mark their
spiritual progress. From them historians have been able to
deduce the qualities most valued in women during that period.
By the eighteenth century, diaries were not only more numerous but more secular, full of memorabilia and detailed
daily experiences, most of them written by upper class, educated women but some reflecting the lives of "ordinary" women.
By the nineteenth century, women with only a modicum of
education joined the host of female autobiographers since the
personal documentary had become a popular female endeavor
and a sign of "gentility." As diary writing became popular, it
developed into a distinct literature, its style and content creating
a genre of its own.[9]

Unlike most other literary forms, diary writing is structured
mainly by chronology. Spontaneous and unrestrained by literary conventions, it is first-draft reporting without the artifice
or embellishment of more traditional literature. That is its
primary value to historians. The diary is also an honest, self-

revelatory portrait where the "best face" is not always the one portrayed. Sometimes a letter describing an event might differ sharply from a diary entry describing the same event, the diary usually reflecting the truer image of the reality. A day in Madge Preston's life illustrates this dichotomy. On New Year's day in 1867, Madge, a well-to-do Baltimore matron, wrote a cheerful, encouraging letter to her daughter, May, who was away at school. She mentioned that her husband was at home all day because of the holiday and that her niece Theodosia, who lived with the Prestons and helped with the housework, had returned from a three-week visit with her family. Madge recounted Theodosia's report of her brief visit with May on her way back to the Prestons. Madge also told her daughter about her New Year's day visitors, who included a young man romantically interested in May, along with his mother and sister. She gave May some motherly advice and then ended the letter with expressions of love from all members of the household. The letter was an account of a quiet, pleasurable holiday spent with family and friends with a dutiful word of counsel and encouragement to a beloved daughter—a typical motherly letter.

The diary account, written just before the letter, tells quite a different story. It laments the return of Theodosia, who has evidently been the object of Mr. Preston's affections, as was her sister Rose before her. It sharply criticized Theodosia and Mr. Preston, who amused themselves playing cards together while she was obliged to entertain the visitors alone. It also describes Madge's exasperation, waiting for her husband and Theodosia to retire before seeking solace alone in her room. There Madge was finally able to express the bitter feelings that had been building all day—and long before. "How long, Oh how long," she wrote, "is this fearful life to be endured." Earlier entries indicate that the fearful life that brought such despair included not only the flagrant infidelity of her husband but periodic beatings at his hand, often in the presence of Theodosia. Her shame and humiliation, not to say pain from the abuse, were dark secrets that she quietly locked in her heart—

and confided only to her diary—as any true Victorian woman would be expected to do. Her duty as a wife and mother was to be submissive, cheerful, and self-sacrificing, making her life a charade even for her daughter.[10] Such dual accounts temper the historian's assumptions and validate the complexity of women's lives.

The Mormon practice of plural marriage elicited the same contradictions. In public, women enthusiastically defended the principle; in private they often told a different story. Responding to a critique condemning the practice of sharing husbands as belittling and demeaning, Emmeline Wells, under the pseudonym of Blanche Beechwood, heatedly retorted in the *Woman's Exponent*: "Is there then nothing worth living for, but to be petted, humored and caressed, by a man? That is all very well as far as it goes, but that man is the only thing in existence worth living for I fail to see. All honor and reverence to good men; but they and their attentions are not the only source of happiness on the earth, and need not fill up every thought of woman." A nettled Emmeline also thought the practice likely to benefit a man's character as well. "And when men see that women can exist without their being constantly at hand, that they can learn to be self-reliant or depend upon each other for more or less happiness, it will perhaps take a little of the conceit out of some of them."[11]

At the same time, Emmeline, a plural wife who lived apart from her husband and his other wives and families, confided to her diary: "Oh if my husband could only love me even a little and not seem so perfectly indifferent to any sensation of that kind, he cannot know the craving of my nature, he is surrounded with love on every side, and I am cast out. O my poor aching heart Where shall it rest its burden, only on the Lord, only to Him can I look every other avenue seems closed against me. . . . I have no one to go to for comfort or shelter no strong arm to lean upon no bosom bared for me, no protection or comfort in my husband."[12]

These contradictory texts reflect a need that women of the

past, and maybe of today, often felt to differentiate between public expectations and the private realities of their lives. Duty, devotion to propriety, even a need for self-justification dictated their public persona. Thus Madge did not tell May about the horrendous conditions under which she lived, nor did Emmeline, Daniel H. Wells' sixth wife, publicly convey the emotional deprivation she experienced. These were Victorian women, and only in the hidden pages of their private writings did they acknowledge the pain their marital situations inflicted. The diary enabled a woman to speak in her own voice and to "distinguish her sense of self from the male constructs [or expectations] culturally imposed on her," one critic has observed.[13]

Every diary represents an individual life. Often irregular, incomplete, but always intimate in style, some diaries seem clearly written for an intended audience while others remain more abstract and self-expressive. Though individually unique, women's diaries share common threads that reveal in some measure the reasons why women wrote. First, they wrote because they wanted to express themselves in some permanent form, often because their opportunity for self-expression was so limited. Emmeline Wells, editor and journalist, poet and short-story writer, had much opportunity for public expression, but her compelling need to write carried over to private writing as well, filling more than forty-seven diaries throughout her long life. "There always seems to be so much to write about," she wrote in the *Woman's Exponent*, which she edited for thirty-seven years. "These are some of an author's troubles; thoughts which come crowding up in throngs, harassing the brain, and struggling for a definite existence.... An author's mind ... resembles not an empty tenement, but 'a barn stored to bursting'; it is a painful pressure constraining to write, perhaps involuntarily, memory, imagination, zeal, perceptions of men and things, a crowd of internal imagery, and we write to be quit of them, and not let the crowd increase."[14]

Second, women wrote to record their spiritual growth, an important facet of women's lives in the past. The 1599 diary of British noblewoman Margaret Hoby notes her dependence on such record keeping: "I . . . neclected my custom of praier, for which, as for many other sinnes, it pleased the Lord to punishe me with an Inward assalte . . . and, if I had not taken this Course of examenation [her record keeping], I think I had for gotten itt."[15] As a tangible record of the life of the mind — or spirit — a diary marked each point of progress or change.

Nearly three centuries later, in 1837, Susan Burnham, a young New England school girl, wrote to her friend Zilpa Grant, an advocate of female education and principal of the Ipswich Female Seminary in Massachusetts, of the recent spiritual awakening that had transformed her life. "I never felt the power of the religion of Jesus until about two years ago," she wrote. "I have felt in some degree that I am not my own; that my time, my talents, my influence, and my all belong to Him, who has bought me with his own blood. I feel that my life should be a life of active service, and there is need of my labors in the vineyard of the Lord."[16] Though the confidence was recorded in epistolary form, the level of trust and confidentiality in her dear friend is similar to what she might have confided to a diary.

Mormon women's diaries frequently contained conversion experiences and testimonies gleaned from temple work, healings, and church service. Sarah Studevant Leavitt and her husband joined the Church in Canada in 1837 without the benefit of missionaries but solely from a relative's testimony and a later reading of the Book of Mormon and Doctrine and Covenants. Like many other converts, they were seekers, waiting to hear the restored gospel. "I had a place where I went every day for secret prayers," Mary Leavitt wrote. "My mind would be carried away in prayer so that I knew nothing of what was going on around me. It seemed like a cloud was resting down over my head. . . . If that cloud would break, there would be something new and strange revealed." The account of her conversion is typical: "My husband's sister . . . had heard the gospel preached by a Mormon and believed it and been bap-

199

tized. She commenced and related the whole of Joseph's vision and what the Angel Moroni had said the mission he had called him to. It came to my mind in a moment that this was the message that was behind that cloud, for me and not for me only, but for the whole world, and I considered it of more importance than anything I had ever heard before."[17]

Self-inquiry was another purpose for diary keeping. As with spiritual accounting or preserving significant religious experiences, this purpose often served as a means of self-improvement. Introspection on paper could provide an evaluation of one's present status and an impetus for transformation. Birthdays and New Year's days frequently elicited such self-appraisals as this one of Ellis Shipp, a young woman who became a prominent doctor in nineteenth-century Utah:

"January 20, 1872: Twenty-five years ago as the sun came over the hill I was born. Yes God placed me upon this earth to accomplish some purpose. Twenty-five years—a quarter of a century has elapsed. And what are my accomplishments? Oh very few. There are very few of my weaknesses that I have brought into subjection—but few of my talents that I have cultivated—and I feel but little good I have done. If I did not see such great examples at my age—and even before—of greatness, nobleness, intelligence and worth, I might think I had accomplished all that was in my power, but I believe what *one* can do *another* can, especially a Latter-day Saint who can ask of the Father for his assistance with such unwavering faith and confidence of its bestowal. O what might not be accomplished."[18]

Louisa Greene Richards, first editor of the *Woman's Exponent*, a Primary worker, and young mother in 1879, also hoped for a purposeful life and wondered at her progress: "Today I have been sewing, taking care of 'baby,' reading in the Bible and in Sister E. R. Snow's Poems, and trying to improve myself by reflection and prayer. I have also read a lesson in the Dictionary, which I endeavor to do every day. When I have commenced the week well, it seems to go on well."[19]

Often women wrote to assert their own identity as individuals and to justify their lives, their circumstances, their feelings. "My life matters," they seem to be writing. Lucy Meserve Smith, writing from her home in Provo, Utah, to her husband, apostle George A. Smith, in Salt Lake City, argues to be accepted as she is, without supposition of pretense. "I don't know as you will believe what I say," she wrote, "as Hannah [a sister-wife with whom she lived] says she heard when she was to the city that you said I always pretend to feel better than I did. . . . I feel exactly as I feel whether it is right or wrong I cant help it."[20]

Martha Cragun Cox, an early settler of St. George, uprooted her family to teach school in many early southern Utah communities when teachers were scarce. Throughout her long, introspective reminiscence, she records her struggle to find an identity. As a young teenager, longing to feel independent and self-reliant, she had resolved to be self-sustaining by weaving fabric and then marketing it. Upon hearing her resolve, her father challenged her to "own your own food and clothes or starve"; that proved to be the stimulus she needed. Weaving soon gave way to teaching, a service she felt would enable her to leave something of more permanence behind. Learning "to use only for my support what I earned" was worth more to her, she wrote, than "the wealth of mines."[21]

Emeline Grover Rich, a plural wife of apostle Charles C. Rich and midwife in Paris, Idaho, in the nineteenth century, found diary keeping a means to verbally justify her efforts to support her children and make a life for herself in the almost constant absence of her husband. "Many a day and night have I travelled through storms that were too severe for the Sterner Sex to wait upon the sick. Not altogether for the small pittance received as a remuneration for the same but for the good I could do in relieving the sick and suffering humanity. . . . I have spent the proceeds of my labors in educating my children for their advancement and in so doing have had but one object in mind, ie. that they might make good noble men and

201

women — ornaments in society — and in their turn might be able to transmit to their posterity an imperishable legacy. I am not ashamed of my example set for my children to imitate — feeling that in my humble career through life I have done the best I could according to my judgment."[22]

Yet another reason women found for keeping diaries was to record their observations of significant events. These first-hand accounts intimately detail historical events and show how specific individuals reacted to them. Besides preserving these diarists' feelings and thoughts as such events unfolded, the diaries illuminate the reality of the past from many different perspectives. Mary Ann Freeze, longtime president of the Young Women in Salt Lake Stake, recorded the dedicatory services at the Manti Temple in 1888: "The doors opened [at] 10 a.m. and the services commenced at 11 a.m. and continued four and a half hours. The grandest meeting of my life. The singing was heavenly[;] the Apostles spoke with mighty power. A halo of light surrounded the heads of several of [the] brethren." Her perceptions of that moving occasion include an unusual witness: "But the most wonderful manifestations of anything I had ever before experienced was the privilege of hearing angelic voices singing an anthem. . . . It was clear and penetrating and yet soft and subdued. I involuntarily looked around to see from whence it proceeded, but not seeing anything, concluded it must be the choir practicing in an adjoining room. . . . It was not until the meeting was called to order and the choir arose immediately before me, that I sensed the divine source from whence it proceeded. . . . My gratitude was unbounded that the Lord had by such a heavenly manifestation showed me that I was accepted of him."[23]

Emmeline Wells noted her pleasure when a new Relief Society general presidency was sustained along with a new First Presidency in a solemn assembly in 1902. "It was very gratifying to women interested in the advancement of the sisters," she wrote, "to see the uplifted hands of all the several quorums of the Holy Priesthood raised to sustain them. It was a very grand and impressive spectacle to witness, and the first of its kind on record where women were the officers to be elected."[24] For a woman who was dedicated to advancing women in all aspects of their lives, as Emmeline Wells was, this was indeed a marked occasion in Church history.

General Relief Society president, Zina D. H. Young, friend and associate of Eliza R. Snow and one of the Church's most beloved women, was a sporadic diary writer. Yet her Nauvoo diary, however brief, proves her to be an attentive witness, coloring her observations with the hues of her own feelings about what she was observing. Following the slaying of the Prophet Joseph, she records these events: "July 1, 1844: I washed Joseph and Hiram's clothes. August, 1844. I went to meeting in the afternoon. Thanks be to Him who reigns on high, the majority of the Twelve are here. Brigham Young spoke and the Church voted that the 12 should act in the office of their calling next to Joseph or the three first presidents. November 17, 1844: This day long to be remembered. Emma Smith, the wife of Joseph Smith the Martyr, had a son born, in the morning. O may the choicest of heaven's blessings attend the child. May it grow into manhood, and may it walk in the way of its Father, be a comfort to its friends and be the means of performing a mighty work to the glory of god and prince forever. March 14, 1845: Business moves rapidly, all things in union among the Saints. Some are leaving that do not feel to fellowship the present authorities of the Church but God knows and the Saints know. We are in the sure way."[25]

Every entry in her occasional diaries is an expression of confidence that she had indeed found the sure way and that her life was inexorably tied to the fortunes of the religious movement she had espoused as a young girl just a few years after the Church was organized.

As scholar William Mulder pointed out, Mormon diaries are a subliterature that helps us understand history. "In them," he wrote, "we find something of the daily living and dying of men and women both weak and valiant. Their story is not epic except as life and many days together give it sweep — it is the sweep of daily existence, the great movement that is the result of countless little movements."[26] Perhaps the most universal thread throughout women's diaries is the daily accounting of the many unheralded moments that made up their lives. A primary reason for most women to keep diaries was to hold on to these little moments that, tied together, gave form and substance to their lives. For Louisa Greene Richards, Friday, January 31, 1879, was just another busy day. Of her voice lessons she noted, with some dismay, "Sickness with first one member of the family and then another, has prevented my attendance at the class so much that I shall not venture to start for another term at present." The pressures of family responsibilities have a way of encroaching on private plans. Then she added, without commentary, what must have been a troublesome and inconvenient piece of news. "Sister Lyon, whose house we are occupying wants us to vacate it, that she may move in herself." She ends the entry for the day with what is surely the most ubiquitous diary entry of that time, a medical report: "I have news from my mother, that the folks down there are getting better of the chills."[27]

Mary Jane Mount Tanner, a Provo Relief Society president, devoted diarist, and would-be poet, found her attempts to write frustratingly interrupted by the demands of her young family. "I am trying to write some today," she wrote the day after Christmas in 1877, "but I always find it tedious work owing to the annoyance of the children. If I sit in the room with them they play and talk to me," she discovered, "and if I sit in another room they are continually coming to the door for something and keep me answering their questions every few minutes. It is always so, and for that reason, as well as many others, I am not able to accomplish much in the literary line."[28] Her complaint could fit comfortably on the pages of any mother's journal. The daily impediments to writing fell upon one another with such regularity that the reader is as happy as Mary Jane when her book of poetry is finally completed.

Winter Quarters spurred many women to record the details of each day if only to share them later with absent husbands or to hold on to a singular time in their lives. Finding pleasure in the company of other women, sharing their loneliness and apprehension of the future, and enjoying the dances and other social gatherings of the winter encampment, these women recorded a busy time of social interaction and anticipation for the further move westward. Mary Haskin Parker Richards waited in Winter Quarters while her husband served a mission in England. Except for reference to a tent, her diary entry for January 29, 1847, belies the temporariness of her situation. "We had little snow," she records for that day. "After getting breakfast & doing up my work I went up to our Tent. Found a good fire in the stove. Was there all alone for several hours, writing a letter to my far absent husband. Felt very lonely although it seemed good to be alone awhile communicating my thoughts to that dear absent friend who is dearer to me yes far dearer than all others. About 5 PM I returned to Janes [a sister-in-law]. Got supper and then went with Elsy Snyder to the Singing School. On our way called at Maria's. Found her about ready so we all went together. There were more of [at] C[h]oir tonight at the Council house than had ever been seen together since we left Nauvoo. We sung for about an hour & 1/2 then danced till 1/2 past 11. . . . It was the Anniversary of the night I was married and I told some of the Sisters that I was celebrating it &c."[29]

Finally, diaries served as a silent confidante, a willing receptor of private thoughts and emotions. Confiding one's feelings to a mute page frequently brought a needed catharsis. Few women's diaries of the nineteenth century escaped mention of the loss of a child, often an infant. Though a common experience for women in those years, the heartbreak was nonetheless acute. Jane Baxter Gunnell of Cache Valley, Utah, retreated to a quarantine house on the outskirts of Wellsville when her third child and only daughter, in a family that eventually numbered six sons, became ill with diphtheria. Though

205

pregnant with her fourth child, she was left to nurse her little daughter alone. She had "fumigated" her sons with an antiseptic and sent them to live with her sister-wife Emma before leaving her home. "I didn't have much to doctor her with," she regretted. "I prayed for two days and nights, but it wasn't to be. She died in my arms as I rocked her watching the sun coming up over the horizon. . . . I was expecting my fourth child and how I wanted another little girl, but it was a boy."[30]

When Ellis Shipp, a wife and the mother of three children, started off for Philadelphia Woman's Medical College in 1875, she was armed with a little money, her husband's support, and her own enthusiasm about the new venture, though deeply saddened at leaving her children behind. When she returned to Philadelphia for her second year of study, however, she did so pregnant, penniless, and against her husband's wishes. "I have parted from my darlings before," she lamented, "but never under such circumstances. Oh, Heaven help me to endure this agony. Oh, I pray my Father to preserve them, keep them safe till I return. My dear, dear husband and my darling children — oh, how fondly do I love them. How can I live from out their presence. I have been urged on by a something, I know not what, to take this step. Heaven grant that it may prove a wise one."[31] It was, indeed, a wise step, for when she returned to her home in Salt Lake City, she was able to provide much needed medical service and became one of Utah's most prominent early woman doctors.

Polygamy exacted a heavy emotional price from its adherents. Women suffered loneliness, understandable jealousy, and a psychological and cultural dislocation that frequently left lifetime scars. Emily Wells Grant, plural wife of apostle Heber J. Grant, spent the first six years of her marriage separated from her husband because of the anti-polygamy crusade of the 1880s. In exile in England, she wrote many diary-like letters in which she recorded her attempt to make the best of a situation that was oppressive and disheartening. Always exhibiting the self-sacrificing demeanor expected of women of her time, she nonetheless occasionally gave way to the emotional pain this irksome situation caused. "I don't believe it is as hard for you as for me," she wrote to her husband, "but don't ever imagine for one moment that I have a regret—other than that I can't be your wife and realize the true happiness of home life as you now do. I envy every girl I know her cozy little home with her children and husband, besides the comforts of life." Then, in a sardonic comment on the anti-Mormon vendetta, she adds, "I guess the present crusade is doing good if it is a benefit to people to suffer."[32]

Emmeline Wells also suffered from the separation that plural marriage inevitably caused and often mourned her husband's seeming indifference and lack of visits during the early period of their marriage. Years later, when her life was filled with pressing commitments as a general officer in the Relief Society, an active suffragist, and editor of the *Woman's Exponent*, her husband, Daniel H. Wells, invited her to visit him in Manti, Utah, where he was presiding over the temple. The reunion of this husband and wife, so long physically and emotionally apart, was like that of long-lost lovers. He was seventy-six and she was sixty-two. "O, the joy of being once more in his dear presence," Emmeline confided to her diary. "His room is so nice and we are so cozy by the large grate and such a comfortable fire in it. We are more like lovers than husband and wife for we are so far removed from each other there is always the embarrassment of lovers and yet we have been married more than 37 years. How odd it seems. I do not feel old, neither does he—we are young to each other and that is well."[33]

And so women wrote—for themselves, for others, to be "rid of the crowd" of ideas and feelings that filled their minds and hearts, or to give validity to their existence and weight to their experience. While early Mormon women's diaries were not necessarily unique as diaries, they displayed some distinctive characteristics. First, they conveyed a strong historical consciousness. These first-generation Mormon women were well aware that they were on the cutting edge of a new gospel dispensation and that their lives had historical significance. Conversion was a major act of self-assertion that for women often meant a stronger break with tradition and family moorings than it did for men.

Second, most of the diaries exhibit a strong sense of self-worth or a self-conscious effort to develop it. Women often expressed attitudes of humility and inadequacy and a desire to improve, but few were truly self-deprecating. They knew their lives counted for something and for most a sense of purpose was clear and unequivocal. Moreover, their diaries exhibit a deep conviction of the nobility of sacrifice, far surpassing the usual selflessness attributed to women. Whether the sacrifice meant sharing a husband, abandoning a home, leaving loved ones through conversion, paying tithing, spending years working in women's organizations, or forging new settlements out of hostile environments, dedication to a larger cause meliorated the losses, the hardships, the disappointments. Consecrating their all to building the kingdom, they—time after time—answered the call to give without reserve. The intense loyalty and obedience to authority so evident in their private writings clearly signal their faith and allegiance to a cause transcending self-interest.

Though only a few women's diaries focused on gender issues, all were gender-conscious. They noted the close female relationships that resulted from their kingdom-building tasks just as fervently as their family and domestic ties. This commitment to kingdom building dramatically enhanced the ordinary; even the most mundane activity noted in the diary seemed to play an important role in the greater drama being staged about them. Certainly their other-worldly focus, which promised eternal association with loved ones and eventual advancement to godhood, imbued every act with an eternal consequence. Their diaries display their firm conviction of what they were about, as individuals and as a people.

Finally, Mormon diaries conveyed a deeply internalized

group consciousness and an individual identity taken from membership in that group. Though they were busily engaged in raising their own families, earning their own living, and attending to their own affairs, what they were doing related directly to the purposes of their Mormon affiliation and their identification with its mores as well as its mission.

Women have long been recognized as preservers, determined to find ways to hold on to the past and link it to the present and future. Maybe in their role as creators of life they feel more keenly the continuity of generations and seek to connect them through a shared memory, either through artifacts lovingly passed from generation to generation, or through oral and written means, whereby traditions and customs as well as thoughts and experiences are carefully transmitted.

Moreover, through their personal writings, women have recorded and preserved an entire female culture, rich with its own values, traditions, and language that has always existed alongside the dominant male culture but has been long rejected as historically irrelevant. Though ignored by traditional historians, women's written history has quietly existed in this private form that has kept women's lives from being irretrievably lost, though long hidden and unseen. These gendered texts enable us to view the human experience from a different angle of vision that broadens our perspective and enhances our understanding of the past.

One literary critic has compared the "super subtle design" of diary writing to that of a quilt, both of them symbols of women's rich but unrecognized culture. The quilt is made up of hundreds of "incremental stitches," she wrote, that eventually define the pattern.[34] So, too, the diary has a pattern of "language, content, and narrative structure" that gives it shape and form. Not until the last stitch in the quilt is made or the last entry in the diary written is the pattern complete and the design fully revealed. In its unplanned, sometimes incoherent, and often haphazard pattern, the diary acquires a life of its own, even as it transcribes the life of its author. Unique yet universal, it both instructs as history and delights as literature.

Notes

1. "The Old Garret," *Woman's Exponent* 17 (1 October 1888): 67.
2. Carl N. Degler, *At Odds: Women and the Family in America from the Revolution to the Present* (New York: Oxford University Press, 1980), pp. 308–9.
3. Ann Douglas Wood, "The Scribbling Women and Fanny Fern: Why Women Wrote," *American Quarterly* 23 (1971): 3–25.
4. For historical uses of women's diaries see, for example, Nancy Cott, *The Bonds of Womanhood* (New Haven: Yale University Press, 1977), and Carroll Smith-Rosenberg, "The Female World of Love and Ritual: Relations Between Women in Nineteenth-Century America," *Signs, A Journal of Women in Culture and Society* 1 (1975): 1–29. For literary uses see Elaine Showalter, ed., *The New Feminist Criticism* (New York: Pantheon, 1985), and Ellen Moers, *Literary Women: The Great Writers* (New York: Doubleday, 1976).
5. John Schilb elaborates on the value of using personal diaries and journals in traditional literature classes in "The Usefulness of Women's Nontraditional Literature in the Traditional Literature-and-Composition Course," in *Women's Personal Narratives: Essays in Criticism and Pedagogy,* ed. Leonore Hoffmann and Margo Culley (New York: The Modern Language Association of America, 1985), p. 117.
6. An interesting modern analogue is the self-defined "sacred community" of a group of orthodox Jewish women which has "consciously rejected the male, secular culture" and celebrated gender differences as natural and eternal. The "highest levels of spirituality," they claim, are reached through "female life-cycle experiences." See Debra Renee Kaufman, "Engendering Family Theory, Toward a Feminist Interpretive Framework," in *Fashioning Family Theory,* ed. Jetse Sprey (Newbury Park, Calif: Sage Publications, 1990), pp. 107–35, esp. p. 120. I am indebted to Marie Cornwall for drawing my attention to this article.
7. Judy Nolte Lensink explores the use of diaries to explain women's culture from a literary perspective in "Expanding the Boundaries of Criticism: The Diary as Female Autobiography," *Women's Studies* 14 (1987): 44. Historians Nancy Cott and Carroll Smith-Rosenberg describe and analyze women's culture of the past in *The Bonds of Womanhood* and "The Female World of Love and Ritual," respectively.
8. The term is William Mulder's in "Mormonism and Literature," in *A Believing People: Literature of the Latter-day Saints,* ed. Richard H.

Cracroft and Neal E. Lambert (Provo, Utah: Brigham Young University Press, 1974), p. 209.

9. Harriet Blodgett, *Centuries of Female Days: English Women's Private Diaries* (New Brunswick: Rutgers University Press, 1988).

10. Virginia Walcott Beauchamp, "Letters and Diaries, The Persona and the Real Woman—A Case Study," in *Women's Personal Narratives*, pp. 40–47.

11. "Why, Ah! Why," *Woman's Exponent* 3 (30 September-1 October, 1874): 67.

12. Emmeline B. Wells Diary, 30 Sept. 1874, Harold B. Lee Library, Brigham Young University, Provo, Utah.

13. Blodgett, p. 261, n. 16.

14. "Why Women Write," *Woman's Exponent* 3 (15 March 1875):159.

15. Margaret Hoby, 10 Sept. 1599, as quoted in Blodgett, p. 76.

16. 8 Dec. 1837, ms., Mount Holyoke College Archives, quoted in Keith E. Melder, *Beginnings of Sisterhood: The American Woman's Rights Movement, 1800–1850* (New York: Schocken Books, 1977), p. 36.

17. Kenneth W. Godfrey, Audrey M. Godfrey, Jill Mulvay Derr, eds., *Women's Voices: An Untold History of the Latter-day Saints* (Salt Lake City: Deseret Book Co., 1982), p. 30.

18. Ellis Shipp Musser, ed., *The Early Autobiography and Diary of Ellis Reynolds Shipp, M.D.* (Salt Lake City: Deseret News Press, 1962), pp. 94–95.

19. Louisa Greene Richards Diary, 31 Mar. 1879, typescript copy, LDS Church Archives, Salt Lake City, Utah.

20. Lucy Meserve Smith to George A. Smith, 15 June 1854, Provo, Utah, George A. Smith Papers, LDS Church Archives, Salt Lake City, Utah.

21. Reminiscences of Martha Cragun Cox, typescript copy, pp. 94–99, LDS Church Archives, Salt Lake City, Utah.

22. Emeline Grover Rich Diary, Jan. 1892—Dec. 1893, Paris, Idaho, LDS Church Archives, Salt Lake City, Utah.

23. Mary Ann Burnham Freeze Diary, 21 May 1888, Harold B. Lee Library, Brigham Young University, Provo, Utah.

24. Bathsheba W. Smith was sustained as the new general president (following the death of Zina D. H. Young) with Anna Taylor Hyde and Ida Smoot Dusenberry as her counselors and Emmeline B. Wells as general secretary. Relief Society Record, Nov. 1902, LDS Church Archives, Salt Lake City, Utah.

25. Zina D. H. Young, Nauvoo Diary, LDS Church Archives, Salt Lake City, Utah.

26. William Mulder, "Mormonism and Literature," p. 209.

27. Louisa Green Richards Diary, 31 Jan. 1879, LDS Church Archives, Salt Lake City, Utah.

211

28. Mary Jane Mount Tanner Diary, 26 Dec. 1877, Marriott Library, University of Utah, Salt Lake City, Utah.
29. As quoted in *Women's Voices*, pp. 179–80.
30. Jane Baxter Gunnell, Life History, typescript copy in possession of author.
31. In Musser, 27 Sept. 1876, p. 240.
32. Emily Wells Grant to Heber J. Grant, circa June 1887, copy in possession of author.
33. Emmeline B. Wells Diary, 13 Mar. 1890, Harold B. Lee Library, Brigham Young University, Provo, Utah.
34. Judith Nolte Lensink, p. 41.

"This Boke Is Myne":
Medieval Women and Their Books

CATHERINE CORMAN PARRY

The period of European history between the fall of Rome and the advent of the Renaissance is frequently called the Dark Ages. But while the time suffered the turbulence of conquest and the distress of life without modern medicine and technology, it did not lack the illumination of scholarship, religion, and literature. Indeed, the term *dark* more accurately describes our understanding of the period than it does the period itself. Histories of the world in general, and of the Middle Ages in particular, have tended to focus on conspicuous wielders of power and to ignore the seemingly less significant contributions made by those excluded from the power structures — such as women. Recently, however, scholars have begun reassessing notions of how history is perceived and written, resulting in our clearer understanding of women's role in their society.

Most of us grew up with the notion that literacy in the Middle Ages was mostly confined to men, and that women, even when they could read, certainly did not compose books. We also learned that the painstaking hand-copying of books was undertaken by generations of monks hunched over manuscripts in poorly-lighted scriptoria. Even if we emend that conception to include professional copyists outside the monastery, we still consider book production a male province. But although men dominated the bookish world, many women

Catherine Corman Parry, a native of California, earned her master's and doctoral degrees at the University of California, Los Angeles. She teaches Old and Middle English language and literature at Brigham Young University and serves as the Laurel advisor in her ward.

213

recognized the power intrinsic to the written word. They, too, read, wrote, and made books, prized them for their beauty, sought them for knowledge of the sacred and secular. Perhaps because of their exclusion from the circles of authority and centers of learning, women empowered themselves through their association with books and wielded the word as effectively as men wielded the sword.

The new Christian religion spread to central and northern Europe even before the collapse of the Roman Empire, as early as the late second century A.D. When the ascetic movement — the separation of consecrated men and women into self-contained religious communities — arrived there, local bishops encouraged their parishioners to become part of these centers of learning and devotion. Because women in secular life had little autonomy or opportunity for education, those with religious aspirations often found even the restrictions of the convent more bearable than the "freedom" of secular life.

These women and men spread Christianity to the local people and provided the foundation for missionary efforts far away. Although the nuns, unlike many monks, did not travel the countryside preaching, they did provide goods and services vital to the missionary effort: they made wool and clothing, offered shelter and food to wandering missionaries, and produced books containing scripture and doctrine. The legacy of these pioneering female scribes was eventually felt as far away as England. When a Frankish princess, Bertha, was given in marriage to the non-Christian king of the Anglo-Saxons in Kent, she opened the way for Pope Gregory to send a missionary delegation that eventually spread the Christian message throughout England. We find records of stalwart Anglo-Saxon women establishing abbeys, which serve as refuges of devotion and learning in a turbulent time. A woman named Eadburg directed one such abbey in the mid-eighth century.

According to contemporary accounts, Eadburg possessed remarkable abilities, including an unremitting zeal for knowledge. We know her mainly through her correspondence with

Boniface, a remarkable man who spent most of his life converting heathen tribes and reforming the church in Germany. Unfortunately, all of Eadburg's correspondence has been lost, and we must rely on Boniface's letters for a picture of this venerable woman. They tell us that Boniface turned to Eadburg and her women for much of the spiritual and tangible aid he needed for his work. In one letter, for instance, he requests that she make him a book written in gold, containing the letters of the apostle Peter, in order that he may place "the honour and reverence of holy writ before mortal eyes" while he preaches.[1] In the same letter he acknowledges other books and gifts that Eadburg's community has sent, remarking that "books and vestments, the proofs of your affection, have been to me a consolation in misfortune."[2] This letter not only suggests the devoted energies and mutual affection of those engaged in God's work but reveals that women engaged in the scribal arts. Writing in gold on parchment required more than even the usual skill, and Boniface's request suggests that Eadburg's nuns did it well. In fact, Eadburg herself must have been known for her writing, as one of Boniface's companions sent her a silver style used for writing on wax tablets.

Some three to four hundred years after Eadburg, Diemud, a nun at Wessobrun between 1057 and 1130, copied more than forty-five books (according to the list that remains). Unfortunately only fifteen of these survived to the nineteenth century. Diemud's production "exceeded what could be done by several men," and was "most skilful . . . in a most beautiful and legible character both for divine service and for the library of the monastery."[3] Descriptions of her manuscripts mention Diemud's small, elegant writing and her ornate capital letters. But Diemud was not the only female scribe in Bavaria. Leukardis, for instance, used her knowledge of Scotch, Greek, Latin, and German to aid her copying, and the nuns at Admunt were praised for neatly mending their parchment leaves with silken thread. And an abbot named Emo not only encouraged his men to write but "taking count of the diligence of the female sex he set women who were clever at writing to practice the art assiduously."[4]

Herrad, abbess of Hohenburg in the twelfth century, forms a bridge between women who copied and women who authored. She compiled a massive, encyclopedic work which she called "The Garden of Delights." The book was ostensibly a history of the world as the Bible presents it, but it also contained numerous digressions on philosophy, customs, and moral speculation. Herrad apparently created *The Garden of Delights* for her nuns' education, for in it she says: "I was thinking of your happiness when like a bee guided by the inspiring God I drew from many flowers of sacred and philosophic writing this book called the 'Garden of Delights'; and I have put it together to the praise of Christ and the Church, and to your enjoyment."[5] Amazingly, the entire book, all 324 leaves, appear to be Herrad's work. Scholars mostly agree that the compilation and synthesis of the material, as well as the actual writing and drawing, are all Herrad's own, though the coloring of the illustrations may have been done by others. As one scholar expresses it, "the work was wonderfully complete in plan and execution — the conception of one mind, which labored with unceasing perseverance to realize the conception it had formed."[6] The entire work burned during the bombardment of Strasburg in 1870, so we must rely on the notes and drawings of scholars who studied the manuscript before then.

The abbey at Helfta also produced some remarkable female writers. From 1251 until 1291 the Abbess Gertrude of Hackeborn oversaw more than a hundred women at Helfta and devoted her energies to creating a pious house of charity, learning, and prayer. She promoted both literary and scriptural study, believing that if the former were neglected, the latter would suffer, and consequently went to great lengths to procure books for the abbey's library.[7] Three of the most renowned mystics of the medieval church lived and wrote at Helfta during this period: Mechthild the sister of Abbess Gertrude, Mechthild

216

the beguine, and Gertrude the Great (not to be confused with Abbess Gertrude).

We find in each woman a reverence bordering on passion for the Lord, love for her fellow human beings, and amazement that God would choose to speak through her. All recognized that despite their learning, their position as female recipients of God's special grace opened them to the skepticism and ridicule of their male associates. As Mechthild the beguine exclaimed, "Ah Lord, were I a learned man, a priest, in whom thou hadst made manifest this power, thou would'st see him honored, but how can they believe that on such unworthy ground thou hast raised a golden house? . . . Lord, I fail to see the reason of it."[8] Later, her fears of unworthiness and presumption led her for a time to stop recording her visions, and it took the counsel of her priest combined with God's strong rebuke to reassure her that writing was her special calling.

Gertrude the Great's reaction to her own visions and abilities echoes that of Mechthild. A younger contemporary of the Abbess Gertrude and the two Mechthilds, Gertrude entered Helfta when she was about five years old. As we have noted, the insistence on study in that house resulted in a thorough, if strenuous, religious education, and this left its mark on the young Gertrude. In her youth she pursued liberal arts, but after receiving a vision of Christ when she was twenty-five, she devoted the entirety of her studies to religion. After mastering the scriptures — which she never ceased to expound to the edification of those around her — she collected passages from the writings of Church Fathers, and apparently gathered these into books. Gertrude occupied her entire days translating religious works from Latin into German, editing them and adding commentary so that readers could more easily comprehend them. So deep was her understanding and so willing was she to share it that it was said, "[n]one conversed with her who did not afterwards declare they had profited by it."[9] In addition to these many works, she also wrote the *Legacy of Divine Piety*, in which she records her special communion with God.

217

Gertrude and the two Mechthilds are not unique among medieval religious women. Perhaps because of their exclusion from active roles in church government, devout women found an outlet for their fervor in mystical, visionary experience. Hildegard of Bingen, Julian of Norwich, Margery Kempe, and others too numerous to mention here, all recorded their experiences with the Divine in order to convince other struggling Christians of God's unbounded love and tender grace.

The story of women writers is not confined to the abbeys of medieval Europe. Although reading and writing skills in the secular world remained the privilege of individuals wealthy and leisured enough to use or enjoy them, at least some lay women wrote for instruction, entertainment, and occasionally even profit. Christine de Pisan, for instance, came to France from Italy with her parents when her father entered the service of the king of France. The family was quite well off for some time, and Christine apparently received some education. That girls received less instruction than boys caused her much regret, however, and required the mature Christine to supply for herself the lack of learning in her youth. In 1379, her father chose a husband for her, Etienne de Castel, and the two had three children, one of whom died young. Apparently the marriage pleased both parties, for Christine speaks tenderly of the love they shared and writes with conviction of the friendship between a husband and wife. It was, then, a terrible blow when after only ten years of marriage Etienne died of a sudden illness. Christine's father had died earlier, and now the young woman found herself head of a household at only twenty-five.

Perhaps to ease her grief at Etienne's death, Christine wrote a series of twenty ballads. Discovering her gift for writing love poetry, she continued until she had written one hundred ballads. Between 1397 and 1429, in addition to numerous short poems, she wrote more than twenty major works. Some of them were patriotic pieces; others, works of philosophy or moralism. But Christine is perhaps best known for her writings championing women against the misogynist onslaughts of contemporary poets and politicians. For these she won both friends and enemies among the learned men of her day, but even the invective of the latter could not silence her firm and reasonable voice.[10]

Women influence culture, however, not only as writers but as readers. In a recent article Susan Groag Bell suggests that the "knowledge women gleaned from their books and the books' widespread international transportation by their own-ers . . . demonstrates medieval women's considerable cultural influence."[11] According to Bell's preliminary research, a fairly substantial number of medieval European and English noble-women owned books. A little more than half the books they owned were devotional in nature — Bibles, scriptural com-mentary, Books of Hours. The latter, used in private devotions, usually contained prayers, hymns, scriptures, and colorful min-iature illustrations. They received their name from the material and prayers to be read when observing the "Hours," or de-votional periods throughout the day, honoring the Virgin Mary. These beautiful and often lavishly ornamented books seem to have become especially popular during and after the twelfth century.

New books were commissioned in the Middle Ages because of the expense and painstaking effort involved in producing a manuscript. That is, the prospective owner and the book pro-ducer would agree on such matters as cost (based on length, quality of materials, and ornamentation) and what the book would contain. We may infer from this process, then, that the women who commissioned books selected the material within them, which was mostly devotional in nature. Bell suggests two reasons for that. Initially, women's need for the private spiritual sustenance offered by books may have been greater than that of men because of the former's inferior position in medieval Christian thought and their consequent exclusion from church circles of learning and influence. Secondly, their role as child-rearers led women to select material of the high-est moral import for the instruction of their children. This instruction applied to both boys and girls; however, the ownership of books, at least in some cultures in Europe, appears to have been a special matter between mother and daughter. For instance, a collection of Saxon custom laws compiled around 1215 lists the household items that were generally inherited by a daughter from her mother, including household furniture, linens, clothes, cooking utensils, and books, specifically religious books.[12] A Dutch Book of Hours contains the names of six generations of women owners, and in numerous wills mothers bequeath books to their daughters.[13] Such a custom undoubtedly affected the way women perceived themselves, as they received the lessons hand-picked for them by their mothers and grandmothers and in turn selected the lessons their own daughters would learn. It also must have influenced books themselves, since the material women chose in one book influenced the production of other books.

The influence of women is also demonstrated in the use of vernacular languages. Most devotional literature, including the Bible, was written in Latin. Because women outside the abbey were conscientiously not taught Latin, those who wished to read religious works had to have them translated into their vernacular languages. Booklists, descriptions in wills, commentaries on the times, as well as the surviving manuscripts themselves, all attest that religious works were indeed translated from Latin into the languages women could read, despite the church's qualms about putting scripture in the hands of those ill-equipped to interpret it. Anne of Bohemia, first wife to Richard II of England, arrived in England with a trunkful of books, among which were a Bible in her native Czech and one in German. She commissioned an English translation also, prompting John Wycliffe, the great English reformer, to point to her as an example in his effort to legitimize an English translation of the Bible.

If we remember that the medieval custom of arranged marriages frequently sent women across vast distances to make their homes, we can begin to perceive how vast must also have been the influence of the books they brought with them. Bell suggests that women's subtle role in the translation and dissemination of the Bible and other religious works may have sped reformist movements that led to the Reformation: "Scholars agree that one of the key issues in reformist movements throughout the late Middle Ages was the public's greater familiarity with the teaching of the New Testament — a familiarity obviously deepened by the spread of literacy and the invention of printing, but first and foremost by the translation of scriptural texts into the vernacular. Women played an important role in teaching, in translating, and in loosening the hierarchical bonds of church control through their close and private relationship to religious books."[14]

As we assess, then, medieval women's relationship with books, we can see how our approach to history may have clouded as much as illuminated our understanding of the past. If we are to "see life steadily and see it whole," we must not focus exclusively on the conspicuous wielders of power, but rather we must explore the contribution of all segments of society in shaping values. Further, an understanding of how medieval women perceived themselves can aid in our assessments of our own selves. They, too, sought appropriate outlets for devotional energy and influence in a patriarchal culture; their responses to their situation can say much to us regarding our own.

Notes

1. Lina Eckenstein, *Women under Monasticism* (Cambridge: Cambridge University Press, 1986), p. 122.
2. Ibid.
3. Ibid., p. 236.
4. Ibid., p. 237.
5. Ibid., p. 255.
6. Ibid., p. 243.
7. Jeremy Finnegan, O.P., "The Women at Helfta," in *Peace Weavers: Medieval Religious Women*, vol. 2, ed. John A. Nichols and Lillian Thomas Shank (Cistercian Publications, 1987), p. 212.

8. Eckenstein, p. 336.

9. Ibid., p. 347.

10. Angela M. Lucas, *Women in the Middle Ages: Religion, Marriage, and Letters* (Harvester Press, Ltd., 1983), p. 169.

11. Susan Groag Bell, "Medieval Women Book Owners; Arbiters of Lay Piety and Ambassadors of Culture," in *Women and Power in the Middle Ages*, ed. Mary Erler and Maryanne Kowaleski (Athens, Ga.: The University of Georgia Press, 1988), pp. 149–87.

12. Ibid., p. 157.

13. Ibid.

14. Ibid., p. 179.

Outside Cultural Comfort Zones: Four Italian Women

CINZIA DONATELLI NOBLE

All of us have surely felt, at some time in our lives, that the world is against us, that we hopelessly fight to have our rights or abilities recognized, and that others control our condition in the world. From many examples throughout Italian history, I have selected four exceptional women who found it difficult to expose their ideals and abilities but had the courage to face opposition and bring about change. Of course, their success depended on extensive preparation, as does ours. Accomplishment and influence do not come by chance but are always the result of sacrifice, study, work, and courage.

One of the very few women to be remembered from ancient Roman history is Cornelia, the daughter of Scipio Africanus, a famous general. Born sometime between 195 and 190 B.C., she became the mother of the two Gracchi, the first reformers of land laws and privilege.

In her teenage years she married Tiberius Gracchus, a man of approximately forty who was involved in politics, wars, and a brilliant career. She gave birth to twelve children, of whom only three survived to adulthood. Her husband died when she was still in her thirties, and she chose never to remarry, even

Cinzia Donatelli Noble, lecturer of Italian at Brigham Young University, received her Laurea in Lettere Classiche from the Università G. D'Annunzio, in Chieti, Italy. She has published two books, Cesare Pavese e la letteratura americana *and* Pronuncia e fonetica dell'italiano, *and has written several articles on twentieth-century Italian literature and linguistics. She has served in the Young Women, Relief Society, and Primary organizations. She and her husband, Randy, are the parents of two children.*

to the king of Egypt, Ptolemy IV, who pursued her hand incessantly. Instead she invested her life and pride in raising her family; she devoted herself completely to her children.

In Roman society it was usually the father who supervised the education of the sons, but after she was widowed, Cornelia undertook completely the task of educating Tiberius and Gaius. She chose their teachers from among the most famous Greek scholars, even though at the time Greek culture was considered immoral, tainted by Oriental influences, and certain to lead to the destruction of Roman values. Cornelia herself had an intellectual disposition and was an excellent writer; she knew firsthand the philosophical and oratorical excellence of Greek culture and wanted her sons to be well and fully educated. Their education prepared them to be unusually moral and enlightened leaders. Not surprisingly, when her sons grew to manhood, Cornelia had enemies who accused her of maneuvering her sons in all their social and political reforms and of even hiring men for seditious activities in the city. Contemporary opinion, however, recognizes Cornelia's honesty and perseverance. In his speeches, her son Gaius often mentioned his mother's good name as a credential in his behalf, because Cornelia was widely known as a woman with old-fashioned, strong Roman morals.

She was convinced that the *mos maiorum*, the customs of the ancestors, were the safeguard against modern decadence. Cornelia, who loved her children above all, taught them to fight corruption, even to the risking of their lives. She sacrificed, suffered, and lost much when first Tiberius and then Gaius were killed by mobs incited by the upper classes, who feared losing their special privileges. She is still remembered as she would have wished, as a woman and mother of high moral standards, who devoted herself completely to her children. A statue was erected in her honor in the city, bearing this inscription: "Cornelia, Africani f. Gracchorum," that is, "Cornelia, the Mother of the Gracchi." It was a monument to motherhood and to a woman who did not wish to be remembered in and of herself but only in recognition of her children.[1]

Another woman who influenced her times was born in Siena in 1347, well over a thousand years later. Her name was Caterina. In many ways her spiritual life may seem extreme and unfamiliar to us, but we cannot help but admire her courage during trials, her perseverance in her ideals, and her willpower.

The twenty-fourth of a wealthy family of twenty-five children, she was during her infancy the delight of her family and relatives: a wise, lively, and active little girl. She was born at the end of the Middle Ages, when the soul was still regarded as more important than material acquirements. The Tuscan cities in her region were nonetheless bustling with life, engaging in commerce, and growing in power and wealth. It was an age of changes, when religion was still the dominant force and concern in life, but the dawn of the Renaissance and the rise of solely secular power were on the horizon. In Caterina's time the pope still wielded both secular and ecclesiastical power. Wars and battles were commonplace even in the ecclesiastical domain.

Caterina was an observant girl, sensitive to the struggles of her time. She felt the importance of closeness to Christ and understood remarkably early in her life that there were corrupt bishops and cardinals in the Catholic church. She decided that there was a need to return to a purer obedience to the laws of holiness and the rules of the Church. She was only six years old when she claimed to have had her first vision, with Christ the Lord inviting her to repentance, obedience, and sacrifice. She was seven when she devoted herself to those ideals. At first she began spending most of her days and nights in prayer, defeating all of her family's attempts to persuade her to listen to reason or return to reality. Although her family's alarm is understandable, I also understand how, at a time when the true Church had not yet been restored, Caterina would feel a need to initiate change in the Catholic Church and a strong desire to be an active part in the "cleansing process," as she called it.

She chose the only possible way she knew of. In those days, a woman did not have much freedom; she was usually married by her family, did not have any rights, and could not travel freely. Caterina overcame all these obstacles. It was the custom for girls to marry at only twelve or thirteen years old. Despite her mother's efforts to arrange a marriage, Caterina devoted her life to the service of the Lord and became a Dominican nun in the order of the Mantellate when she was only sixteen years old. As a nun, she enjoyed respect and power that otherwise she could not have had.

Her major resource was prayer. She spent innumerable hours praying to the Lord, not ceasing until she received the asked-for inspiration. Endowed with unusual patience, she endured many struggles. As she later wrote: "O sweet patience, full of joy and happiness! . . . [Through it] any sorrow becomes sweet, any ominous weight becomes light."[2] In every trial of her life she always turned to the Lord, and envisioned him as a God of love, "Our sweet Lord, who doesn't want anything but love from us."[3]

By age twenty, Caterina had already drawn a large group of disciples, who recognized her spiritual maturity and great wisdom. As an ambassador of peace, she traveled extensively throughout the Italian peninsula, to Florence, Pisa, Rome, and many other cities. She rushed to Siena, her hometown, and later to Varazze, when the black plague was ravaging the land. There, Caterina risked her life by visiting the sick. She consoled mourning relatives and shared her inner peace and hope with all. The love she felt for the Lord became an impetus to good works because, she explained, "Love is never idle, but always endeavors to reach greatness."[4]

In 1376, she traveled to the papal court in Avignon on a dual mission. First, she interceded for the people of Florence, who were suffering the pope's interdiction, which was destroying the Florentine markets. Second, and of great historical significance, Caterina was eminent in exhorting the pontiff to return to Rome to avert the influence of corrupt French bishops. She was not afraid to address the pope directly and sternly, telling him, as I paraphrase her words, "If you are, as you say, the bishop of Rome, you must go back to your sheep, and take care of your fold, as a good shepherd." Impressed by Caterina's wisdom and courage, the pope listened. A few months later, he at last returned to Rome, where he called her to be an advisor and spiritual counselor.

In Rome Caterina continued her life of prayer and service. Neglecting her already weak body, she consumed herself with continuous fasting and penitence. Finally, at age thirty-three, she departed from her mortal body, recommending to the Father her soul and spirit. In 1461 Pope Pio II canonized Caterina as a saint; in 1866 she was declared protector of the city of Rome; in 1939 protector of Italy, together with St. Francis of Assisi; and in 1970 she was named doctor of the church.

Saint Caterina of Siena was a woman who always strived, within the limits of her means and age, to achieve truth. In her message of faith she stated that we will one day know eternal truth "in the knowledge of ourselves, seeing that God has created us in His image and likeness, and through the fire of His Charity. This is the truth: that he created us, so we would share of Him, and we could enjoy His eternal and highest goodness."[5]

As years and centuries went by, the cultural atmosphere of Italy and Europe changed. Men started to enjoy and cultivate beauty, to study the ancient Roman and Greek classical works of art and literature, to exchange new ideas and philosophies, and to study the sciences. The new era sprouted eagerness, desire, and pride in all that human intelligence and talent could do.

In 1752 Eleonora de Fonseca Pimentel was born in Rome to Portuguese parents who had moved to Italy. When she was eight years old, her family went to Naples, where they settled and her brothers started their military careers. At an early age,

Eleonora distinguished herself for her intelligence and live-liness. She studied several subjects, such as the sciences, juris-prudence, economy, and literature. She wrote a book on fi-nance and several poems and became known as the "musarum regina," the queen of poetry, for her ability to write verses in both Italian and Latin. Well known in the cultural circles of Italian scholars, she corresponded often with Pietro Metastasio, the most renowned Italian poet of her time. Her verses reflect the fashion of the times, being very formal and filled with rhetorical figures.

At age twenty-five, she married a Neapolitan army officer and had a baby boy. Her son died when he was scarcely two, and Eleonora wrote several despairing poems in which all the artifice of rhetoric was lost in her pain. "Son, my dear son, alas! This is the hour / When I used to turn to you," she mourns, remembering the sweetness of nursing her firstborn. Her grief is voiced simply yet eloquently as she recalls how, as she cradled him,

> . . . you lifted toward me
> Your tender hand, giving me
> The first tokens of love: this memory brings
> Sorrow to my heart.[6]

Eleonora was also moved by the poverty in her beloved city; she deplored the gap existing between the governing class of the aristocracy and the common people who were confined to lives of ignorance and misery. Inspired by the French Rev-olution ideals of freedom, equality, and the brotherhood of all men, she believed that a kingdom should not be considered a tangible object — a possession to be transmitted as an inher-itance — but rather it should be regarded as an administrative responsibility, first, to defend the public rights of a nation and, second, to defend and preserve the private rights of citizens by the means of laws that are just and equal for everyone. She joined the Republicans against King Ferdinando of Borbone and participated in the founding of the free Neapolitan Republic during the revolution of 1799. As a member of the central committee, she became the major journalist of the new regime, editing the newspaper *Monitore Napoletano*.

Eleonora devoted herself to this political cause and wrote tirelessly of the hopes, struggles, and programs of the young republic. She believed in a pure republican ideal, to be shaped on the model of ancient Rome, in which loyal and uncorrupted citizens could lead a just and free nation. Eleonora also tried to educate the people, to offer opportunities and social development to everyone. But the French revolutionary army soon removed its support, and Borbone again conquered Naples. She was immediately arrested and condemned as a traitor.

Eleonora never denied her beliefs, and she confronted death with courage and nobility. Dressed in black, she was taken to the gallows, the last of her group to be executed. She looked upon the fallen bodies of her companions and pronounced the Latin words: "Forsan et haec olim meminisse iuvabit": "Perhaps one day it will be of use to remember even these events."[7] She was hanged on August 20, 1799, a martyr victim of a revengeful tyrant — but her sacrifice was "of use." Other Italian patriots and heroes, inspired by her writings and example, devoted themselves to deliver their country from foreign bondage. Since 1861, Italy now stands as a free country because of such men and women.

In 1909, a little more than a hundred years after Eleonora's death, twin girls were born in Turin. They were of Jewish descent, although the family did not practice the religion. Of the twins, Rita was the shy one, the one who was afraid of adults, especially her father. She seemed to have little self-esteem. Her father, with his blue eyes, aquiline nose, and thick mustache, was prone to sudden bursts of anger, which frightened this little girl. He was a very strict man whose belief that specialized education was not for women reflected the ideas of the times. Women were to be content with the general study of literature, art, and music; their education was intended to be ornamental rather than useful, in keeping with their prospects. We can imagine his reaction when Rita, at twenty years old, asked permission to continue her studies; she wanted to become a doctor. To her surprise, however, after explaining at length all his doubts about the wisdom and propriety of such a decision, he consented to support her desire.

At the university she found a mentor: a professor, also Jewish and with a character remarkably similar to her father's, who took a special parental interest in guiding her studies. Together they shared the persecutions of the Fascist era, were expelled for racial reasons from the university and forced to hide in Turin, Florence, and then Switzerland to continue their medical studies and experiments. Finally in 1946 Rita emigrated to the United States, invited by a German Jewish scientist who had escaped Hitler's persecutions. She remained in America for thirty years. At Washington University in St. Louis, she discovered the "nerve-growth factor," now known as NGF, a locally acting hormone that causes some types of nerve cells to grow. NGF, because it affects cell growth, proliferation, and differentiation, has become an invaluable tool in cancer research.

In 1986 Dr. Rita Levi Montalcini was awarded the Nobel Prize for medicine. She had dedicated her life to research, renounced many of the gifts life can give a woman, and overcome poverty and racial persecutions in her pursuit of scientific truths. Her choice to develop her intellectual resources has blessed the world.

Cornelia, mother of the Gracchi; Saint Caterina of Siena; Eleonora de Fonseca Pimentel; Dr. Rita Levi Montalcini: these four Italian women developed and used their talents to bless the world. Through trials and persecutions, despite fears, they pushed forward in their vocations. They never felt diminished nor accepted limitations simply because they were women, even in times when problems and obstacles were daunting. Each one sought learning and preparation, whether in scientific, political, spiritual, or maternal pursuits. Each followed her convictions of what was true, what was just, and, equally important, what was worth doing—even when to do so led far outside cultural comfort zones.

Notes

1. See Alvin Bernstein, *Tiberius Sempronius Gracchus: Tradition and Apostasy* (Ithaca, N. Y.: Cornell University Press, 1978); Henry Boren, *The Gracchi* (New York: Twayne, 1968).
2. Caterina da Siena, *Le cose più belle* (Roma: Logos, 1979), p. 18. All translation from Italian to English by Cinzia Donatelli Noble.
3. Ibid.
4. Ibid., p. 42.
5. Ibid., p. 25.
6. Benedetto Croce, *La rivoluzione napoletana del 1799* (Bari: Laterza, 1926), p. 16.
7. Ibid., p. 59.

Elizabeth Barrett Browning's Sonnets in Our Cynical Century

STEVEN C. WALKER

At the time of their publication in 1850 Elizabeth Barrett Browning's *Sonnets from the Portuguese* were widely—and wildly—popular. They sold almost five times as many volumes, for example, as *Men and Women* (1855), the most popular volume of poems by Elizabeth's famed husband Robert Browning. Critics of the time, too, were far more excited about Elizabeth than about Robert. She was thought to be "after Shakespeare . . . the equal of any,"[1] "ranked side by side with Milton and with Wordsworth."[2]

But by the turn of the century, Elizabeth Barrett Browning's flourishing reputation had withered more than most Victorian poetry under the critical glare of the twentieth century. And now, a century and a half after first publication, Elizabeth's shrinking artistic reputation can be traced in anthologies, reduced from a randomly sampled average of sixteen poems in pre-1990 to an average in 1990 anthologies of one. *Sonnets from the Portuguese* have become a kind of Rodney Dangerfield of poetry: they get no respect. The "sophisticated twentieth-century reader" considers them "awkward, mawkish, and indecently personal—in short, embarrassing."[3]

Steven C. Walker is professor of English at Brigham Young University, where he teaches Victorian and modern British literature as well as courses in the Bible as literature and Christian fantasy. He has been honored as Maeser Distinguished Teacher and Honors Professor of the Year. He received his Ph.D. from Harvard University and is author of Seven Ways of Looking at Susanna *and co-author of* A Book of Mormons. *He has served on the general Church Relief Society writing committee and in three bishoprics. He and his wife, Ardith Walker, are the parents of three children.*

Cultural opinion may be right in having demoted Elizabeth Barrett Browning from a major to a minor poet. But I'm not sure that is so much a considered opinion as a sociological phenomenon. And I've a nagging suspicion, if that is so, that we may be missing something in those fifteen Elizabeth Barrett Browning poems we no longer read. I've a nagging suspicion that Elizabeth Barrett Browning's decline in cultural respect may have less to do with aesthetics than with politics.

In today's literary world, of course, aesthetics *are* politics. But Mrs. Browning got herself in critical trouble way before we raised our consciousnesses and found subtler ways of putting women down. The first mistake she made was writing poetry—a womanly sort of a thing to do, even when done by men. Not satisfied with that female indulgence, she wrote on a woman's subject: love. And she took a woman's perspective on love, discussing not good old masculine lust, but the feminized version, the domestic variety of love. And she wrote that womanish stuff in a feminine sort of age. Victorian values are for us too domestic, too sentimental.

So today we tend to see Mrs. Browning, and her poetry, and her literary age, in such insulting terms as "sentimental," "soft"—in a word, "womanly." That unspoken accusation of womanliness has led to serious doubts about the quality of her poetry. English readers for a century have enjoyed a love-hate relationship with the love sonnets of Elizabeth Barrett Browning. My own schizoid reaction may be typical.

On the one hand, Barrett's poems inspire in me ridicule. I have but to hear the words "How do I love thee? Let me count the ways" and I begin ticking off on my fingers the failed possibilities while gazing befuddled into space—as if, having anticipated a flood of reasons for loving the beloved, I am dumbfounded when not a single one materializes. My routine mimics the many cartoons I've seen suggesting that Barrett exaggerated the ease of listing the qualities of the beloved.

On the other hand, I have framed above the bed where my wife and I sleep the forty-third *Sonnet from the Portuguese:*

I love thee to the level of every day's
Most quiet need, by sun and candle light.

I am indeed schizoid about Elizabeth Barrett Browning's poetry. On the one hand I laugh at her poems; on the other hand, I enjoy them deeply. Publicly I ridicule; in the privacy of my own home I come close to revering.

My ambivalent personal reaction reflects the general response to Elizabeth Barrett Browning's sonnets. Critics studiously ignore her: seventeen biographies but only two book-length critical assessments of her voluminous and undeniably significant—at least historically significant—writing. Public familiarity with her work seems to have bred contempt for it among literary critics. Yet for all that aloof critical silence, the public continues to buy *Sonnets from the Portuguese*. Elizabeth Barrett Browning's sonnet cycle outdistances even *The Rubaiyat of Omar Khayam* as the bestselling Victorian poetry in our century.

How did we arrive at that split in our communal aesthetic psyche? Have we somehow decided that anything as popular as Barrett's love poetry cannot by definition be any good? Is it a sad truth that only the semiliterate public who lack our cultivated tastes can enjoy romantic love lyrics in our day? Or are we being mulishly antiwoman in one of the few places we still dare? Does that split reaction of the twentieth century to Barrett's sonnets imply there are two *Sonnets from the Portuguese* — on the one hand, the cultural phenomenon the book has become; on the other, the personal experience of the poems?

Twentieth-century critics haven't experienced the poems much. Yet all evidence indicates that lovers continue to experience the sonnets passionately. Love being blind and lovers notoriously focused upon matters other than the rhyme schemes of sonnets, lovers may not be the most reliable judges of literary quality. On the other hand, critics who have assumed *The Sonnets from the Portuguese* would quietly expire under the weight of their own sentimentality weren't seeing too clearly either.

So which half of our corporate brain reads her best? The leftbrain highbrows who studiously refuse to read her? The rightbrain lovelorn who persist even in our unsentimental century in giving her book as a Valentine gift? The rational "masculine" reader, or the emotional "feminine" reader? To put the question more practically, is Elizabeth Barrett Browning worth reading? And if so, how should she be read? As a poetic misfortune? As a relative of Robert Browning? Is there any possibility of reading her as a real poet?

On the outside chance that we in cultured circles may have been training ourselves to dislike, on principle, popular literature such as Elizabeth Barrett Browning's sonnets, I've tried a simple experiment with my Victorian literature classes over the past decade in an attempt to identify the source of the critical disdain of Barrett's poems. If the major critical case against *Sonnets from the Portuguese* is that they are popular, then the best-known, easily recognized sonnets will tend to be the least liked. That is exactly what seems to happen.

I identified a hierarchy of familiarity among a sampling of *Sonnets from the Portuguese.* Ninety-two percent of my students, for example, recognized as Barrett's her Sonnet 43: "How Do I Love Thee?" (The other 8 percent were asleep.) About half, 48 percent, identified "When Our Two Souls Stand Up." Only 18 percent spotted Sonnet 20 as one of Barrett's: "Beloved, my Beloved, when I think. . . . That thou wast in the world a year ago."

And sure enough, my students' assessment of the quality of these poems was inversely related to their awareness of Barrett's authorship; the less certain they were that she had written the poem, the better they liked it. Sonnet 20 had a 62 percent approval rate, Sonnet 22 came in at 58 percent approving, and the infamous Sonnet 43—"How Do I Love Thee?"—was approved by only 23 percent.

What we have here looks very like kneejerk aesthetic snobbery. There has been little direct critical devaluation of Barrett's poetry. It's more as if we would not deign to discuss anything so unutterably common. The poems have not been officially blackballed so much as effectually shunned.

The familiarity of public acceptance seems to have bred critical avoidance of *The Sonnets from the Portuguese.* That phenomenon can be seen clearly as soon as we move from the supersaturation of "How Do I Love Thee" to the less well-known lines of "When Our Two Souls Stand Up": we get educated people liking the latter poem better. A case could be made for Sonnet 22 as more sentimental than Sonnet 43. Sonnet 22 appears in *Love Story,* that tear-jerking movie in which the young wife dies gracefully in her husband's arms. In that super-sentimentalized atmosphere, dark-eyed Ali MacGraw plights troth to virile Ryan O'Neal through a reading of Sonnet 22:

> When our two souls stand up erect and strong,
> Face to face, silent, drawing nigh and nigher,
> Until the lengthening wings break into fire
> At either curved point,—what bitter wrong
> Can the earth do to us, that we should not long
> Be here contented? Think! In mounting higher,
> The angels would press on us and aspire
> To drop some golden orb of perfect song
> Into our deep, dear silence. Let us stay
> Rather on earth, Beloved,—where the unfit
> Contrarious moods of men recoil away
> And isolate pure spirits, and permit
> A place to stand and love in for a day,
> With darkness and the death-hour rounding it.[4]

My students, less certain of that poem's origin, like it better than "How Do I Love Thee?" And when they get as far afield from familiarity as Sonnet 20, almost totally unaware of its source, they begin to take it seriously as a poem though it may lack the poetic texture of 22 or even 43. I'm not suggesting a literary plot against Elizabeth Barrett Browning, but I do think there is at least a "familiarity breeds contempt" principle at work here that may be causing us in the twentieth century to look too superficially at the *Sonnets from the Portuguese* when we are looking at all. Even our long overdue resurrection of women writers has failed to resurrect Barrett, perhaps because, paradoxically enough, her public popularity has kept her alive.

However that may be, we respond to the poems of Elizabeth Barrett Browning as to a cultural cliche, and that kind of homogenization makes me suspicious. There may be nothing of lasting poetic value in the sonnets of Elizabeth Barrett Browning. But if there is, we're missing it. We might do well to take a more individual look, a more intimate look, a more up-to-date reader-responsive look.

When I urged them to look more closely at Barrett's sonnets, my students concluded Sonnet 43 suffers the tragic flaw of having become too well known. A greeting card staple, the poem strikes the educated readerly eye about as freshly as last Monday's newspaper at the bottom of the birdcage. Her "How do I love thee" first line has been parodied so many times it sounds like self-parody.

But when it came to describing exactly what wasn't liked about the poem, the specific objections seemed to say as much about the readers as about Barrett as a writer. My students had three main objections about the sonnet. The first was that the poem was bland, not sufficiently intense. When I suggested that their reading might be bland, not sufficiently intense, they retreated to their second objection: "overgeneralization." They accused Barrett of being too highblown, of being too "cosmic" in her "overwrought abstractions," of "overexalted" "talking about love intellectually," of too many "superlative" generalizations that fail to produce "a mental image." As one snidely put it, "How, with all these emotional ultimates, Elizabeth will manage to love him better yet after death is difficult to imagine." "How Do I Love Thee?" was viewed as a "list which, for the most part, is neither meaningful nor memorable." "It all sounds very fine," they said, "but what does it mean?" The third perceived problem with the sonnet was interesting because I thought it directly contradicted the second: the poems were seen to be—often by the very individuals who objected to their "unvarying exalted tone"—as "too varied in their imagery."

That they particularly objected to Sonnet 22 on these same grounds is intriguing because it seems apparent that Barrett plays here deliberately upon the tension between angelic imagery and sexual imagery.

The poem is about as bluntly sexual as could be sneaked by the Royal Attorney in 1850. If those two "souls" standing up "erect and strong" were any more anatomical I'd be embarrassed to talk about it in 1990. All that female "orb"like "rounding" imagery in connection with all that male "stand up" and "point" imagery goes beyond suggestive to "erect"ly direct, amid the friction of a shocking amount of being "press[ed] on" and "mounting higher."

Yet its sexual directness is not the most striking of its realisms. Barrett confronts pointblank the rarity of our most intimate loving moments but refuses to give up her conviction that the oneness of sexual union can make earth's hard realities—"contrarious moods," "the death-hour"—not merely tolerable but preferable to dwelling with angels. Her lovers, besieged by time, find infinity in it. The angel imagery in the poem compounds that eroticism not only through those rejected overperfect angels who disturb our "deep, dear silence" with their "perfect song," but in the angel-like lovers themselves, those "pure spirits" at the conclusion of the poem. "Lengthening wings break[ing] into fire/At either curved point," too, are decidedly angelic at the same time they are evocatively sensual. If you can see them, as one reader does, as the wings of the cherubim surrounding the ark of the covenant, what we get here is angels making love in the Holy of Holies. Barrett takes her paean to loving so far here as to suggest that if angels don't make love, then the place to be is earth, because it is the loving that makes any place sacred.

If her imagery is fuzzy-edged, it is fuzzy-edged to a purpose. Whatever the poem may lose in precision it gains in expan-

238

siveness. And the poem is about expansiveness. In facing "darkness and the death-hour" at its end, the sonnet reaches out with quiet courage, farther than our realistic century tends to reach, unsentimentally to the dark brink of our very lives, to confront death and the unknown head on. Here for me is a lovely "rounding," a completing of the kind memorialized in *The Tempest* in "our little life is rounded with a sleep" (4.1.158). Sex here transcends into spirit and refuses to be content with spirit; love reaches to the stars and decides to stay where it is on the Robert Frost principle of "I do not know where it is likely to go better."

That's a nice Jungian balancing of extremes. Neither the appeal of the chaste angelic life nor the lure of the lively world of men are enough for the fullness of life love nourishes. When those souls "erect and strong," approach each other "face to face," the intimacy intensifying as they draw "nigh and nigher" and their wings climactically "break into fire," the climax is not just sexual, but emotional, intellectual ("Think," she implores us), and not just sexual and emotional and intellectual but (as such a Spiritualist as Barrett might have welcomed our saying) spiritual. Love, says the poem, allows us to hold in our arms as much of eternity as we can handle. And its very transitoriness, that ephemeral quality we feel so hauntingly in physical love, makes us value it the more: "To love that more," as Shakespeare puts it, "Which thou must leave ere long."

Maybe I'm overstating her understatement. I would not want to give the impression of wordiness where Barrett is concise. My point, put simply, is: This is pretty good stuff. It would be a shame if such profound and moving and compelling things were there in the sonnets of Elizabeth Barrett Browning and we were to miss them.

How do we manage to overlook those subtleties? Is it because Mrs. Browning is a "Mrs.," a woman? Could it be that she is too much woman for us? Could it be that Barrett is too delicately understated for our age with its fixation on that coarseness we call "vividness"? Leigh Hunt thought the sonnets "grand in the manifestation of power withheld,"[5] a quality I think we ought to appreciate.

Could it be, as one of my students who actually liked Sonnet 43 claimed, that in their apparent contradictions the "sonnets are an accurate record of our own tendencies toward a mild form of schizophrenia in our expressions of love," that they might have the capacity to "reveal us to ourselves in all our inconsistency"? Could it be that in our fast-paced society we are prone to overlook the kind of quiet depths where Elizabeth Barrett Browning speaks most profoundly? Could it be that her style of loving goes deeper than we are willing to go?

Could it be that in the twentieth century we want love that says not

> I love thee with the breath,
> Smiles, tears of all my life

but

> I love you like boiled onions, girl, buttered?[6]

or

> The pain of loving you
> is almost more than I can bear[7]

or

> I fought with her, she fought with me,
> and things went along right merrily[8]

or

> We merged our fleshes, I and she,
> in mutual indignity[9]

or

> I know now how life is cheap as dirt,
> And still the hungry, angry heart
> Hangs on[10]

or

> Go to bed, the God of the paramecium . . .
> will goad your complex evolution[11]

Our closeup statements may mean more for us, but we wouldn't want to limit ourselves to nearsightedness. We should not overlook that "I love you like boiled onions, girl, buttered," however more vivid than "I love you with the breath/ Smiles, tears of all my life," is less inclusive—it means to say less, and succeeds in that. For us, less has become more. We tend to be reductive, deliberately minimalistic. It might extend our narrowing horizons to read someone as expansive as Elizabeth Barrett Browning.

And it may be that the kind of love she so wholeheartedly extols didn't altogether fade away after 1850. Maybe there's some still around. Maybe there would be more if we were to read more *Sonnets from the Portuguese*, or at least to read more expansively, more as if poetry somehow related to life and life, especially in its loving aspect, mattered. I'm not really proposing we regress to 1850. But I am hoping that, laying aside the blinders of our twentieth-century reductive perspective, Elizabeth Barrett Browning's sonnets will prove worth our reading, "to the level of everyday's / Most quiet need, by sun and candle light."

I wouldn't be so foolhardy as to attempt to defend a poem that has become a cliche for sentimentality. But it might be worth our while to notice that even Sonnet 43, this much-laughed-at poem, moves well: beginning with that overture of the measured measurelessness of her love, "the depth and breadth and height / My soul can reach"; expanding her love to a new dimension with each line; reaching the climax of the crescendo in "I love thee with the breath, / Smiles, tears, of all my life"; then resolving those gentle rhythms in quietly transcendent closing lines and, in quiet passing, relating passion to grief and to faith as few have dared. Mere summation though it admittedly is of her sonnet cycle, it has its poetic moments.

Romantic love has a built-in tendency to sentiment. Should we eliminate that from our vocabulary of feelings? When I was sixteen years old and first fell in love, I memorized Sonnet 43 from *Sonnets from the Portuguese* "as naturally," as Keats would say, "as the leaves come to the trees." So did a lot of people. If we were to forget it, we would have lost something, something valuable. In fact, I would almost say, judging by my male difficulty in fully grasping the understated passion in the delicate wildness of these sonnets, we may have already lost something uniquely feminine.

Notes

1. George Barnett Smith, *Elizabeth Barrett Browning, Poets and Novelists* (1875), p. 97.
2. William T. Arnold, *The English Poets*, vol. 4 (1880), p. 566.
3. Dorothy Mermin, "The Female Poet and the Embarrassed Reader: Elizabeth Barrett Browning's *Sonnets from the Portuguese*," *The Critical Perspective*, vol. 7, ed. Harold Bloom (New York: Chelsea House, 1988), p. 4333.
4. Elizabeth Barrett Browning, *Sonnets from the Portuguese* (Garden City, N. Y.: Hanover House, 1954), p. 36, is the most readily available version. The preferred scholarly version is *The Complete Works of Elizabeth Barrett Browning*, ed. Charlotte Porter, 1900.
5. Leigh Hunt, *The Book of the Sonnet* (Boston, 1867), unpaginated introduction.
6. Judson Jerome, "The Superiority of Music," *The Honey and the Gall: Poems of Married Life*, ed. Chad Walsh (New York: Macmillan, 1967), pp. 120–21.
7. D. H. Lawrence, "A Young Wife," *Look! We Have Come Through!* (New York: B. W. Huebsch, 1920), pp. 46–47.
8. Robert Creeley, "Ballad of the Despairing Husband," *For Love: Poems 1950–1960* (New York: Scribner's, 1962), pp. 76–77.
9. X. J. Kennedy, "The Aged Wino's Counsel to a Young Man on the Brink

of Marriage," *Cross Ties: Selected Poems* (Athens: University of Georgia Press, 1985), p. 63.

10. Howard Nemerov, "The Vacuum," *Howard Nemerov: New and Selected Poems* (Chicago: University of Chicago Press, 1960), p. 50.

11. Chad Walsh, "Nuptial Hymn," *The Honey and the Gall: Poems of Married Life*, ed. Chad Walsh (New York: Macmillan, 1967), pp. 104–6.

ABUSE IN WOMEN'S LIVES

"Blessed are those that mourn for they shall be comforted."

—Matthew 5:4

The Savior is the ultimate healer, but that does not mean that there is no pain or that solutions come easily. We need each other to move the healing process along. Acknowledging the reality of abuse and our communal vulnerability begins to move us toward wholeness.

—Grethe B. Peterson

The Problem

GRETHE B. PETERSON

In January 1984, ABC television broadcast a movie called *Something about Amelia.* It was unlike anything a major network had produced and presented on prime-time television. It was the story of a white, middle-class, teenage girl who had a sexual relationship with her father. *Something about Amelia* was carefully crafted and sensitively portrayed and contained a message that child protective workers throughout the country had been trying to convey for years: sexual abuse of children in America is not uncommon, and it is not bound to class or culture. When the show was over, child-abuse hotlines across the country began to ring. The number of calls was not in the hundreds and thousands, but in the tens of thousands. Some of the callers were victims, some were concerned family members, and some were friends of friends. All were asking for help and direction.

A year later, in 1985, the Los Angeles *Times* conducted a survey on sexual abuse by which the following statistics were established:

38 million Americans were sexually abused as children

Grethe B. Peterson earned her bachelor's degree in history at Brigham Young University and graduated from the Radcliffe management training program. She has served as vice chair of the Governor's Commission on Women and Families, chair of the Utah Task Force on Sexual Abuse, and chair of the Utah Endowment for the Humanities. She has served as a member of the Young Women General Board, as a ward Young Women president, and as a Relief Society teacher. She and her husband, Chase, are the parents of three children and the grandparents of three.

1 out of every 4 women has been sexually abused by age 18 years

1 out of 7 men has been sexually abused by age 18 years

That is a national statistic. What about Utah? Aren't we different here? Our church and our culture place great emphasis on the sacredness of the family. Certainly there must be less abuse!

The 1990 statistics indicate that the cases of sexual abuse have nearly doubled in Utah since 1983:

The number of sexual abuse victims in 1983 was 611.

The number of sexual abuse victims in 1989 was 1,846.

It is difficult to know if there has been an actual increase in sexual abuse or if more cases are being reported because people are better educated about what abuse is. But, whether or not sexual abuse has increased, the number is staggering. And furthermore, we know that more than 80 percent of the abuse that is reported takes place in the child's home.

Not all abuse is sexual abuse. These statistics do not index the other types of family violence we are all aware of. Comforting the victim/survivor is part of the healing process. We can extend compassion, support, love, and the assurance that we will be there for each other. The Savior is the ultimate healer, but that does not mean that there is no pain or that solutions come easily. We need each other to move the healing process along. Acknowledging the reality of abuse and our communal vulnerability begins to move us toward wholeness.

Helping the Victim of Abuse

TAMMY B. HEATON

Abuse is an unsettling topic. It is easier to believe the statistics must be exaggerated or that abuse only happens to those we do not know than to deal with the feelings of fear and impotent anger that hearing of abuse may arouse in us. Yet abuse affects members of every social class, race, religion, and geographical area. Current statistics indicate that one of three females will have been sexually molested by age eighteen. One of eight males will have been sexually molested by age sixteen. I mention these statistics not to shock or upset anyone but to point out the reality of sexual abuse. It is simply a fact that all of us are probably in contact with survivors of sexual abuse, and sometime in our lives we will probably be in a position to offer aid to a victim.

My experiences have taught me that the better we understand our personal feelings about an abusive situation, in addition to understanding the dynamics of abuse, the better we are able to support the victim of abuse. For example, you may feel you would be powerless to do anything. Or you might be fearful of making a mistake and hurting the victim deeper. Then again, you may simply fear the unknown repercussions of involvement. Acknowledging these feelings gives you the power to take steps toward changing. For instance, you can actively find out about programs in the community that can aid the victim of abuse directly or train you to help such victims.

Tammy B. Heaton is a homemaker and a graduate student at Brigham Young University. She earned a bachelor's degree in accounting from BYU and has recently completed a second undergraduate major in psychology. She is pursuing graduate training in this field. She and her husband, Tim, are the parents of four children.

A good place to start is by calling your state Social Services office or the local police station or abuse shelter.

Even becoming informed takes emotional courage, so let me give you a list of *should do's* in providing support to victims of abuse.

Recognize that support is necessary for the victims of abuse to heal. You are an important part in the transformation from victims to survivors—people who can acknowledge the abuse they experienced and process it in a way that allows them to change and grow and not remain victims of unjust, traumatic life events.

Supporters need to understand that past experiences shape present behaviors. Thus, as a result of abuse, victims often develop attitudes and behaviors that helped them survive at the time but which are ultimately unhealthy. A child, for instance, may learn not to trust. A deep-seated lack of trust will probably pervade in detrimental ways all his or her subsequent relations, from school teachers and religious leaders to friends and spouse. Given the chance to process the abuse they experienced, victims can discover how it has affected their subsequent behaviors and attitudes and become able to choose between attitudes they now wish to retain and those they wish to change. A supporter who encourages a victim to "forget about it and get on with life" may hinder the victim's growth into a survivor. Supporters not only allow victims the opportunity to unload the burden of memory they carry but also serve as a sounding board in a process of healing and growth.

So what is it that you need to do to support victims of abuse?

Listen! I cannot emphasize that enough. Allow victims to talk as *they* desire and about what *they* want to talk about. So that you will know what to expect, I might add that they will, if given a chance, talk . . . and talk . . . and talk. Abuse is a denial of the victims' rights: their right to control their own bodies; their right to protection, and in the case of incest, to love from parents; their right to feel good about themselves; their right to esteem themselves. Your listening to them confirms their right to be themselves and feel *however* they may now feel about what happened. Your validation of their right to have their own feelings will help restore and feed their self-esteem. At times listening will require great patience on your part; I implore you to hang in there for their sakes, to encourage the healing process.

Give them lots of reassurance. What I usually say — and I believe this to be absolutely true — is, "If you've survived this far, you can be guaranteed you have the strength and inner resources within you to heal the pain you now feel." Also it is important to reassure victims of protection from further abuse. To do so, you may need to request assistance from the police, social services, or whatever authority is appropriate in the situation.

Try to understand not only what has happened but also, and this is even more important, how victims feel about what happened. Pay close attention to their perceptions of the abuse from within the boundaries of their experience. In other words, listen for their feelings about themselves and their reactions to the abuse. That is crucial, because not only is this their experience but it is also their healing. You may be thinking that if you were in the same situation you would have done something else, but the past is irretrievably past. The present reality of the abuse is *now* in the mind and heart of abuse victims, and therein lie the clues for helping. You must tune in to their *interpretation* of what happened in order to respond correctly to their needs.

Nor is there one standard interpretation or pattern you are likely to encounter. The ways such traumatic experiences reverberate in a person's life are not the same for everyone. Most victims, for instance, illogically assume guilt for crimes perpetrated against them, yet the way each victim copes with that mistaken burden of guilt varies. Some may respond by becoming self-destructively promiscuous; others may become aloof and frigid; yet others may develop some other coping behavior. Thus, just as we cannot categorize women into one personality type, neither can we do so with victims of abuse.

There are as many potential differences as similarities. Abuse victims are as individual as we are. We each have a right to our feelings, whatever they are. Only you can know your fears or courage, joy or pain. Feelings are neither right nor wrong. So, avoid denying or minimizing the victim's experience or feelings in any way. This is particularly important since abuse, by definition, denies the victim's feelings.

Understand your own feelings about abuse, about the victim, and about the abuser. So much of your ability to aid a victim ultimately depends on that understanding. How do we come to understand our feelings regarding abuse and thereby enhance our support? There seems to be a similarity between the feelings that the victim of abuse has and the feelings that we will experience.

Victims feel *confused*. What happened? Why does he/she treat me this way? An LDS victim might wonder, "I pray, but my prayers don't seem to help. Maybe I'm at fault. What should I do? Should I tell someone?"

Perhaps abuse is confusing to you too. Do you wonder who to contact, or even if you should contact someone about a situation you are aware of? Is your uncertainty enhanced by worry over what the reaction will be? Will your involvement put you at risk? Are you unsure of what to say to the victim or how to help? Perhaps you are unsure about how to define abuse. What is permissible and what is clearly abusive behavior?

Answering such questions as these and identifying the feelings can help both you and the victim as you sort out problems and then decide how to address them.

Victims are *fearful*. They are afraid of further abuse. They may be afraid to walk down the street alone, even in daylight. They are afraid of your reaction, of not being believed, when they tell you what happened. Sexual abuse of a child by a trusted person is a betrayal of the child's trust. The child and later the adult may then be fearful of trusting others, which hampers relationship building. Fear may be combined with the sense of powerlessness victims feel when they are denied the right to control their own lives.

Fear is a natural emotion for a potential support giver to feel as well. You may feel powerless to help. You may fear repercussions from getting involved. Rather than turn away from what you fear, contact authorities. They can help you decide the next step to take and how to do it. They can also assure you of the consequences of your behavior. Three books that are excellent both as an aid for the victim in healing and also as an aid to your understanding of abuse are *The Courage to Heal: A Guide for Women Survivors of Child Sexual Abuse*,[1] *Why Me? Help for Victims of Child Sexual Abuse (Even If They Are Adults Now)*,[2] and *Soul Survivors (Male and Female)*.[3]

Victims feel *guilt* and *shame*. Those emotions often prove a significant deterrent to their ability to solicit our sympathy and aid. Victims feel dirty and stigmatized because of the abuse. They all too often believe, "A decent person would not have this happen to them! God blesses good people, so what about me?" If we, by shying away from a disturbing problem, reinforce that kind of erroneous thinking, then we help to prolong their victimization.

Frankly, many people feel so uncomfortable in discussing or dealing with sex that they find it difficult to support victims of sexual abuse, sometimes even to the extent of blaming the victim for the abuse rather than the abuser. We must take care not to transfer the fault from the perpetrator of abuse to the victim as a means of reassuring ourselves that it could never happen to us.

By understanding your feelings about abuse, you can aid victims in their struggles to escape abusive situations and heal their lives. It is my sincere hope that you will recognize your importance as a supporter for the abuse victim, that you will extend your heart and ears to these people who need you. There is great joy to be had in participating in another's triumphing over adverse circumstances.

Notes

1. Ellen Bass and Laura Davis, *The Courage to Heal: A Guide for Women Survivors of Child Sexual Abuse* (New York: Harper & Row, 1988).
2. Lynn B. Daugherty, *Why Me? Help for Victims of Child Sexual Abuse (Even If They Are Adults Now)* (Wisconsin: Mother Courage Press, 1984).
3. J. P. Gannon, *Soul Survivors (Male and Female)* (New York: Prentice-Hall Press, 1989).

Becoming a Survivor

LYNDA N. DRISCOLL

For some years I have been president of Network Against Child Abuse. It is much easier to speak in that capacity or on any other subject than to speak about my own personal experience. On my own journey from victim to survivor, I'd often say to my therapist, "I'm not going to make it, am I?" And no matter how often he assured me that I was going to make it, I had a nagging doubt inside until I talked to another survivor who had been through the abuse I had been through, who had also been through the journey into the dark woods and had come out the other side. Her assurances — "I felt that too," "This is what you'll probably find next," and "You're right on track" — helped me to take each blind next step in faith. I hope that I can offer a reassuring hand to some of you who are victims, who are struggling to become survivors — whether or not you know that you are victims.

"Know the truth and the truth shall make you free." (John 8:32.) That is my husband's favorite scripture. After joining four different religions, I finally joined The Church of Jesus Christ of Latter-day Saints. I thought that I had at last discovered the

Lynda N. Driscoll is a convert to the Church, the wife of University of Utah professor Jerry A. Driscoll, and the mother of five children. She is president of Network Against Child Abuse, Inc., a nonprofit organization stressing education and legislation and offering speakers' panels and support groups. A member of the statewide Task Force on Child Sexual Abuse and the Committee on Ritual Abuse, she has recently coauthored a professional paper, "Survivors of Childhood Ritual Abuse: Multigenerational Satanic Cult Involvement," the results of a year-long study throughout the United States and Canada.

truth—and so I had, doctrinally. But that is not the only truth upon which you base your life. I had built my self-image and my life on lies—personal lies. Lie number one: my father loved me. Every child needs to believe that she or he is loved. Lie number two: since he loved me, the horrifying things that happened to me as a child must have been my fault. If only I was bigger or "gooder" or smarter or something. In reality I wasn't bigger because I was born prematurely. Beginning life at only two and one-half pounds, I hadn't caught up to my own age group yet. It would have been impossible to be a "gooder" child: I was trying to be the perfect child. I wasn't smarter because I continuously daydreamed through school about the things that had happened to me at night. In reality none of the abuse or the bad grades or my small size had anything to do with me. Nor was there anything I could do to fix it. But that was not what I believed—I believed everything was all my fault.

As I grew I began to repress my conscious awareness of the abuse. Eventually I had no memory of it whatsoever. But I did not forget the lies, and I continued to build my life around them. What was my life like? First of all, I had terrible self-esteem. I thought of myself as the thirteenth article of faith in reverse. Second, I was always in a crisis. If there wasn't one, I made one. I had become addicted to adrenalin rush at a very young age, and I didn't feel alive unless I was experiencing one. Third, I was constantly overinvolved. I was a human doing instead of a human being.

I was never still a moment. To relax was to be selfish or lazy. This constant movement had several rewards. First, I held the world's record for unfinished projects. Second, I could feel superior. After all, I could move three times as fast as anyone I knew, and *they* told me so. I believed that my self-worth depended upon what I could accomplish and how fast I could accomplish it. Third, I never had time to allow myself to recognize or feel the pain and anxiety that lived inside of me. My busyness was an attempt to avoid the memories of a childhood I could not face. But it didn't work completely. For one thing, my life didn't contain time for me, and in truth I really resented that and felt angry about it. For another, though I didn't remember the abuse, it came out in other ways. I felt chronic, misplaced, inappropriate anger. A slip of the tongue and the offender became the target of all my anger from the time I was three years old. I had chronic, varying problems with my health—one after another after another. I experienced wide mood swings and deep depressions. But rather than address these problems, my solution was usually to just work harder and faster.

Finally, it became apparent to me that I could not go any faster, and my defenses against despair began to collapse. I reasoned, "If I'm not good enough now, and I can't go any faster to be better, then there is no reason to live." My wish to be dead and my suicidal thoughts heightened. The constant unhappiness I felt even after I joined the Church—in fact, *especially* after I joined the Church—became proof to me that I must be a wicked person. I knew deep inside that I must be inherently faulty, unfixable, and unlovable even to God.

"God moves in a mysterious way his wonders to perform." (*Hymns of The Church of Jesus Christ of Latter-day Saints,* 1985, no. 285.) Ironically, my next escape into nonstop crisis and busyness finally led me to face my real problem. A dreadful case of sexual abuse came to light, and a ward member who had abused many children in our ward was convicted of six counts of first-degree felony. When after only seven months he was let out of prison on bail pending appeal, I began a campaign which was the founding of Network Against Child Abuse. Although I did not yet remember my own abuse, that was the beginning of my healing process. For the first time I was fighting back. I was big enough, I was smart enough, and I was definitely angry enough to do something about the injustice on behalf of innocent children I knew and loved. The more I learned, the more I realized the problem of abuse was enormous. The angrier I got, the harder I worked and the

longer the hours. I was sleeping two to four hours a night. I was falling asleep at the wheel of my car. I even fell asleep pushing a grocery cart in the store and ran into a woman. (Had she pressed charges, it might have been the first lawsuit in the history of the state for injury dealt by a grocery cart!) In short, I was obsessed.

I read everything I could find. I wrote to everybody in the state — I'm sure you all got a letter. And finally after two years of nonstop activity I began to realize, "Hey, I have a problem. It's not the ward's problem. It's not the children of the state of Utah's problem. It's something within me." So finally I went to a therapist. Of course, I had been to therapists before. In fact, I had been to therapists off and on for twenty-five years — most of my adult life. We had coped with lots of problems, but we had never delved down to the core issues.

"To every thing there is a season, and a time to every purpose under heaven." (Ecclesiastes 3:11.) This was my season to remember and to learn the truth so that it could set me free. I had remembered some inappropriate fondling by my step-father, so I thought maybe that was it. Or maybe there was something else that I was repressing about him. My therapist decided to pursue the matter through hypnosis. When he took me back to three years of age, however, and I began to remember the abuse by my biological father, I nearly came out of the trance. That began two years of grueling, fracturing, torturous memory work. Besides individual therapy I enrolled in a ten-week group therapy for AMAC (Adults Molested As Children). I took a class at the University of Utah on interpreting dreams. I started an on-going self-help support group for AMACs, which offered a much-needed sense of community. Yes, I was pursuing this matter with my usual all-out effort and intensity, but the multidimensional approach helped me to move quickly through my memories.

Let me warn you, however, the process certainly did not feel like healing. As a matter of fact, it hurt more than you can imagine. But as with any festering sore, the poison must first be let out before the wound can heal. Without the hurting, there can be no healing. You cannot simply forget the past and go on from here—not with severe childhood abuse by a primary caregiver. I had to face the horrifying truth. My father did not love me. My father did not know how to love. My father used me for his own sick agendas, and it did not matter a bit to him how much it hurt me, physically, sexually, emotionally, or spiritually. And I had to face the lies. I had always been told that my mother was strong, and I believed that. My mother wasn't strong—not then. It took her until I was five and a half to get me out of that abusive situation and only then because my life was in peril. It was hard for her, just as it is hard for many women today to make the decision to leave their husbands in order to protect their children. And there will always be women who cannot make that decision. I am very grateful my mother got me out when she did.

There were many days while living the pain that I wondered, "Why am I doing this?" I wanted the pain to stop. I wanted it to stop *right now,* but there was no way out and no end in sight—no light at the end of the tunnel—and no way to go back either. But by facing the lies and the truth, I was finally able to put the blame where it belonged. It wasn't my fault. And if you are a victim, it wasn't your fault either. It was my father's fault. There was nothing inherently wrong with me.

To heal you have to grieve first, and you have to be at last angry, enraged at the wrong done to you. That is not easy because we are so often told that we shouldn't be angry and that we should forgive and forget. But I had to get the anger out so that I could let love in. Among other things, I spent a lot of time with hot angry tears, yelling and even swearing at my dead father. I even found it helpful, if somewhat hazardous to my reputation, to go into the forest and beat the heck out of dead trees, with an ax, a shovel, a tree limb, anything I could find.

"Let each man learn to know himself / To gain that knowledge, let him labor." (*Hymns*, 1950, no. 91.) Now that I have dealt with the lies, the truth, the grief, and the anger, my life has at last begun to change, and I am learning to know myself in a new way, as a human being rather than a human doing. The inappropriate chronic, intense rage is gone. I can now walk through the crystal department at ZCMI without having the urge to sweep every piece of crystal on the floor and break it into a million pieces. A pot can fall out of the cupboard without my wanting to throw it across the room. The constant anxiety has diminished. My husband can actually be late from work without my believing he has abandoned me.

I am no longer a crisis-aholic. I do not need to feel an adrenalin rush to know that I am alive. I'm no longer a workaholic. I can slow down — I can even stop. I do not feel damaged or dirty or inferior any longer.

I'm trying new things. I went to the beach in California for two weeks and soaked in the waves and sun. I meditate an hour each day. I walk when weather permits. I sleep. I find things I enjoy doing, like taking long, luxurious baths and manicures and pedicures — two new words in my vocabulary. Sometimes I sculpt; sometimes I read for fun. No abuse books or Networks . . . right now. My boundaries are weak, and I can't listen to the horror stories of others without being drawn back into pain, anger, and anxiety. So for now I must rest from the battle in order to heal. And when I try to stick my nose back into the fight, which is very easy for me to do, my friends in the Network gently remind me that they can handle it and they do.

It is still sometimes hard to hear others in lessons and in testimony meetings express gratitude for how the Lord has blessed them with wonderful parents, when I know much of my own life has been totally devastated by childhood abuse. But I am now realizing that the free agency of unrighteous individuals, not God, permitted what happened to me as a child and what is still happening to children in Zion. And I know it is the Lord who has given me strength to become a survivor and to find help for myself and for others.

Aiding the Victim of Abuse: What One LDS Stake Has Done

WARREN R. NIELSEN

I want to discuss aiding the abuse victim from a church leader's point of view. I have served many years in bishoprics and stake presidencies. (I am currently serving in the third stake presidency.) I would like to focus on what a stake can do by describing what one Provo student stake has already done.

I could list for you a score of qualifications that explain my interest in this problem. Let me tell you the most important: we have been through it as a family. A few years ago two of our children were sexually abused by a young man we had taken into our home as a foster child. Between 3:00 and 5:00 this afternoon I spent two hours with a therapist and one of my children working through some unresolved pain. So I want you to know that even though I don't understand it all, as a family we have been there.

A little over a year ago, a delightful young woman, recently returned from a mission, came to my office for a temple recommend interview. We discussed all of the questions, and everything in her life was absolutely in order. But after we finished the paperwork, I couldn't seem to end the interview.

Warren R. Nielsen, professor and chair of the Management and Quantitative Methods Department at Illinois State University, received his doctoral degree from the University of Illinois. He served as assistant administrative vice-president of human resources at Brigham Young University. He has written extensively about human behavior, leadership, values, and change. He has served the Church in various callings, including regional representative. He and his wife, DeAnn Davis Nielsen, are the parents of four children.

Something felt incomplete. Finally I paid attention to that sense of unfinished business and said, "Tell me, Sister, have you ever been sexually abused?" After many tears and further discussion, she was able to admit, "Yes, I have." We talked about a lot of things, but what concerned me most was what she told me about her conversation with her mission president. She told me that her mission president was the only other person she had spoken to about the abuse, but he talked with her for only "about three or four minutes." Puzzled, I asked her, "What did he say to you?" She replied, "Well, he said, as long as I kept working hard and if I did the things I was supposed to, some day I would know when I was forgiven."

I had to stifle my anger. I asked her, "Tell me, have you been forgiven?"

"No," she said. No, she felt that she had not been forgiven.

"Have you prayed about it?" I asked.

"Yes."

"Well," I asked, "why do you think you haven't been forgiven?" Her sad answer was, "Well, I guess I haven't done enough yet for Heavenly Father to tell me that I have been forgiven."

"Let me give you another explanation," I volunteered. "You have your Heavenly Father between a rock and a hard place. There has been no transgression; there is no sin. As you pray for forgiveness, if your Father in Heaven tells you you have been forgiven, he would be acknowledging that you have transgressed. He would rather not tell you that you are forgiven if it means letting you believe that you have transgressed. So as of tonight, don't you ever again in your entire life ask to be forgiven for this. If you want to ask your Father in Heaven to help you with your hurt, your confusion, that is another thing. But don't you ever again ask to be forgiven."

I'm sure that there are a number of you who read this who are also burdened wrongfully with a sense of guilt. I tell you as I told her: if you are praying for forgiveness, stop. Absolutely stop. There is no sin. There is no transgression. There is nothing for which you need to be forgiven.

My experience that day, as well as my own family interests, led me to introduce this topic when I met with the stake president of a BYU stake. As it turned out, I wasn't the only member of the stake presidency to have had such an experience in a temple recommend interview. I was far from alone in my concern. So as a stake presidency we determined to deal with this issue and deal with it out in the open. We were not going to turn our faces away and assume that it was not our problem. We were going to help.

Here is what has happened since that time. Perhaps you can go home and talk to your bishops and stake presidents; or, if not, at least you can take courage that something is being done somewhere. First of all, we held a number of training sessions with our bishops. We started out with the Church pamphlet on sexual abuse. By the way, it is a very good pamphlet. It would be a major step forward if we could get all our bishops to read it.[1] The Church pamphlet on abuse states clearly, unequivocally, that victims are not guilty of sin or transgression and have no need to repent.

Next, we arranged a session with a therapist who worked with us closely. He spent a long time talking with the bishops, helping them understand abuse—primarily sexual abuse, because that is our student stake's most frequent concern. The therapist explained to our bishops what abuse is, how it happens, the impact on young peoples' lives and so forth. When necessary, I had some sessions with the bishops myself to deal with specific items and special cases.

After these bishops training sessions, I was sent out on the circuit—which meant that I visited every Relief Society in our stake at least once and sometimes twice in an attempt to reach every young woman in our boundaries. I spent about an hour and a half in every Relief Society. I told them up front, "I am here because some of you have been abused. Some of you have roommates who have been abused. Many of you will be mothers who may have abused children. And we want to start talking about it." I talked about the impact of sexual abuse: the feelings of absolute, total lack of self-worth; the inability to trust people. I cited the example of the bright, accomplished, nice young woman who turns down the elders quorum president when he asks her out. Why does she choose instead the young man who has been excommunicated twice, is now back in the Church but on probation again? Why is he the one she goes out with? Because that is the one she feels good enough to go out with. That is how she feels about herself.

We talked about the sexual problems that follow abuse. Often the abuse victim becomes promiscuous. And if a leader doesn't understand what is going on, he or she may really come down hard on these kids, labeling them as morally unclean. In actuality, the out-of-control behavior may all be tied to the original abuse, the present immoral behavior arising not from flawed character but from the unresolved impact of past sexual abuse.

One absolutely essential point that we had to help our bishops understand was that they couldn't deal with immoral behavior as isolated incidents. That is always true, but especially in the case of victims of sexual abuse; they had to deal with it as a package. So if a bishop had a nineteen-year-old girl in his ward who was being promiscuous, and she had been sexually abused at thirteen, then at nineteen, he is still dealing with what happened to her as a thirteen-year-old. And furthermore, he could not effectively deal with her behavior as a moral issue — it was an abuse issue. We would then talk openly about dealing with these old wounds to her sense of self-worth rather than focusing only on her present sexual behaviors, which violate Church standards.

We also talked both to the bishops and to the Relief Societies about the Church's position. The truth of the Church's position, however, is especially hard for the victims of sexual abuse to believe. Many of you can understand this. If you have been abused, people can tell you that you are not guilty and that you are just as clean as anybody else, but you don't believe it at all. It's a matter of the heart; but at least we can try to communicate to everyone what the Church's position is about abuse. The Church's position is very clear: for the victim of abuse, there is no sin; there is no transgression; there is no guilt. We may feel guilty, but there is no guilt.

The wounds from abuse are not easily healed. Another step our stake found essential was to establish close ties with some reliable therapists. And when we've referred young people to therapists, we've helped them get there. We have told them, "Therapy is appropriate, it's valuable, it's necessary. Let us get you there. Let us help you with it."

Let me draw your attention to one last concern. Many of you are in Young Women programs and Relief Societies. We really make it tough for a young woman who has been abused. I do not advocate changing our Church programs, but if a little girl has been abused at age ten, she is really in for a tough row to hoe. She has to sit through standards nights for years. She has to sit through discussions about temple marriage and about being morally clean. She has family home evenings to face. And if she has a dad like I was, we frequently talked about moral cleanliness in our home — not knowing that I had children sitting there dying inside. So when you have standards nights and discussions on temple marriage, be sensitive. Keep in mind that at least a third of those young girls in your class have probably been abused and are thinking that they are already immoral and unclean. All you will be doing is heaping more confusion and guilt on them.

A young girl who has been sexually abused is every bit as clean as any girl on the face of the earth and just as worthy to go to the temple as anybody. We all know that in this life where Satan has dominion, bad things — truly horrible things — can happen to good — truly, truly good — people. How I wish I could tell you of my experiences giving blessings to these youngsters. These young women who have been abused are more than just "not bad" — they are among the best of the best of the best.

266

I have laid my hands on young people's heads in the last year, young people whom I know were valiant spirits in the pre-mortal existence and beloved of the Savior. That's who they were and that's who they are. Don't you dare scare them away from the Church and the gospel in standards nights and in discussions of temple marriage. Don't do it. Be sensitive in your meetings. Be careful in your family home evenings. The most important thing is to love them. Sometimes they are very hard to love. Please remember who they are.

Note

1. "Child Abuse: Helps for Ecclesiastical Leaders," The Church of Jesus Christ of Latter-day Saints, 1985.

Index
_____

Index

Domestic chores: sharing, in marriage, 96–100; dividing, according to ability, 104; reasons for sharing, 104–5

Dominion, righteous versus unrighteous, 58–59

Dreams: of childhood, 147–48; abandoning, through fear, 150–54

Eadburg, eighth-century abbess, 214–15

Emotional problems, children from families with, 187–88

Enlightenment, the, 75–76

Equal Rights Amendment, 85

Equality in marriage: in sharing domestic chores, 96–100; developing attitude of, 101–3; based on mutual respect and decision making, 110; varying definitions of, 116

Erickson, Beth, 13

Evaluation, honest, of self, 139

Eve: traditional blaming of, for origin of sin, 49; name-title of, 53–54; eternal marriage of, to Adam, 54–55

Everyday activities, joy of, 18, 138–39

Expectations, unmet, make people unhappy, 101

Fall of Adam and Eve: unity of couple suppressed by, 55–56; as shared transgression, 56; judgments following, as statements of cause and effect, 56–57, 61; blessings of, 60

Fall of Icarus, The, 149

Families, American: modern, problems of, 69; diversity in, 70; in seventeenth century, 70–73; in eighteenth century, 73–75; changes in, following Enlightenment, 75; in nineteenth century, 76–83; burdened with contradictory theories, 83–84; lessons about, from past, 88

Family history, postcards direct mother's efforts in, 43–44

Farnsworth, Ella and Bill, 93–94

Fear: abandoning dreams through, 150–54; avoiding change out of, 171; of helping abuse victims, 249–50; felt by abuse victims, 252–53

Featherstone, Vaughn J., 143–44

Filene, Peter, 87

Fitzhugh, William, 72

Flower bulbs planted by friend, 42

Freeze, Mary Ann, 202

Freudian theories, 83–84

Friedan, Betty, 87

Friends, viewing all others as, 165–66

Future, productive attitude toward, 19–20

"Gallant Ship Is under Weigh, The," 8–9

Garden of Delights, The, 216

Gender roles: in nineteenth century, 78–80; changing perceptions of, 87; views of, preserved in women's writings, 195

271